The Spotted Bride

Rachelle C. Hood

Visit our website at www.freedomlinebooks.com.

Dedication

... to our Bridegroom

ACKNOWLEDGMENTS

To my precious daughter Ryan:
God knows, I could not have run this course without you.
Wait for me at the finish line!

Suzanne—Long live THE QUEEN!
Jeri—You shall go out with joy!

CONTENTS

PART THREE: LIVING THE MESSAGE

Prologue: "Tell the Story!"

On Tuesday, May 15, 2012, while working out at the gym, the Lord spoke to me about a dream He gave me the day before. In the dream, I had written a book about my life as an executive in Corporate America. Since I had not written such a book, I recorded the dream in my journals, out of obedience, and left it.

The Lord then reminded me of another dream He had given me that morning. In it, the time had come for me to graduate. I was designated the "most achieved" student among a body of White students. However, the school leaders decided a young man would be given the honor, because I was Black. I warned everyone that I would interrupt the ceremony if they proceeded with the plan.

While I saw shades of my past in the dream, I disregarded it. *Lord, this stuff is ancient history to me now—long buried. Why are You digging it up?*

Instantly, the Lord brought to mind a Strengths Test I had taken three days earlier and connected it to the two dreams. I had participated in a behavioral-personality assessment as a part of a women's Bible study. I sacked the test because I did not agree with the results. The Lord later revealed the evaluation was correct, and I should not have written it off.

Among other things, the test identified me as an achiever. *Go back. Look at your top five strengths from a Kingdom perspective. Rewrite them,* His Spirit counseled. When I did, I saw clearly that I had been hardwired from the womb to achieve a divine purpose related to my strengths. But what was it?

I discovered my five dominate areas of strengths were: Strategic, Achiever, Adaptability, Belief, and Input. (A detailed discussion of these areas is appended for reference.)

As I worked out on the treadmill, I pondered the five areas. Our strengths tie to a God-given purpose. Then it hit me like a freight train. My pace slowed on the treadmill.

Oh, no! Lord, really? Are You sure? Do You really want to do this? Apparently, the time had come. *How much do You want me to reveal?*

He spoke three words: "Tell the story!"

The next day, I began writing, not really knowing the direction the Lord would take me. Over the course of the next 18 months, I wrote three books that became *The Spotted Bride Series.* The Lord had deposited within me an end-time message for His beloved bride.

For years, He had shown me things in dreams and visions that I committed to my journals. Only a handful of people knew what He had revealed. Now He wanted the message to move beyond a handful. The Lord called me to warn His bride, to share with her what He has revealed to me over the years about the coming judgment on the United States of America and the rest of the world. Herewith, is the first part of the three-part series.

Note:

The names of some people
have been changed to protect their identities.

PART ONE: THE GROUNDWORK

Chapter 1
The Mark

I was born December 16, 1953 in Detroit, Michigan to Earl and Gloria Hood. I was born with a large black spot on the right side of my nose, traveling just underneath my right eye. My mother told me the blemish was a birthmark. I now know God marked me at birth for a future call. In the fullness of time, I would walk out the destiny of Christ's spotted, blemished bride during the last hours of the last days as a harbinger to His corporate bride of things to come.

God required me to become the message I was to deliver to His spotted spouse. I would have to walk out everything by faith just as she would—the glorious and inglorious—before I could tell her anything. My journey would serve as a testimonial and a blueprint for her. It would also give her hope.

Although the process of preparing me for this call began in early childhood, it wasn't until the latter years of my life I began to experience an explosion of dreams, visions, revelations—even divine encounters—accompanied by intense spiritual warfare. The Lord used these wonders to detach me from the world and all that hindered my walk with Him. I lost nearly everything, but I gained the most wondrous relationship a human being can have with her Creator.

Still, God had a greater purpose for upending my life. The time for Him to remove His bride from the earth was fast approaching. Yet, she was still spotted, blemished. She would have to be made ready. Like me, she had to be refined. He was returning for a bride without spot or blemish.

Chapter 2
My Family

I was my father's fourth child. He previously had been married for eight years to a woman named Amy. They had two daughters together, Nanette and Nancy. I was my mother's second child. My mother was nine years younger than my father and had never been married.

My stepsisters, born in Detroit, spent time in Europe after their mother remarried a man named Mr. Butler, a captain stationed in Germany. My earliest recollection of my stepsisters was a black and white photograph of them, standing on a balcony there. They wore simple, lovely print dresses, white anklet socks and black, shiny shoes. Nanette stood a foot taller than Nancy, and they were both smiling. Germany seemed a million miles away—a whole other world. But it did not look much different from anywhere else I had been; I had not yet been anywhere.

My father divorced Amy for reasons no one likes to talk about. Everyone whispered infidelity. Nanette was eight and Nancy was five at the time. He was serving in the Marines while stationed in the South Pacific, and Amy "played around." That is all I heard. So, after my father's tour of duty, they parted.

My father met my mother in Buffalo, New York. Although my mother did not know her father well as a child, she moved to New York when she was 19 years old to work in his restaurant. That is where she met my father. Day after day, he came to the restaurant to pester my mother for a date. She barely got her work done because of him.

Late one night, well past midnight, he asked her to attend church with him the next morning. Desperate to get rid of him, she agreed. She was confident he would not show up the next morning, but he did. He looked quite dapper in his suit and tie. From there, the relationship quickly blossomed. They dated four months. Then they married.

Together, they had three children in rapid succession—Arlene, me, and Earl, followed by a stillborn son. A year later, they had one last child, my brother Carl. I remember how excited we were when my mother brought him home from the hospital. He did not resemble the rest of us. His complexion was light like our mother's.

Nanette and Nancy were like full sisters to us. We all grew up together. They adored my mother and loved her as though she was their biological mother. I believe this is one of my mother's greatest accomplishments. Nanette and Nancy trusted her and confided in her about many things. My mother often counseled them on constructively working out their differences with their own mother. At various points, they lived with us because of friction with Amy, whose difficult personality was common knowledge.

My parents also adopted a third son Rook when he was 3 years old. He originally had been adopted by my mother's father, Grandpa Yaak and his common-law wife, Naomi. He was nearly the same age as Carl. After my grandparents died suddenly, one after the other, my parents could not bear the thought of Rook becoming a ward of the State, so they adopted him.

Our three-bedroom, one-bathroom two-family flat was located at 4011 W. Philadelphia, on Detroit's Westside. It was like Grand Central Station because my father and mother had large hearts. Over the years, my family took in many relatives, helping them get on their feet. We learned early in life how important it was to share what we had. This was a particularly difficult lesson for me because I distinctly remember being a stingy child, especially when it came to food. My ice cream was *my* ice cream! My cookies were *my* cookies! I shared nothing.

My Mother's Family

My mother was born into abject poverty in a tiny, tilted, two-room wood-frame house in Clarendon, Arkansas. A small town of fewer than 300 people back then, Clarendon had only one stop light. Folks often joked, "Don't blink riding through, or you'll miss it." My mother had one brother, a stepbrother, my Uncle Odis. High-spirited and always congenial, I liked him a lot. Every day, he consumed a 12-pack case of Coca-Cola and smoked a carton of cigarettes.

My Uncle Odis fancied himself a ladies' man. He fathered numerous children by several different women throughout his lifetime. To this day, I do not believe I know all my cousins. His father, my mother's stepfather, whom she always referred to as Mr. Schaffer, was a nice man. Although he favored my uncle, he was kind to my mother and grandmother. He let my uncle, born to him late in life, run wild. My siblings and I did not have many dealings with Mr. Schaffer. I only remember him as gentle and quiet. He died when we were young.

I knew my mother's mother, Grandma Lillian, better than all my grandparents. She was sweet to me and Arlene, but Earl claimed she was mean to the boys in our family. My grandmother could be easily mistaken for a White woman and often was. Her mother had been raped by a Jewish doctor, who employed her as a maid.

My grandmother was the oldest of a long string of children, but she was the only one with fair skin, long silky red hair, and blue eyes that turned gray when she was angry. She never attended school. There was always too much house and field work to do.

When Grandpa Yaak, who people say was "black as shoe leather," was passing through Clarendon to help construct a bridge over the White River near town, he took one look at this fair maiden and asked for her hand in marriage. Never having been wooed by anyone in the small town of Clarendon, she accepted. The marriage did not last long because my grandfather could not get my grandmother to leave town. But it did produce my mother, who was also considered a beautiful woman in her day.

My Father's Family

Unlike my mother, my father and his eight brothers and sisters were raised in a large house on an acre of land in Ferndale, Michigan. My Grandpa Fisher Hood—after whom my dad and Earl derived their middle names—grew cherry, peach, apple, and walnut trees on his land. He also cultivated a vineyard on the side of the house that produced plump juicy grapes. Arlene and I used to pick and eat those grapes all day long. We also picked strawberries and raspberries from the bushes out back, which Grandma Lena made into delicious homemade jams.

As a little girl, I loved visiting them. Their home felt a little bit like paradise. I remember my grandfather, a Baptist minister with only a sixth-grade education, taking my sister and me for rides on his rickety tractor and secretly buying us ice cream. "Now don't tell Lena!" he would whisper on our return trip home. He was more laid back than my Grandma Lena, who, although loving, was quite stern.

I was always amazed at the fact that she and her three sisters went to college—Clarke College, in Atlanta, Georgia. Black women attending college was a rarity in the late nineteenth century! My great-great-uncle Martin, who owned several businesses, including a grocery store, funded their education.

My dad once asked my grandmother how she, a college-educated woman ended up with my grandfather. "Earl, your Daddy is a *good* man," she responded. The fact that my grandfather was noble and kind was more important to her than anything else. I think my grandmother was often misunderstood because she rarely smiled. But she was also good and honorable.

My father and his siblings lived and went to school with Whites. I was surprised when I first saw a photograph of my father's graduating high school class. It was Lincoln High School's Class of 1940. My father was one of only six black faces—two women and four men—in a sea of White students. Remarkably, he grew up experiencing very little discrimination.

That changed, however, when he entered the military. The difference in how the armed forces treated its Black enlistees versus its White ones was a cold slap in his face. When he joined the Montford Pointe Marines, the first regiment of Black marines in the United States, they were not allowed to live in the same barracks or fight alongside White soldiers.

One of his regiment's first duties was to cut down trees to build their own barracks. However, the disparate treatment he experienced in the Service did not poison his attitude toward Whites. He had too many positive experiences with White classmates, teachers, and neighbors to let resentment darken his heart. As anyone who knew him could attest, his heart was much too big, much too generous for that.

Chapter 3
My Earliest Memories

"Look Mom, There's Jesus!"

My mother and Aunt Lorraine, who was my mother's aunt and my great-aunt, told me time and again, I began to have "Jesus sightings" at an early age. I remember only one episode, confirmed by my mother.

One day, she put my sister Arlene and me down for an afternoon nap in our back bedroom. We both slept in the same twin bed by a long row of windows. We could see the rooftops of many neighborhood homes because we lived on the top floor of our two-family flat.

Suddenly, my mother heard yelling. She burst through the door to find me standing on the bed, pointing. I was beside myself with excitement!

"Look Mommy! There's Jesus!" Tucking me back in bed, she tenderly explained the man was not Jesus, but a roofer working on a roof.

She often reminisced about the time she took Arlene and me on our first bus ride downtown to go shopping. In those days, my parents owned only one car. My dad used it for work, so we rode the bus.

She herded the two of us onto the bus, holding our hands on either side of her. My sister entered first. She climbed the stairs and began walking toward the back.

The minute I boarded the bus, I exclaimed in earshot of everyone, "Mommy, look! There's Jesus!" I pointed to an Orthodox Jewish Rabbi sitting near a window. Everyone chuckled, including the Rabbi. Mortified, my mother scooped me up in her arms, apologized to the good Rabbi and raced to the back of the bus. And so, it went.

Decades later, I still saw Jesus in everybody and everything, albeit in different ways. Later in life, I found myself searching for Him, literally, in places all over the earth. A distant call, I heard. The searching was programmed into my spiritual DNA. But who could have known it at the time?

"God Made the Trees"

I remember the first time God ever spoke to my consciousness. I was on a ride in the family car. I could not have been more than 4 years old. The car was packed. So, I found a place on the ledge beneath the rearview window, fitting my head and feet snuggly against either side of the car. Lying on my back, I gazed skyward.

I watched the passing treetops as my father drove. As I gazed upward, a truth entered my young heart, and I recited it to myself as though I was telling someone my name. "God made the trees." Instinctively, I knew with complete and utter certainty that no man could make a tree. Only God could do that.

"I Ain't Kissing No Boy!"

Another one of my earliest childhood recollections was being invited to a birthday party three blocks from my home at a house I had never visited. I was about 5 years old. My mother dressed me up in a pale-yellow dress with a big bow tied in the back. I wore white anklet socks and white shoes. She dropped me off at the birthday party and left.

There were hordes of children at the party. The girls were dressed like I was, and many of the boys wore suits, some with short pants. The kids engaged in all kinds of games and activities as the adults looked on. I am not sure why I was invited because I did not know one child at the party. I walked through the rooms, watching the other children play. I had no desire to join them. I was satisfied just to watch.

Suddenly, we were all gathered into one room and told to form a large circle on the floor. I did not know why. Curious, I obeyed. A lady stepped into the middle of the circle and began to spin an empty coke bottle. The next thing I knew, one of the girls was being pushed to the other side of the circle to kiss a boy! Everyone laughed, especially the adults. I was aghast. They spun the bottle again, and my little heart raced. I held my breath. The bottle stopped. I dodged another bullet.

I decided I had enough. I got up and made my way to the exit. I held the banister tightly as I slowly descended the steep staircase of the two-family flat and walked out the front door. No one saw me leave. It never dawned on me to ask permission. Walking in the general direction of my house, I eventually found my way home.

"Yes, yes. It's okay!" I heard my mother's voice on the phone as I climbed the front stairs. "I think I hear her coming up the steps now. Yes, thank you for calling."

"I ain't kissing no boy!" I burst through the door. I poured out the whole disgusting tale to my mother, my little arms flailing.

She never scolded me for leaving the party. Instead, she was astonished I had found my way home alone. While it was too early to draw conclusions, this kind of fierce independence, fearlessness, and aversion to all forms of romance would emerge, time and again, in the years to come.

Eight years later, Reginald Diggs, a boy who lived across the street and was a year older than I, gave me my first kiss. He stole it. I had played with him and some other neighborhood boys all day. When it was dusk and time to go inside, he leaned over and kissed me on the left cheek and ran. The other boys laughed. I was stunned. Then, incensed, I balled up my fists and stomped upstairs. I went straight to the bathroom to wash my cheek. I did not speak to him again for weeks.

Chapter 4
Thriving in the Ghetto of Detroit

Close Knit and Hard Working

We did not realize it at the time, but our parents instilled in us a love for one another and a strong work ethic that would serve us well in the years to come. Both our parents worked, so we had a lot of daily chores. We knew to complete our homework and work assignments before going outside to play. It did not matter whether our parents were home or not. We never received an allowance for doing our work because there was no money for that. We were raised to know our bedroom and the whole house had to be kept clean. They were our responsibility.

My mother did all the cooking. She would call from work every day to instruct us on what to take out of the freezer for dinner. We would have the table set when she arrived. Every evening after dinner, Arlene washed the dishes, and I dried them. Every evening, Earl took out the garbage.

I also made sure the beds were made every day, which I liked to do. My sister and I both knew how to wash clothes in the wringer-washer machine in the basement, four flights down. We took turns washing the clothes on Mondays. On Tuesdays, she ironed and folded the clothes, including the sheets and pillowcases. I put them away. Once a week, my sister mopped the kitchen and bathroom floors on her hands and knees after I swept. It was my job to vacuum the living and dining room floors. We liked to rearrange the furniture, which was dusted twice a week.

We reshuffled the worn living room furniture often to surprise our mother when she came home from work. She always fawned over our rearrangements, which delighted us to no end. When we had money, we enjoyed spending it on her. We brought her gifts at the "Five and Dime" on Grand River Boulevard. The three of us—Arlene, Earl, and I—would walk those aisles forever with our hands full of quarters, dimes, and nickels, until we could agree on just the right gift. My mother graciously accepted and displayed every gift we gave her.

Practically everyone on our block kept a nice yard back then, and we were no different. We helped my dad keep the front lawn looking manicured. The backyard and the yard on the side were another story. My father would cut the grass and trim the edges and the hedges every other week while we pulled weeds with my mother. Every evening, we took turns watering the lawn and shrubs that lined the front of the house.

In autumn, the whole family raked the fallen leaves. As kids, we took great pleasure playing in the piles of leaves. I treasured the smell of them burning after the job was done. I hated the day the City Council banned the practice of burning leaves. We also helped my dad shovel snow in the wintertime, which was my favorite time of the year as a child.

For the most part, we were an obedient bunch. When the streetlights came on in the evenings, we knew to drop our bikes where we were and hightail it home to prepare for dinner. The next day, our bikes would always be where we left them. We all ate together around a large dining room table as we discussed the happenings of the day. We all talked at once, over one another, yet no one missed a beat. To this day, I converse this way.

Sundays at Our House

Every Sunday, like clockwork, we piled in the family car and headed to the First Baptist Institutional Church, a modest place of worship, which my grandparents help found in Hamtramck, Michigan. We looked like little ducks following my parents into the brick building.

As much as I liked learning, I do not remember being enthralled with Sunday school. Big church was always a challenge for my brothers and me. We did not know how to sit still for two and a half hours without ripping the pews apart. The best part of church was when it was over, and we learned if we behaved well enough to avoid a spanking.

My favorite part of the day was Sunday dinner. Almost every Sunday, we had fried chicken, mashed potatoes and gravy, green beans, and rolls. One of my fondest childhood memories was the smell of my father's cigar smoke wafting through the house as he watched the Sunday football games. He yelled at the television screen while we waited for dinner to be prepared.

My mother always sang the same song, "Blessed Assurance," as she cooked. I can still see her in her pearl necklace, a crisp white apron draped over her Sunday frock, singing: *"This is my story. This is my song, praising my Savior all the day long."* That song still has the power to transport me back to my childhood.

I was not particularly attuned to God as a child. I knew He existed, and He made trees. I thought this business about suddenly dying and not being ready was something I could not do too much about. So, I did what I could do. I said the same prayer every night: "Now I lay me down to sleep, I pray the Lord my soul to keep. If I die before I wake, I pray the Lord my soul to take."

When I was 12—just after I had been baptized because everyone else was doing it—I made a decision. One night, I told the Lord that I was tired of praying to Him. It seemed to me, after 12 years, we had this thing down pat.

"Just keep me out of trouble from here on out," I asked Him. That was it. I didn't talk to Him again until I was 31 years old.

I cannot remember when we stopped attending First Baptist as a family. It seems life just got too busy for my parents. As we grew older, they stopped going to church altogether. (Years later, they would become pillars in their church.) All on our own, we found a Lutheran church about six blocks from our house. It became a second home to us.

We were introduced to the Lutheran Church through its Vacation Bible School. After VBS, we began participating in its afterschool programs. Eventually, we started attending church there regularly without our parents. Earl joined the church's basketball team and became one of its star players. Later, in high school, he became a star track runner to everyone's amazement; he had been born with club feet and had to wear leg braces for years.

It was at Nazareth Lutheran Church that I first memorized the Nicene Creed. I could recite it in my sleep. Also, at the priest's request, I took catechism classes. I did extremely well because I liked to learn, not because I liked God. This local church played a large part in keeping us and a lot of neighborhood kids off the streets and out of trouble. My parents were grateful. We stopped going there when we moved to another neighborhood.

Shades of the Future

I did not realize at the time that I was an odd, precocious child, always serious and contemplative. These traits would become even more embedded as I grew older. Once, as a little child, I overheard my mother and father discussing our bills in the dining room. The conversation grew louder and louder. My mother sounded distressed. I walked into the dining room where they were.

Papers covered the table. I pulled back one of the tall dining room chairs and managed to climb onto the seat. I rested my chubby arms on the table, just barely. They had not noticed me. I watched my father speak, then my mother, then my father. I listened intently for a few minutes. I interrupted.

"So tell me, exactly, how are we going to pay all these bills?" They both looked at me momentarily stunned. "Well?" I raised my arms, looking first at my father, then my mother.

After another moment of silence, my mother slowly rose from her seat, pulled back my chair from the table and uninvited me to the conference. She shuffled me off to my bedroom. "This is between your father and me. You do not have to worry about a thing. Are your things put away?"

By "things" she meant my one tea set, comprised of four plastic cups, four saucers, and two spoons. As a little girl, I did not have a lot of toys, nor did I play with dolls. I tried at first, but I did not like it. I did not see the point.

I asked my mother for pencils, paper, and books. In my spare time, I liked to play "office" by myself. Alone, in the front bedroom when no one else was present, I would boss myself around. I played all the roles. I was the boss and the staff. I would change my voice and my physical position, depending on who I was.

Sitting on the edge of the bed, I would ask nicely: "Where is that report?"

I would jump off the bed to the chair and answer: "It's not ready yet. I've been so busy."

Jumping back to the bed, I queried: "So when will it be ready?"

Where I got this from, I have no idea. No one in our family had an office job, and I certainly did not get it from television. At that age, I only watched cartoons after school. I love cartoons to this day.

Mighty Mouse was the first cartoon I ever loved. I decided when I married, I wanted Mighty Mouse to be my husband. He always rescued the other mice from the mean cats. *"Here I come to save the day! That means that Mighty Mouse is on his way."* He was a savior in my little mind. He always made things right.

Then I graduated to *Popeye,* which I watched religiously after school. I could sing the theme song a dozen times a day. *"I'm strong to the finish, 'cause I eats me spinach. I'm Popeye, the Sailor Man."*

This was another seed divinely planted in my young mind. I hated spinach. Years later, I would have to "eat a lot of spinach"—do things I hated—as God slowly trained and prepared me for my call.

As I grew, I also became a big fan of *The Twilight Zone.* I liked pondering other-worldly dimensions, beyond the five senses. Who knew what really existed outside our world? How could I have predicted that many years later, I would feel as though I entered my own personal Twilight Zone when things of the spirit began to collide with my temporal world? God and Rod Sterling, the host of *The Twilight Zone,* had laid the early groundwork.

So, when I was not doing homework or watching cartoons, I bossed myself around my play office. My bossiness eventually crossed over into my relationships with Arlene and Earl. Carl, my younger brother, was just a baby at the time.

Whenever anything went awry in the house, my parents lined up the three of us on the living room sofa for questioning. "Okay, who broke the lamp? It will go better for all of you if the person responsible tells us the truth." They would say this, of course, looking at me the whole time.

I made it a general rule, *Look straight ahead. Do not make eye contact*. Although they would question us individually, I was always the usual suspect, even when I was not guilty. They were keenly astute. I was often found to be the behind-the-scenes ringleader of much that went amiss in the house.

I remember once we were all going to get spankings when my father got home from work. I had talked my sister and brother into doing something we were not supposed to do. I had a few hours before my father came home. I felt responsible for the debacle, so I told them to leave everything to me.

I went through the entire house, found all the belts and hid them in the attic. To this day, I do not know how my mother figured out where the belts were or who had hidden them. It did not take her 20 minutes to discover the stash and place me on the sofa for questioning.

I had one girlfriend in elementary school, Molly West. She was a dark, pretty girl. I was short, fat, and content to be totally ignored by boys. It seems over a single summer she became stunningly gorgeous. I would not slim down nor blossom for another four years.

At 12, Molly was tall and willowy. She reminded me of a swan. She had a slender, fluted neck, an elongated waist, and long slender legs; her hair grew long too. Not surprisingly, her interests changed. All she wanted to do was talk about boys and hair products.

I did not have any hair to speak of, and I hated boys. I just wanted us to ride our bikes and discover new things and places. One day, walking home from school, without ever having a discussion, we waved goodbye. I would not see her again until 10 years later when she was a graduate student at the University of Michigan.

My idea of afterschool bliss was settling down with a tall cold bottle of RC Cola, a bag of Cheetos, two chocolate Hostess cupcakes, and the latest issue of *Mad Magazine*. I would devour that magazine from cover to cover, sometimes in one sitting. I did not discover *Mad Magazine* was for boys until I was an adult.

I could never understand Arlene's attraction to Archie Comics, and then later, romance magazines. She was a "Girlie Girl." My Cousin Debbie and I would laugh at those stupid romance stories. We would pick out passages and mimic the love-sick, star-crossed lovers, "Oh, Jack, if you left me, I'd never breathe again." Oh, pleeeeeeeease! I did not have a romantic bone in my body. I was a tomboy through and through.

My express goal in the romance arena was to marry a neurosurgeon. I told anyone who would listen, "I'm going to marry a neurosurgeon when I grow up. I will have lots of money to spend, and he will be too busy to come home." Until that time came, I would play softball with the neighborhood boys on the playground, ride my bike, and climb trees. The scars on my knees and legs attested to that. I looked horrible in a dress.

The one thing I had going for me was my love for school. I enjoyed learning. I adored my teachers. School was my life. I was always some teacher's pet. My mother often spoke of the time when I was in first grade. An overnight storm had blanketed the city with more than 20 inches of snow. The schools were shut down. I would not hear of it! I insisted I needed to get to school. I had things to do. I had projects to complete. What would my teachers do without me?

My mother could not convince me the schools were closed, so rather than fight with me, she stuffed me into my red hooded snowsuit—leggings and all. She put on my white snow boots, wrapped my head and face in a long scarf, so only my eyes showed and sent me on my way. I looked like the Michelin Man.

Trudging through freshly fallen snow, almost past my thighs, I made it as far as the corner. We lived in the second house from the corner. The mailman spotted me, picked me up, tucked me sideways underneath his arm and carried me home like a little statue. Had he not, I would still be trying to get to school.

I often carried a fresh apple to school for my favorite teacher. It had to be big, red, and shiny. I would ask to stay after class to erase the blackboards. I just wanted to be helpful. My teachers loved that about me. I was one of the four highest ranking students when I graduated from Angel Elementary School in 1966.

My insatiable appetite for learning cost me dearly when I entered McMichael Junior High. It was not cool to be smart in a ghetto school. I did not get the memo. My mother used to lament: "She has a lot of book smarts but no street smarts—absolutely no common sense!" I was always first to raise my hand. I always had the right answers and could pontificate on a matter until the teacher stopped me.

It is understandable that I had only one friend in middle school, Delores Johnson. She was the only child of a single mother, who was bedridden and dying of cancer. She bore Delores late in life. That may explain why Delores always wore two-piece suits to school and red lipstick. Her mother frequently gave her $2 to buy lunch for herself and me in the school cafeteria. I always looked forward to Fridays when they served fish fillet sandwiches. I would smother mine in tartar sauce.

At 5'9", Delores towered over all the other students, including the boys. We were both misfits in our own ways. But we liked each other. We were joined at the hip. People said we looked like the number 10, walking the halls together.

I had no idea how much the other students resented me, until one day when the Social Studies teacher stepped out of the classroom. When he did, a girl named Lessie, who sat in the front of the classroom turned around and spewed a bunch of profanities in my direction. I looked behind me to see to whom she was talking. Only after she finished, did I realize she was talking to me! Following that tirade, she and two other girls bullied me for most of the school year. One day, they took turns pushing me in the small of my back as I walked the eight blocks home from school.

The boys also teased me about my large breasts. I would hear, "44s!" ... "62s!" ... "77s!" whenever I boarded the bus to go to my piano lessons after school on Tuesdays. It took me a long time to realize they were making fun of my bust size. I ignored them. The one positive outcome of those Tuesday bus trips was after seven years of piano lessons I learned to play rather well.

My first piece of sheet music was *Beautiful Dreamer*. Years later, the Lord would use this song to awaken me in the wee hours of the morning to talk with Him. In my spirit, I would hear the gentle lyrics *Beautiful dreamer wake unto me; star lights and dew drops are waiting for thee.*

I could not be provoked into fighting. I learned my lesson in grade school. I had a clash with a girl named Velma Gilmore. I lost the scrap, but later won a friend. I still bear physical scars from that brawl. I vowed I would never again engage in a physical conflict. I would break the vow two decades later when I married my first husband.

I never told anyone at home about the harassment at school. I did not want to worry my mother. She had too many other things to deal with, so I quietly endured it.

Chapter 5
Growing Up Black in America

Some of my most poignant memories growing up revolved around summer visits to my mother's childhood home in Arkansas. My father would drive us down, and we kids would stay for two months. It was like entering a different world. I had never seen such poverty.

Where to stop and eat, while driving south, was always a gamble. Some restaurants would serve us and some would not. We would wait patiently as a family at our table. If the waitress never came over, we left. Eventually, my parents learned to pack our meals and snacks and carry them with us in the car.

Although we could purchase gasoline on our trips, frequently we were barred from using the public restrooms. "Out back there, yonder" was code for "You can do your business in the woods" at the rear of the station. After my first trip "back yonder," I resolved to hold mine as long as I could.

For some strange reason, the prejudice angered my mother more than my father. Living in the South, she grew up experiencing far more racial bigotry than he. But after every stop for the next 10 miles, we would hear, "Oh, so they can take our money, but we can't use their toilets, huh? Who do they think they are?" My father would reach over and pat my mother's knee, "Calm down, Gloria, calm down. It's okay. Let's just keep going. We'll be there soon."

Not being allowed to use the restrooms like everybody else was just the tip of the iceberg. Racial intolerance ran deep in Clarendon, Arkansas. At the town's only movie theater, Black customers were not allowed to sit on the main floor with White patrons. We had to sit in the balcony. My two cousins, Billy and Shirley, once pulled me out of a long line of people waiting to buy tickets to see a Hayley Mills movie. It did not occur to me that everyone in the line was White, and I was Black.

Amused by my ignorance, my cousins escorted me to a side entrance, where we could purchase our tickets and buy popcorn and large sour pickles. I never understood the pickle thing, which both of them bought. That day, I liked the idea of sitting in the balcony. After we settled in, we had the whole place to ourselves, and we did not have to wait in a long line in the hot sun. The injustice of it flew right over my adolescent head. Later, I would marvel at the ignorance of it all.

Generally, we could patronize public places like the local diner, but we had to order at the back door. We were never allowed inside. We would place our order at the door and wait until it was done. Then we would take it home or eat it on the way.

Getting adjusted to my Grandma Lillian's shack of a house was no easy feat. I was astonished at how we could see the ground through the large cracks in the floorboards. At night, we could also hear the mice running through the walls behind the old, flowered wallpaper. That always frightened us out of our minds. Arlene, Earl, and I would cuddle together with the covers over our heads, terrified that one would find its way into the room and into our bed, although that never happened.

The outhouse—a hole in the ground with a dingy, badly chipped toilet seat on top—was where we used the bathroom. I hated going to the outhouse, but I especially loathed using it at night. The stench was almost unbearable. And trying to shoo away big crawling bugs and flying insects from the seat was sometimes more than I could stomach.

I remember one morning my Grandma Lillian asked if we wanted fried chicken for breakfast. I thought that was a splendid idea—fried chicken in the morning *and* in the middle of the week! At home, fried chicken was reserved for Sunday dinner only.

As much as I liked fried chicken, I started to have doubts when I saw my grandmother out in the backyard chasing down the chickens. She grabbed one. She stood in the middle of the yard and swung that chicken over her head like she was readying a slingshot. Then, with a single flick of her wrist, the chicken's neck snapped off. Its headless body flew across the yard and ran in circles for what seemed like an eternity. I could not believe my eyes. She scooped up its lifeless body and headed for the kitchen. I was paralyzed where I stood.

Under burning hot water that would have scalded less calloused hands, my grandmother plucked the feathers from the chicken in less than two minutes. After sprinkling it with generous amounts of salt and pepper, she floured it. Then she deep fried it. When that little fried chicken leg hit my plate, I could hardly stand to touch it. It looked nothing like the plump chicken legs I used to see up North, purchased from a store. My grandmother insisted we were looking at the natural size of a chicken. Picking at it, I slowly succumbed. I was surprised at how good it tasted.

On our return trip home, it seemed my father always brought back one of my mother's relatives—an uncle, an aunt, a cousin—someone trying to escape the poverty and cotton fields of Arkansas. He would bring them to live with us in our small, cramped two-family flat. They were attracted to Detroit's thriving auto industry.

After my father helped one get on his feet, he would send for another. One by one, they came to live with us. One time, we took in an entire family—a husband, wife, and their two children. The third bedroom off the living room was always taken by relatives. Sooner or later, they all got jobs, moved out, married if they were not already, and raised families of their own. I grew up knowing relatives on my mother's side best, largely because of this.

My father worked two and three jobs to support us. At one point, he would drive to Flint, Michigan, nearly 70 miles away, to work second shift on a second job. In addition to working regular jobs, he always picked up odd chores, like painting houses or pouring concrete to bring in extra income.

He was highly entrepreneurial and dreamed of owning his own business one day. When I was in high school, we had a family gasoline station, but that turned out to be a bust. Later, my father opened his own auto parts store, and after that, a dry-cleaning business.

He ran the auto parts store for years and then turned it over to Earl to run. In due course, my brother bought out my father and converted the auto parts store into an auto repair shop. It was the same with the dry cleaners. My father started that business at age 65. He ran it for five years and then turned it over to Carl, who still runs it today. At 89, my father still helped Carl run the business.

Similarly, my mother always held a job. She worked hard in and outside the home. Well before I was born, she and my father, along with my Uncle Clayton and Aunt Essie, owned a restaurant on Detroit's eastside.

As I was growing up, my mother worked as a cashier at a local grocery store. She would take the bus to and from work. She worked eight to ten hour shifts every day, sometimes six days a week. Then she would come home and work. She did not like to work outside the house, but she had no choice. We needed the money.

One hot summer afternoon, my mother came home early, lugging bags of groceries in both arms. It was a two-block walk from the bus stop to our house. My sister, brothers, and I—along with a half dozen neighborhood kids—were having the time of our lives playing. We raced back and forth across our front lawn and the lawns of our neighbors. Running on these green manicured lawns was something we were not supposed to do. We were so engrossed in our play that we never saw her approaching.

When I finally spotted her, I saw her eyes grow large and her jaw drop. The grocery bags hit the pavement. She broke into sobs. She just stood there with both hands pressed to her face. We stopped dead in our tracks. *What? It's just grass!* Finally, I gathered the courage to run to her, "Mom, what's wrong?" The more she looked at us, the harder she cried.

Only later could she explain the heartbreak of not being home to supervise us. That day, each of us had fastened a sanitary napkin to our forehead. We attached a rubber band to each end of the napkin and looped the bands around our ears. We had no idea what these pads were for, but they made wonderful sweatbands. In fact, we had made sweatbands for all the neighborhood kids.

In time, my mother left her minimum-wage cashier's job and joined Chrysler Corporation. She spent 10 years at Chrysler, working her way up from an assembly line worker to middle management. She joined General Dynamics when it purchased Chrysler Defense in 1982. My mother rose from an administrator to a middle manager at General Dynamics and retired there after nearly 20 years of service.

I will never forget what she told us about her first job interview at Chrysler. She weighed less than 110 pounds. She knew she did not meet the weight requirement for a plant job. The day of the interview, she filled her purse with rolls of coins. She held onto her purse when weighed by the Company nurse. She passed and was hired that day. My cousin, Helen, who went along with my mother, in hopes of snagging one of those sought-after assembly plant jobs, tried the same tactic. But the nurse spotted her purse and asked her to put it down. Since she was even smaller than my mother, she was not hired that day.

I would not call my parents "political" or "activists" by any stretch of the imagination, although they always voted and encouraged us to do the same when we got older. Too many people had sacrificed too much for us to dismiss this precious right. In the 1960s, I marched alongside my parents through the streets of Detroit when Dr. Martin Luther King Jr. came to town. That was as close to activism as they would get.

I never heard a racist remark spoken by either of my parents. We were taught to accept (or reject) people on their individual merits. My father was fond of saying, "Never judge a book by its cover." After Dr. King was assassinated, riots broke out, and large sections of the city went up in flames. Most of those neighborhoods were never restored.

While our neighborhood was not touched by the riots, the unrests made a deep impression on me. For the first time, I became conscious of the gross inequities that existed in the world, and I understood their ability to incite rage in some people. But despite the social injustices that touched my young life, I never grew bitter. I was simply mindful, aware that life was not fair.

Finally, the time came to leave McMichael. I was ecstatic. Lessie and her friends could no longer bully me. Despite the torment, I graduated at the top of my class with high honors. I was immediately accepted into the college preparatory honors program at Mackenzie High School, which was in a completely different school district.

By the end of my senior year at Mackenzie, I was President of the National Honors Society and the Spanish Club. I was also Vice Editor of the school yearbook. My peers voted me "Most Likely to Succeed." Of all the students graduating that year, I finished second, and as Salutatorian, I was asked to give the commencement address. I never learned why Mildred Morton, the Valedictorian, was not given the honor.

Growing up poor and Black in Detroit's inner city and seeing the value of hard work firsthand fortified and prepared me for my future in ways I could have never imagined. I understood what it was like to be dirt poor and still have dignity. In years to come, I realized my journey allowed me to grasp class and racial subtleties way beyond my years. It was college that prepared me to negotiate with ease the world of privileged, White America.

Chapter 6
The Opera in My Mind

Raised in the Motor City, we were surrounded by Motown music—the "Motown Sounds." Debbie and I went to more than one Motown Review, where we saw live, on stage, the likes of Gladys Knight and the Pips, The Four Tops, The Temptations, Stevie Wonder, Smokey Robinson and the Miracles, Martha Reeves and the Vandellas, Mary Wells, and Marvin Gaye—just to name a few. I now realize my great love of music was one of God's grand designs in my life. He would speak to me through it, although I did not realize that was happening until much later in life.

I did not discover my love for music until I was 12 years old when Arlene received a record player for her thirteenth birthday. With it, she also received two albums—one by Dionne Warwick and one by The Impressions. After a week of listening to Warwick's *Walk on By* and The Impressions' *Keep on Pushing*, she was done. She put the record player away, and I picked it up.

Music captured my imagination like nothing else. Every spare dollar I received found its way to the local record shop on Grand River Boulevard, where I bought my '45 discs. I had to be one of their best customers. I spent hours listening to music in my room behind a locked door. My parents always knew where to find me. "Don't you ever get tired of listening to the same tunes over and over again?" my father asked. He had no idea the things I saw in my mind when I listened. No one did.

Something mystical happened. An opera unfolded. I saw visions of people, places, and events. I did not know it then, but I was seeing remnants of my own life that would play out 43 years later! I did not know I was looking into the future. Through music, I came to know things about the spirit realm that I could not have possibly known without a relationship with Christ. My relationship with the Lord did not develop until many years later. Decades would pass before I understood the significance of the visions or "daydreams."

Following are two excerpts from my prayer journals, recorded 12 years apart, as I gradually learned that what I had experienced at such a young age was supernatural and prophetic:

May 11, 1997

Scenes from the Other Side

The truth, "all the world's a stage," is an idea God has been forming in my mind for decades. I can now recall countless daydreams regarding this spiritual fact. For years, strange scenes unfolded in my mind as I listened to music.

I began having day visions at age 12. They tapered off when I left college at 23; they had all but stopped by the time I married at 27. The scenes were extraordinary since I was not born again until age 31. Prior to that time, I knew extraordinarily little about God and nothing about the opposing forces of evil.

There were two worlds in my daydreams. They existed in two different dimensions. One world was cognizant of the other, but the other did not realize there was another dimension. This was because that dimension was invisible. The inhabitants of the invisible world "spirited" people away into their world. ("Spirited" was the term I used back then.) It was never clear how this was done. In an instant, a person would just disappear and then reappear on the other side.

Interestingly, all the inhabitants of the invisible world were males. Their captives were females. A captive's physical appearance would change slightly when she crossed over. It seemed only she knew that she was not quite the same as she was before. Residents of the other side considered these women trophies. They were sought out for their extraordinary beauty. The invisible beings always desired new trophies. They would go to considerable lengths to capture them.

While the women who were spirited away had some measure of freedom when they crossed over to the other side, they were prisoners. These hapless victims were often given any and everything they could possibly want because the unseen creatures were extraordinarily wealthy. Many of these women roamed around in rambling estates. However, one striking feature of all the hostages was that they were deeply unhappy. These joyless women seemed to have everything their hearts desired, except the one thing they longed for most—freedom.

They sadly "played their parts." The women did what their oppressors required. This now reminds me of lost people on earth taken captive by Satan and his minions, who reside in the spiritual realm. Their captives have everything the world says they should have, but they are not free in Christ, and therefore are oppressed, harassed, and tormented.

Sometimes the women had social gatherings—parties, picnics, teas. Unbeknownst to them, they were being watched the entire time. They were oblivious to their captors' reconnaissance. These tyrants observed all their discussions and actions from places far and high. They heard and saw everything. Nothing the women said or did went unnoticed.

Astoundingly, the imprisoned ones never plotted an escape. Later, I realized they did not know the way to freedom. Their tormentors took extreme precautions to guard against any escapes. There were times a knowledgeable detainee would try to inform others of a secret way out. The captors listened intently for such messages and squashed them.

If one tried to get away, their harassers dropped everything and chased after her to bring her back. It was difficult to escape. Fugitives always seemed to get recaptured. Recaptured runaways were then observed more closely. Sometimes they were locked up or confined in places with bars. For the most part, the women resigned themselves to their fate and tried to make the best of their new home.

Sometimes the captives performed on a literal stage. Oddly, these scenes included both males and females. Many of them had extraordinary artistic gifts and abilities. Some were dancers, some pianists, some vocalists. They could do astounding things with their bodies and voices. They performed to please their audiences.

The inhabitants of the invisible world loved to watch them. However, they were always watchful for rebel performers. Rebels surreptitiously communicated coded escape messages in their performances. They were considered dangerous and were dealt with swiftly—confronted, reined in, and more intensely observed.

In my day visions, I frequently saw a woman they always referred to as "the dark one" because of her skin color. The mysterious beings were always searching for her because she spelled trouble for them. She had been a captive but had escaped. She knew their dark secrets, and she was determined to set others free.

Whenever she sang or performed, some who heard her broke free from their bondage because her songs were encoded with instructions on how to flee. Her performances infuriated the invisible creatures. They wanted the dark one locked up and out of the way. Occasionally, they would spot her in various places and go nuts. They would radio comrades higher up in the system, who would rush to where she had been spotted. But they could never capture her. She always evaded them.

In the theater, these unseen bullies watched the performances of their unsuspecting prisoners from high balconies, which were invisible to the performers. The more gifted the artist, the more desirable they were to the furtive observers. In fact, they fought amongst themselves for the choice ones. The higher ranked officers usually secured the most popular entertainers.

There was terrific contention in the group when someone in the lower ranks attracted and caught a highly coveted actor or player. Each used lavish gifts to lure a prey to his domain. A person's talents, gifts, and skills seemed to determine their desirability. The more accomplished, the more sought after one was.

In the invisible world, there appeared to be many ranks. There was always someone higher up (and farther off) than the next. When the inhabitants of the invisible world showed themselves on rare occasions, they appeared to be extremely prosperous and handsome. But this was a deception. They were, in fact, hideous beasts, who transformed themselves to appear attractive to the human eye. This was why they chose, for the most part, to remain hidden.

Sometimes they wanted to observe a potential captive up close. They would be in the same place with the person and just stare from across the room. Sometimes they would follow them from room to room, through walls, observing. In some of these settings, they made themselves visible to the person. While they posed as admirers, I knew they were vicious, ruthless. Some victims were flattered by the attention, some were apprehensive, and some were adversarial.

Ultimately, the captors observed to imprison. Once imprisoned, the hostage became the property of her huntsman. She lived in his domain. Over time, the creatures made their prey commit terrible, lustful acts. Some captives came to enjoy their descent.

The unobserved rulers talked amongst themselves, but rarely, if ever, directly to their quarry. They seemed to know all languages, although they spoke little. Often, they would go off to war to fight forces that were never identified. They were warriors. They rode horses and dressed in ancient vestments and lived in castles and palaces high in the mountains or other lofty places. Some were kings, some princes, and others just horsemen.

I can recall a rebel captive disappearing after causing much upset in the unseen world. Something happened, and she was never heard from again. The rumor was someone helped her escape, once and for all, to the other side. The secret beasts hated the woman and would forbid her name to be spoken ever again in their realm. They wanted to wipe out her memory. They sought to paint her as a myth—a fairy tale, a fable. But many refused to believe it. Others took up her mantle to set captives free after she left.

At age 24, I made a concerted effort to put the music aside. Its importance in my life waned, and the visions stopped. I would not truly enjoy music again until I was 43 and much to my surprise and delight, the Lord was ready to speak to me again through it, but this time for His personal pleasure.

It would be decades before I fully understood I was glimpsing the spiritual realm in these childhood visions. I was seeing scenes that would play out in my life and in the lives of others many years later. I came to realize I had been a captive at one point. I also began to suspect I was the rebel who would set many free and one day disappear.

September 29, 2009

Setting Captives Free

In the wee hours of the morning, I felt a deep pain in the sole of my left foot. The pain woke me up, and I knew it was the Lord. He wanted to talk. We talked for a while and then it came to me—a revelation from Him about what happened Sunday evening, after I came back from church!

I arrived home from church just in time to have a scheduled telephone conference with my cousin, Lydia. She and her family are facing some serious challenges, and she wanted Biblical counseling. She may have to leave her husband.

Lydia is a beautiful African American woman who lives in a massive home, in a wealthy suburb of Detroit. Her house is valued at nearly $1 million. She lives with her husband and two children. She looks like she has everything in the world. Yet, she does not have two red pennies to rub together.

Her insurance business is failing. And her mother, who is one of her employees, cannot help. Lydia's cell phone has been cut off. For years, she alone provided for her children and herself. Now she cannot.

Her wealthy husband, who is beset with spirits of covetousness and greed, provides only for himself. Although he is an extremely successful businessman, he pays the mortgage and nothing else. He is also unfaithful. He engaged in an illicit affair just 24 hours after they were married. Lydia hinted that he asked her to engage in perverted sexual acts to keep him interested in her. She discovered he had four other children after they were married. He provides for none of them.

Lydia and I talked and prayed for an hour. She received solid Biblical instruction, which she greatly appreciated. We agreed to talk again next Sunday at 4:00 p.m. We decided to confer every Sunday at the same time, until Christ took her through to the other side of the mess she was in.

As soon as I was done with Lydia, my dear friend Marci called. She was desperate for me to call her daughter Rebecca who, at that moment, was crying hysterically. Rebecca is a stunning woman of Jewish and Latin descent. She used to be a model.

She lives with her wealthy husband and two children in an expensive neighborhood in South Florida. They reside in a million-dollar home. Her husband practices criminal law.

After years of defending wealthy clients—some reported to be quite unsavory—in Colombia, South America, her husband has grown very rich. But Rebecca describes him as a controlling, selfish, tight-fisted man. Rebecca, 20 years his junior, is his trophy wife.

Married nearly a decade, Rebecca recently discovered her husband has been having a year-long affair with a Colombian woman. He refuses to leave his mistress, but also refuses to let Rebecca go. He, too, asked Rebecca to engage in perverted sexual acts with him and others to keep him. Rebecca wants out of the marriage.

Rebecca and I talked and prayed for a good while. I counseled her from the Scriptures. She was immensely grateful. Her husband was on a flight home from Columbia after she went ballistic upon learning about the affair.

I cautioned her not to be provoked into an argument. "Cry out to God, lean on Him, and ask for His direction and guidance. Then do whatever He instructs." I told her to quietly obey the Holy Spirit and not to announce her plans to the world. I assured her God would bring her out. I invited her, as I have on other occasions, to call me anytime, even in the wee hours of the morning if she had to.

Not more than an hour later, I was on the phone with another woman Sally, who was on the verge of suicide. A ministry partner gave me her phone number on Thursday and asked me to reach out to her. "Women need to talk to women!" he said in frustration. "I don't know what else to say to her."

I quickly learned that after 28 years of marriage, Sally's husband wants out. He has wanted to leave her for two years. She thought they had a good marriage. Presently, they live under the same roof, but he is hostile toward her. "He hates my guts," she wept.

Sally is a blonde, blue-eyed beauty from St. Thomas, Virgin Islands. She confessed to me that she is in shock and filled with anger, fear, and a deep sense of abandonment. She is scared about what the future holds for her. When I called her, she was on the Internet looking for a job. She must go back to work, but where and doing what?

After about 45 minutes of talking, Sally sobbed: "People keep talking to me about God, but all they say just bounces off my head. I don't know what to do with it. Tell me, what do I do with all this? I don't know what to do!"

Her inability to grasp godly instruction suggested she did not have a relationship with Christ. I explained the beautiful gift of salvation that Christ offers. I asked to lead her in a prayer. We would ask Christ to take hold of her life now. She agreed. Near the end of the prayer, she stopped reciting after me and took over. She asked God to help her, to heal her, to show her His way for her life.

At the end of our conversation, Sally was different from when we started! I could hear a lilt in her voice. She was no longer drowning in despair. She even laughed a few times. I gave her my telephone number and email address. That very night, I emailed her a pamphlet on how to develop her relationship with God. I told her I hope we become friends. She liked that.

Days later, as I thought about these three women, God began to connect the dots. All three women were physically beautiful, lived in large estate homes (mansions in two cases), and had been wooed, seduced into marrying wealthy, worthless husbands. The demonically inspired men were not husbands in any real sense. They were abusive, greedy, selfish, and in two cases, actively trying to lure their wives into becoming as perverted as they. Despite having it all, the women were profoundly unhappy, in deep bondage, and did not know the way to freedom.

I had seen these women before ... and many others like them! Where? Then it hit me—IN THE VISIONS THE LORD GAVE ME AS A CHILD! At the time, I thought it was all make-believe, just the meandering mind of an imaginative adolescent. I now realized the Lord was giving me glimpses of actual people in my life at age 55!

While I knew these invisible beings were hideous without ever seeing one, as a child I did not realize they were demon spirits. Nor did I recognize that the women these creatures were hell-bent on enslaving, defiling, and ultimately destroying, represented the bride of Christ!

But the biggest shocker of all was the sudden realization that I was "the dark one!" There was only one feature about the dark lady that I clearly remember from my childhood days. On occasion, she pinned up the sides of her long, dark hair in a swoop just above each ear. That was the same hairstyle I wore the Sunday I spoke to Lydia, Rebecca, and Sally! And, it was the exact same hairstyle I wore in a dream the Lord gave me four days earlier! I found it memorable because I almost never wear my hair that way.

The Lord was trying to help me understand that I was now living in the time I used to see in my childhood visions. He was also alerting me to the fact that I was the dark one. I was the rebel escapee He would use to set many captives free!

Chapter 7
My College Years—
Glimpsing My Hidden Benefactor and Protector

During my last year of high school, there was some doubt if I would go to college. No one in my immediate family had ever been. My teachers and counselors whispered among themselves, "It would be a shame if this one didn't go." After winning the state competition for creating a promotional ad to sell a line of refrigerators, I became the star of my co-op education class. As the top student, I was awarded one of the highly valued cooperative retail assignments.

I worked after school for Federal Department Stores as part of my business co-op class. I was placed in the men's underwear department. Selling men's underwear was not exactly what I had in mind when they offered me the job. The first time I ever saw a jock strap, I did not know which end was up. I was at a complete loss. For the life of me, and to the utter frustration of my supervisor, I also had trouble mastering the cash register. I never felt more incompetent. After three weeks, I quit.

The benefit of that job, though, is that it opened my eyes. I knew, come hell or high water, I had to go to college. I was not yet ready for the world of work, at least not that kind of work. If I did not go to college, I would surely starve to death.

I was obsessed with becoming an advertising executive. In the eleventh grade, I completely misinterpreted a book I read for my economics class, *The Hidden Persuaders* by Vance Packard. It was a negative book on the advertising industry. But I was utterly enthralled with the idea of making a living by "manipulating the minds of consumers." I applied to Michigan State University, known for its advertising program.

More than 40,000 students biked or walked the tree-lined paths of Michigan State. It was, and still is, a picturesque campus. In my day, few African Americans made it to this level, despite Affirmative Action. I was one of them.

Up until that time, I did not realize I had no real-life interactions with people outside my own race. All I knew about White people came from a handful of White teachers and television. The very first phone call back to my mother was a sad, revealing indictment on race relations in the United States: "Mom, you won't believe it! Guess what? White people curse!" Until I saw it with my own eyes and heard it with my own ears, I did not know White people did bad things.

I never saw them on the news getting arrested. They were always positively, wholesomely presented in the television shows I watched. I was flabbergasted to learn they used profanity. I had only heard Black people curse. Somewhere in my subconscious mind, I thought only Black people did bad things. I was 19 years old for goodness' sake!

I soon learned my White friends had been equally scammed. They were amazed I was smart and came from a loving, in-tact family. We began to explore one another's world. Several months into the school year, some closest to me timidly asked, "May I touch your hair?" I sported a short afro during four of my five years at MSU. Others confessed the only Black person they ever interacted with before me was the maid.

For the most part, my five years in college were one, big fat miracle after another. But I would not realize just how miraculous this period of my life was until many years later. The first miracle was to be accepted into college with an SAT score of 740! The only stipulation was that I had to take remedial reading and math courses during the summer before starting my regular classes in the fall. I passed those courses with flying colors.

There was a reason for the low SAT score: no preparation. I did not know students could prepare for SATs until many years later when I saw how my own daughter was prepared at her exclusive private school in South Carolina. She took SAT primers in the ninth, tenth, and eleventh grades. By the twelfth grade, she was ready and scored well.

In my case, we were told one day after class to show up at a specific address the next day with two, sharpened number two pencils. That was it. When they opened the double doors, we were all herded into a big room with other students from around the city. A man at the head of the room gave us a few instructions about the test, and we were off and running. I had no idea what I was doing.

The test was one big guessing game for me. It was amazing I even scored 740. I did not realize points were deducted for wrong answers. Years later, while reading a SAT primer in preparation for my daughter's first test, I realized I should not have guessed.

College expenses were provided through a whole series of inexplicable miracles. My family had no money to send me to college, so I applied for student loans and government grants, which I received each year. But I also received many private scholarships that I never applied for. They simply came to me, out of nowhere when I needed them.

During the third term of my freshman year, I applied to become a resident assistant, which was unheard of then. Those positions were reserved for juniors and seniors. But I was determined to become an RA, so I could receive free room and board. The loans, grants, and scholarships were not enough to cover all my expenses—tuition, books, housing, food, and other costs. My parents could not afford any of it, so I needed the job. Everyone was thrilled when I was chosen.

I was assigned to the Honors Floor in Case Hall. This floor was reserved for brainy, studious girls—mostly freshmen. Residents on this floor had to abide by certain rules. For example, there was no talking in the hallways after 8:30 p.m. This created a quiet environment for study.

Honors Floor??!! Those were some of the wildest, loudest young women I had ever seen in my life. Many of them did not go to bed until dawn. After a year of being awakened in the wee hours of the morning with, "Ray, you've got girls drinking on the roof again. Get 'em down ... NOW!"

I decided the free room and board was not worth the aggravation. I would have to find another income source, and I did.

My job as an advertising sales representative for the campus newspaper, *The State News*, funded a considerable share of my college education. It was one of the highest-paying jobs a student could get on campus. In my junior and senior years, I won a summer internship with one of Detroit's two daily newspapers, *The Detroit Free Press*. I sold advertising space to local retailers. Those internships proved to be quite lucrative, covering a substantial portion of my school expenses those years.

During my last year of college, as a graduate student, I was offered a summer internship with an advertising agency in Chicago—D'Arcy MacManus and Masius. Although it did not pay as much as the *Detroit Free Press,* and I used most of the money I earned that summer to live in Chicago, the experience was invaluable.

During the school year, I worked as an assistant to a professor in the Communications Department. The assistantship paid $400 a month. I remember the job with great fondness because it paved the way for one of the biggest miracles of my life. I still cannot tell the story without crying.

Suffice it to say, I had drifted far from the Lord and the church during my college years. I was deeply hostile toward the things of God. But I did not know it until I accidentally stumbled into a Bible study one night. I never darkened the entrance of a church during my entire stint at MSU, although God gave me profound reasons to seek Him.

Following is an excerpt from my prayer journal, recorded 20 years after I left college, when the Lord finally connected the dots between the extraordinary funding of my education and His call on my life.

May 28, 1997

Two Extraordinary College Memories

During my time alone with the Lord this morning, I thought about two profound occurrences in my life. This was strange because both happened more than 20 years ago when I was in college. I thought about the first time I ever experienced God. Despite this remarkable encounter, I did not associate the event with God until years later.

I also thought about the first time I knew beyond a shadow of a doubt that God saw and knew me. This event was even more astonishing than the first. Yet, it would be another eight years before I finally acknowledged God—cried out to Him and invited Him into my life.

My First Encounter with God

I always kept up with world events. In college, I read the newspaper every day. Although our newspaper was delivered in the morning, on this day, I did not have time to read it until the evening. After I had completed my classes and assignments, I crawled into bed with the newspaper.

I read one heart-wrenching article after another. A couple hung their baby upside down in a closet for days until he died. Hal Lindsey's book, The Great Late Planet Earth, *had just been published. The newspaper gave readers a frightening preview of where the world was headed. By the sixth article, I could not take any more.*

I just wept. I sobbed uncontrollably. I rocked back and forth in my bed. Holding myself, I kept repeating, "I don't belong here! I don't belong here!" The world was just too mean, dark, and evil.

Suddenly, an irrational fear came over me. Terror gripped my heart. I was afraid in a way I had never been before. I looked at the Bible sitting on my nightstand. My mother had packed it in my suitcase the first year I went off to college. I discovered the book when I unpacked my bags. I knew she put it there. During those five years, I moved several times, and wherever I went, I took the Bible out and put it on my nightstand. But I never opened it.

That night, I grabbed it. The book fell open to Psalm 23. "The Lord is my Shepherd; I shall not want ...." I read the whole Psalm once, just once. In an instant, the tears and rocking ceased. Fear fell off. An inexplicable calm washed over me, and I slipped into a peaceful sleep.

The next day, I told my roommate Brenda Flanagan—and anyone else who would listen—about the incident. No one seemed to grasp the specialness of what happened. I could not make them understand how fearful and crazed I was one moment and how perfectly tranquil I was the next. And all I did was read a simple passage of Scripture. What happened? At the time, I had no idea God's Word had spoken to my heart and mind, setting me free from the spirits of fear and despair.

That was my first taste of God. He was making Himself known to me as a gentle Comforter. His consolation was a very real, tangible phenomenon. In our next encounter, a few months later, He revealed Himself as an apt Provider.

May 28, 1997

When I Finally Knew God Knew Me

I was in my senior year at Michigan State. I thought I was going to a party and ended up at a Bible study. I was mad. I was all dressed up to party—rare for me—and walked into a house, where everyone was sitting on the floor in a big circle with Bibles in their laps. I wanted to leave but was talked into staying. I joined the circle. They were studying Malachi 3.

In my lost state, I questioned with utter disdain every exchange. "So, you talk to God, huh? And He talks back? Yeah, yeah ... I see. So, you're telling me God (I spoke His name mockingly) says that if I give back to Him 10 percent of whatever He gives me, He will bless me so much that I won't be able to contain it?" I did not believe any of it.

"God says you can test Him in this and see," a young man named Larry challenged me. By the time I left the study, I had decided to test God. I fully intended to prove them wrong.

For the entire school year, I sent $40 a month back to my mother to give to her church since I was making $400 a month. (Not surprisingly, I did not have a church home in college.) Giving $40 a month did not work on paper. By my calculations, I would always be short the $40 (and more) because every penny counted during those years. I sent the money anyway.

Soon cards arrived in the mail from relatives I had not heard from in years. I did not know they even knew I was in college! They always enclosed cash—$5, $10 or $20. I met every expense the entire school year. I was never short. It did not occur to me that God was in any of it. Sending my $40 tithe to my mother's church became like paying a regular bill. I forgot it was a tithe.

Almost a year from the day I started tithing, something extraordinary happened. I was a financially strapped graduate student, and I needed to register for classes. I sat all day at the kitchen table in my PJs, wondering how I would register the next day with virtually no money.

Hunched over my paper and calculator, I tried to figure out exactly how much I needed to start the process. I included in that figure what it would cost to wash and dry two loads of laundry every other week for the full term. I calculated down to the dollar, being as frugal as possible. I needed something like $3,219—a fortune to me.

Who could help? No one in my family had that kind of money sitting around. With tears stinging my eyes, I finally resolved to drop out of college, find a job, work, save my money, and reenroll the following year. The idea killed me. It was totally against everything I had planned and hoped for myself! Many left colleges and never returned, despite all their good intentions. Would this happen to me?

"Ray, Ray ... what's wrong with you?" Brenda, my roommate, was yelling at me from the back bedroom. "Telephone!" Apparently, she had been calling me. I was so lost in my problems, I had not heard her. I did not want her to see me crying, so I quickly wiped my eyes with my pajama top.

"Hello?" I picked up the wall phone in the kitchen.

"Hi, this is Cindy from the Communications Department. I have good news for you. We decided to increase your assistantship from quarter time to halftime." That meant they had just doubled my time and pay! "We also made it retroactive from the beginning of the year." I could not believe what I was hearing! "If you hurry, you can pick up the check today at the Administration Office. But come here first to pick up the paperwork."

I ripped off my pajama top. Buttons flew everywhere. I changed into my street clothes, jumped in my orange Vega and sped off to the Communications Department.

Cindy gave me a set of multicolored papers to take to the Administration Building. I could see the structure from Cindy's office. It closed at 4:00 p.m. It was just about that time. I jumped in my car and was there in two minutes.

I sprinted up the wide concrete steps. The two big glass doors were locked, but I could see a lone woman inside. I banged on the entrance. She shook her head and mouthed the words, "We're closed." I dropped to my knees with my hands cupped, pleading, begging. She rolled her eyes and came to let me in.

"Thank you!" I kept repeating. I handed her my papers. She took them, went to a tall file cabinet behind the counter and pulled out a folder. She then sat down at her desk and began to type out a check. She put the check in an envelope and sealed it.

"Now, we're closed!" She handed me the envelope. I thanked her profusely as she escorted me to the door and locked it behind me.

I was beyond myself with excitement. I had no idea what to expect. All I wanted was enough money to register the next day. I would worry about the rest later. I raced to my car and ripped open the envelope.

There, before my eyes, was the fortune I needed—$3,219. It was the exact amount, to the dollar, I had calculated hours earlier! I was instantly elated and ashamed in equal measure. I was elated because I knew I would finish graduate school. God would make sure of it. I was *ashamed because I was certain He saw every nasty thing I had ever done. I wept freely on my steering wheel.*

Because of that incident, I became a fervent tither before ever becoming a believer in Christ. God captured my wallet before He captivated my heart. In time, I would invest millions of dollars in His kingdom.

Clearly, the Lord had His merciful hand on my miserable head. But it would have been impossible to convince me of it at the time. In my college days, I thought I was the captain of my ship. I held the reins to my life. If anything good was to come from my life, it would be up to me and me alone to make it happen.

Therefore, it was crucial for me to apply myself. And apply myself, I did. I soared in my studies, completely motivated by fear of failure. I can recall memorizing whole textbooks. Failure was not an option. I would let too many people down—family, professors, and sponsors. There was no room for distractions.

Stephen Collins, an Urban Planning and Development student, whom I met early in college, once asked me on a date. Years later, he told me I informed him "I did not come to college to date. I came to college to learn."

While I had a vague memory of that exchange, he remembered it in vivid detail: "You were dressed in your PJs, preparing for your finals. You'd been reading all day. We were in the study hall on your dorm floor. You dismissed me with a flick of your hand and went back to cramming." He told me I scared away all the young men. I had no idea how unapproachable I was. I was too consumed with my schoolwork to care.

College was highly competitive, and I was determined to finish at the top. Once, I received a "B" on a paper, but I knew I deserved an "A." I poured everything I had into that paper. The lower grade haunted me the entire weekend.

Finally, I made an appointment to speak with the professor. His explanation was simple: "I don't give A's." The injustice of this frustrated me to no end, but I was determined to win him over. I pressured him to give me extra assignments to make up for the lower grade, which he agreed to. In the end, I received a perfect 4.0 in his course.

In 1976, I graduated with the highest honors—in the top two percent of the nation—with a Bachelor of Arts Degree in Communications. I was also named "Woman of the Year." Twelve short months later, when I completed my master's degree in advertising with a minor in marketing, I achieved the same distinction, only this time I was named "Person of the Year."

In graduate school, I deliberately carried twice the normal number of credits, so I could complete my master's degree in one year to save on room and board. Time was money. At the end of it all, my grade point average was 3.98 out of 4.0. My GPA, coupled with my gender and race, made me highly marketable. When I graduated, I had nine job offers.

Clearly, God had plans for my life. He provided for me in countless extraordinary ways during my college years, although I never once acknowledged His provision. He opened doors for me that I could not open for myself. But the Lord was not only a capable Provider in my college days, He was also my Protector.

I was a sophomore in college when, one weekend, I drove to Flint, Michigan to visit my Cousin Debbie. She and I have always been close. She did not go to college. Even though she became pregnant at 16, she managed to finish high school.

She has the most incredible memory. She can still recite our family's telephone numbers, dating back to the early 1960s, or tell me exactly what I ordered in a restaurant 15 years after the fact, or recall what I wore on my fourteenth birthday. I often wondered what she would have become had she not gotten pregnant and had money to go to college.

Debbie and I went to a club that night. We both had a drink. I danced two dances with a guy who appeared pleasant. Unlike most of the other guys, he wore a suit. It was gray and fit nicely. He wore a white, open-collar shirt. No tie.

We were not there long when Debbie decided she wanted to go home. The guy, whom I had just met, promised to take me home when I was ready. Debbie knew him distantly. She gave him her address and left. An hour later, I was also ready to go. I would have to drive back to MSU in the morning. We left. I should have known this guy had more in mind than just a dance when he kept staring at my breasts. I had ignored it.

I did not know the way back to my cousin's house. The man drove leisurely for what seemed like a long time. Unfamiliar with the area, it never dawned on me that he was taking me somewhere else. Finally, I realized something was wrong.

"Where are we?" I asked.

"Take off your clothes," he gently ordered. He had parked the car in an unfamiliar driveway.

"Take off my clothes? Are you crazy?" I balked.

"What if I insist?" he leaned toward me.

"What if you insist?" I repeated, shocked.

"I INSIST!" he screamed.

I nearly jumped out of my seat. Panic set in. He waited a few seconds, then got out and walked to the rear of the car. My mind raced. *Should I try to jump in the driver's seat and get away? I would have to move fast. Should I lock him out and blow the horn? What if he broke the glass before anyone could help me? What if nobody came?* He was now pacing back and forth at the rear of the car in the driveway. *Is he having second thoughts?* Then I had a thought of my own.

No man would rape a vomiting woman. The moment he got back in the car, I starting to choke and gag as if I was on the verge of throwing up. I pretended to hyperventilate. That scared him. I told him only milk could stop it. I do not know why I said that. It just popped into my head. My whole goal at that moment was to get around people. He started the ignition. It was working! We finally made our way to a street populated with pedestrians and cars.

Should I try to jump out at a light? I was sucking and blowing out air at a faster and faster rate. Finally, he stopped, parked the car and ran inside a McDonald's.

Was this my chance? Take the car and go! Go where? I do not know where I am! Will he tell the police I stole his car? Will they believe him or me? He rushed back and thrust a milk carton in my face. I gulped it from the carton.

"You have to take me home," I said in between gasps.

He started the car. Ten minutes later, I was beating on my cousin's door. I was a total wreck. He had dropped me off and sped away. I told her what happened. We talked about how stupid it was to split up and how we would never do that again. I hardly slept that night. In the morning, I drove back to campus still shaken.

I was not prepared for what happened next. Debbie called me at school two days later.

"Rachelle, you know that guy who tried to rape you?" *How could I forget!* "They found him dead last night! He was in a car crash. It was just him. His car was totaled. They found it wrapped around a tree. No one can figure out how it happened."

"Are you positive? How can you be sure it was him?" I asked.

"Trust me. It's him. It's in the paper. I'm looking at it right now." We chatted about other things then rang off.

While I was not physically violated that night, the incident took its toll on me in other ways. For weeks, I only left my dorm room if I had to. For months, whenever I heard the words, "I insist," my stomach knotted and churned. It did not matter who said it or how it was said. Those two words had the power to thrust me back to that night.

A profound gleaning from that unfortunate episode came years later. The lesson was more valuable than anything I ever learned at MSU: *"Do not touch the Lord's anointed ones. Do My prophets no harm,"* meant to treat everyone with the utmost respect because none of us knows who the stranger standing next to us is in heavenly realms. The person could even be an angel. I had no idea who I was becoming in the Lord, nor did this guy. There was a call on my life no one, including I, could have possibly understood.

Looking back, the incident probably played an influential part in my refusal to date during my college years and my intense focus on my studies. With no distractions, I could finish at the top of my class. My grades also won me a prized summer internship with a prestigious advertising firm in Chicago.

My Debut at D'Arcy

My introduction into the real world of advertising was not selling advertising space for the *Detroit Free Press;* it was my summer internship with D'Arcy, MacManus and Masius. I was assigned to the Standard Oil and Gerber Baby Food accounts. I was 23 years old, and I had made it to the big leagues. My dream of becoming an advertising executive was coming true.

It was the American Association of Advertising Agencies that opened this door for me and six other minorities. The advertising business was a closed industry then. It still may be. That meant it was like a country club. A person had to be invited in. So naturally, there were not many African Americans who made a living in advertising.

I had already decided when I graduated with my master's degree the following spring, I would move to Chicago. While Madison Avenue was truly the "Big Leagues" for anyone interested in a career in advertising, Chicago was more my style, my pace—a less expensive, cleaner New York. I easily envisioned living the life I always wanted to live in Chicago. The Windy City was so much more attractive and cosmopolitan than seedy Detroit.

Summer lodging accommodations were made for us on the downtown urban campus of Roosevelt University, which was within walking distance to all the leading advertising agencies. The campus was also close to The Magnificent Mile, where some of the world's finest retail stores and restaurants were located. It was going to be a glorious summer.

I remember my first day at D'Arcy as if it were yesterday. I made a debut I will never forget. I spent the weekend before shopping for just the right suit, my first ever business suit. I settled on an evergreen cotton skirt with a matching jacket. I wore a bright white, starched open-collar blouse underneath. Never had I taken such pains with my appearance. I wanted everything to be perfect for the first day of my first real job.

I was scheduled to report at 9:00 a.m. sharp to Marshall Ottenfeld, the Executive Director of Research at D'Arcy. D'Arcy's offices were in the Standard Oil Building. I knew I could walk to the building in 15 minutes because I had made a trial run the day before. Early Monday morning, with a stomach filled with butterflies, I made my way to the plaza just outside the Standard Oil Building.

As I stood looking up at the building, my reaction was the same as the prior day. I had never seen a taller skyscraper. There was nothing in Detroit to compare to it. I entered the busy lobby from the street level. Mr. Ottenfeld's office was on the eighty-first floor. For the life of me, I could not find the bank of elevators to the eighty-first floor. I only saw even ranges of numbers. No problem. I decided to take the elevator to the eightieth floor. Then, I would just walk up a flight of stairs.

I took the elevator to the eightieth floor. As soon as it opened, and I stepped out, I saw the receptionist behind a large desk. I checked with her first.

"Hello, my name is Rachelle Hood. And I'm here to see a Dr. Ottenfeld." I was all smiles.

"Oh, honey, he's on the eighty-first floor. You'll have to go down and come back up."

As I turned to go back the way I came, I spotted the door to the stairwell. I looked back at the receptionist. She was not looking. I dashed through the door. It slammed behind me. I sprinted up the flight of stairs to the eighty-first floor. I walked over to the door and pulled the handle. It was locked. I looked at my watch. It was now 8:20 a.m.

I decided to go back to the eightieth floor, go down to the lobby, and somehow find the right bank of elevators, which is what I should have done in the first place. I ran back down the stairs to the eightieth floor. I pulled on the door handle. It was locked. I looked at my watch again. No problem. If I ran fast, I could make it.

I started running downstairs, flight after flight. There was no air conditioning in the stairwell. The heat was almost suffocating. I took off my jacket. Down, down, down I went. Completely out of breath, huffing and puffing, I stopped to assess my progress. Seventy-four! I had gone down only six flights! Sweat now poured from my forehead. Running mascara burned my eyes. I could also feel wet drops of perspiration underneath my arms. I checked my blouse. Oh, no—circle stains underneath both arms!

With sudden clarity, I realized I was not going to make it! What had I been thinking? This was my first day on the job! I had wanted it to be so perfect. Surely, they would fire me for being so late or too stupid. I felt I had let down every Black person in America. People like me were not expected to make it, and I just confirmed everyone's expectations. I was beyond despondent. Dragging my jacket on the floor, I started slowly down the stairs, balling my eyes out.

A few more flights down, I spotted a phone on the wall. I ran to it. It had no dial buttons. I put the receiver to my ear.

"May I help you?" I heard a woman's voice. It was music to my ears. I started blubbering in the phone.

"I'm, I'm ... stuck in the stairwell!" I could not stop crying.

"On what floor, Ma'am?" I looked around.

"I'm on the seventy-second floor ... and I'm late! I'm late! It's my first day on the job, and I'm late!" More sobs.

"Someone will be there to get you right away!" Panic replaced her crisp professional voice.

I waited a few minutes. Finally, I heard faint, muffled voices on the other side of the door. They grew louder and louder. Suddenly, the door burst open! A crowd had gathered behind the man with a walkie-talkie. People were straining their necks to see what all the commotion was about.

"Okay, Bill," the man spoke into the walkie-talkie. "Yes! Yes, I found her! I got her!" The security guard escorted me to the odd bank of elevators, located one level below street level. These would take me to the eighty-first floor.

Could you have made a worse impression? I kept asking myself. But guess what? At 9:00 a.m. sharp, I was sitting in Marshall Ottenfeld's office, albeit completely disheveled.

It was in this same office something odd would occur near the end of my internship that I would not understand for years. The strange event was another glimpse into a prophetic call on my life. It was like a bell ringing for me somewhere in the distant future. But at that juncture in my life, the incident was just plain weird.

I was working alone in Dr. Ottenfeld's office, on the opposite side of his desk when suddenly I looked up and spoke aloud: "It's too much!" The three words just spilled out of me. I did not know why I said them or what they referred to. The second I spoke the words, the office door opened. A clerk from Human Resources walked in and handed me my paycheck. I thanked her. She left, closing the door behind her.

I opened the envelope to glance at the check. The words, "It's too much!" again tumbled from my mouth. We were always paid the same amount. But the amount of this check was too much.

I later questioned Dr. Ottenfeld about the new amount. He had his secretary investigate. I learned that taxes should not have been taken out of my previous checks since I was an intern. D'Arcy returned the multiple deductions in one check, making it more than all the others.

For years, I pondered my speaking that incident before it occurred. I rarely spoke about it to anyone. I was at a loss to explain it to myself.

Marshall Ottenfeld turned out to be one of the brightest, nicest men I could ever hope to meet. He worked years on his scientific theory, *Belief Dynamics*, which he felt had the potential to revolutionize the advertising industry. He invited me to help him with his research and was kind enough to include my name as a contributor on the papers that he later published. I was so impressed by his work I chose to write my masters' thesis on the same subject. Basically, the theory is that we act on our beliefs, according to what we believe is true. While Dr. Ottenfeld desired to use the theory to sell products, I learned later that the theory applied to all aspects of human life.

I not only worked directly for Dr. Ottenfeld, I also received numerous assignments from others on his team. His staff was comprised of all women. They took me under their wings and generously poured into me. I learned a lot about advertising and business etiquette. I was included in the social gatherings at their homes. The women were not only smart, but also kind, helpful, and patient. One, Pat Cafferetta, later rose to become President and CEO of one of the most prestigious advertising agencies in Chicago.

My Benefactor used these kind people to introduce me to a professional career in advertising. Their coaching and grooming made my transition from college to the business world smooth.

One night, while lying in my bunk bed at Roosevelt, thinking how lucky I was for my internship, I felt a lump on my right breast. I made a mental note to see a doctor right away. One of the women at the office gave me her doctor's number. He saw me a few days later and confirmed I had a large tumor in my breast. It would have to be removed. Surgery could be done on an out-patient basis to save money. My summer earnings would cover the expense.

The doctor attributed the tumor to birth control pills. It was the stupidest thing. I had been taking birth control pills for six months just in case I found a boyfriend. I had no prospects—not one. I just thought I was due. Surely, one would pop up sooner or later, and when he did, I wanted to be ready. Now this.

The doctor scheduled the surgery. The day of the operation, I was instructed to wait at the corner of two cross streets downtown. A shuttle bus would come to take me to Roosevelt Hospital. I did not tell a soul. I was in the middle of my internship, and I did not want to make waves at work or home. I just took the morning off. My plan was to be back at work that afternoon.

The bus showed up on time. The driver dropped me off in front of the hospital. I checked in with the receptionist. A Black man in green scrubs came out to greet me. He took me to the back. "Okay, change your clothes in there." He pointed to a locker. "And then meet me back here." He handed me a gown and left.

The letter I wrote to my college roommate Brenda about the incident is excerpted below. It explains what happened next:

I opened the locker and got in. I shut the door behind me. There was a little shelf inside. I was barely able to change my clothes in such tight quarters, but I managed to take off everything. I rolled up my panties into a tight little ball and dropped them in a corner. I picked up the gown, and after much effort, managed to slip my arms through it. I tied the strings in a loose knot at the back of my neck. I was ready.

I pushed the door. It would not budge! I pushed again. It didn't move.

"Oh, my gosh! I'm locked in!" I whispered. Don't panic. Don't panic, I told myself. I pressed my face against the slits in the locker. I could see straight ahead, but I had no peripheral vision. I waited for someone, anyone to pass in my line of sight. I heard footsteps.

"Sir! Sir!" I called from the locker. The man looked up, down, and around. He could not figure out where the voice was coming from. He disappeared. I tried again.

"Miss! Miss!" Again, the same thing. "I'm here! I'm here!" I cried. She stopped, looked around. Puzzled, she wandered on. I did not know what to do.

Then I heard over the hospital PA system: "Will Miss Hood please report to surgery. Miss Hood, please report to surgery." Now, I started to panic! What if I missed my surgery?

Suddenly, I saw the man in the green scrubs. Apparently, he was looking for me. I started yelling and kicking the locker as hard as I could. He came over and opened it. He could not speak. He tried, but he just couldn't. He was laughing too hard.

"What, what ... are you doing in there?" He finally managed to ask.

"You told me to get dressed in here!" He shook his head in denial. "Yes, you did," I shrieked.

He eventually got me on the gurney and wheeled me into surgery, where not one but two surgeons and an anesthesiologist were waiting. The anesthesiologist was African American.

By that time, I was a mess. The anesthesiologist injected a fluid to numb my breast. The fluid felt cold inside of me. While I experienced no pain, I was fully aware of the scalpel opening my skin. Looking up at the ceiling lights, I could feel the blood coursing down the side of my breast. It was too much. I could not stop crying. I was too upset. Nothing the doctors could do or say stemmed my tears.

"Your crying is making your blood pump too fast," one doctor complained. "You have to calm down. You have to stop crying."

I wanted to. But I could not. "I have to get my mind on something else," I said. "Maybe if I sing a song," I offered. (Yes, I did.)

"Okay, do that. Do that." The doctors were willing to try anything.

You will not believe the next thing that came out of my mouth: "I need someone to sing with me."

Well, these two surgeons were not about to sing. They both looked at the anesthesiologist. To this day, I cannot believe he agreed to sing with me. He was probably thinking, anything—ANYTHING—to get this over with and get her out of here! But if he was thinking that, no one could tell.

"What do you want to sing?" he asked. He rubbed my forehead as I thought. (Okay, are you sitting down?)

Suddenly, I broke into: "I LEFT A GOOD JOB IN THE CITY! WORKIN' FOR THE MAN EVERY NIGHT AND DAY ... BIG WHEELS KEEP ON TURNING. PROUD MARY KEEPS ON BURNING. ROLLING, ROLLING ... ROLLING ON THE RIVER .... TOOT, TOOT, TOOT, TOOT, TOOT, TOOT, TOOT, TOOT, TOOT, TOOT, TOOT, TOOT!"

Where that came from, I do not know. I did not even like the song. I did not know I even knew the lyrics until I started singing. But he joined me. He and Tina got me through. The anesthesiologist disappeared right after surgery. Bless his heart. I never saw him again.

I left the hospital and went straight to the office as planned. But when the women found out about the surgery, they packed up my things and sent me home. I was not to return until the next day. My mother was horrified that I did not tell anyone about the procedure until it was over.

Only God knew, years after that incident I would leave "a good job in the city" to answer that distant bell that had been ringing for me to "come."

Chapter 8
Ascending the Corporate Ladder

The folks at D'Arcy offered me a job at the end of my internship. I could finish school and return the following spring. As much as I enjoyed my experience there, I turned them down. I decided I wanted to work for Needham, Harper & Steers.

I chose Needham because it had so many prestigious packaged-goods accounts—all well-known, recognizable brands. My starting annual salary in 1977 was $17,000, which felt like a fortune to me since I had been poor all my life.

I found a one-bedroom, one-bathroom apartment at 3600 N. Lakeshore Dr. I turned it into an 800-square foot showplace. I lived on the twenty-sixth floor, overlooking parts of Lake Michigan. I was living my dream. But it quickly morphed into a nightmare.

My official title was Account Assistant. I was assigned to Campbell Soup, working on V-8 Vegetable Juice and Swanson Canned Chicken. I supported two people—both account executives. The first was a young man, less than two years my senior, Grant Castle. He was the nephew of actress Cloris Leachman and a delight. He took me home to meet his family back east after we were snowed in by an unexpected blizzard. A group of us had traveled east to attend a colleague's wedding.

The second account executive was a man named Thomas Branson. Thomas had a previous career in the military. He was married to a stay-at-home wife and mom. Thomas was probably one of Needham's oldest account executives. I quickly realized he and I would have the same title in 12 months if I did not screw up. I sensed I represented everything Thomas resented. I was young, a working woman, and Black—someone who most likely came riding in on the coattails of Affirmative Action.

Thomas did not try to hide his resentment. On his way to lunch, he would slam SAMI Warehouse Inventory Books on my desk and tell me to write a report. Once he rolled his eyes and threw a pencil across the room because I misread some data. Grant showed me how to read and analyze SAMI data. Thomas taught me nothing.

Reporting to Thomas took a tremendous toll on my self-esteem and self-confidence. I dreaded coming to work in the morning. My stomach would tie into knots as I rode the bus to work. The closer I got to the office, the tighter the knots became. I would stay late every night, trying to teach myself new things.

Late one night, by stealth, I discovered that each of my five peers, all White, were offered $18,000 a year to start. Moreover, each had received a $2,000 raise after just six months of service. I came in at $17,000 a year and was given $1,000 raise after nine months.

Was this because they worked on more lucrative accounts? Was it because they came from more prestigious schools? Had Thomas said something to torpedo my career? Or was it ... discrimination? I could not say for sure, but my eyes were permanently opened to the fact that I was somehow perceived as different from the others and of lesser value.

One night, I had all but given up. I sat in the middle of my living room floor and wept. I sobbed like a baby. I rocked and wept and cried out to God. It was not a prayer in any real sense. I just kept repeating as I rocked and wept, "God help me. God help me. God help me."

The next night I stayed late at work again, but this time for a different reason. After months of ill treatment, I decided to act. I gently tapped on Dick Needham's open office door. His father founded the agency a generation earlier. He motioned me in and invited me to sit.

I could not even look him in the eyes. With my head down and in a quiet voice, I told him that I had made a terrible mistake.

"What is that?" he asked.

"I am not cut out for the advertising business," I said. "I'm not sure why I ever thought I was." I told him about my experience at Needham thus far. I blamed only myself.

After I had spoken, he was quiet. For a moment, we sat in silence. Then he said, "I want you to go home and get a good night's rest. Then tomorrow, I want you to come back fresh and ready to work. Leave everything to me."

The next day when I walked through the agency door, I was redirected to another office. I was no longer on Campbell Soup. I had been reassigned to the Wm. Wrigley Jr. account. I would be working on Hubba Bubba Bubble Gum.

Jim Fasules, a spirited, kind-hearted advertising veteran, was the executive vice president over the business. Gene Yovetich, the account director, reported to him. Karen Wagenachnt, my account supervisor, reported to Gene. They continued the grooming started at D'Arcy.

The gum business grew, and soon I found myself making Hubba Bubba commercials out West with The Gumfighter, Don Collier, and veteran actor Dub Taylor. I savored every minute of it. I did not know work could be so much fun.

Two years later, having learned a great deal about commercial production on Hubba Bubba, I was reassigned to the McDonald's Children's account, working for Don Dempsey. He and I became very good friends. My daughter, Ryan, was named after Don's girlfriend at the time, Mary Ryan, who was my best friend at Needham.

Don was a wild, crazy, irreverent man, filled with all kinds of off-the-wall ideas. Nevertheless, Paul Schrage, the head of Marketing at McDonald's at the time, loved him. They were golfing buddies. Everybody loved Don, which boded extremely well for my career.

That first year working for Don, our team produced more than 30 Ronald McDonald television and radio commercials. It seemed I was always in

Los Angeles, being wined and dined by the production houses. In a few more years, I would lose my svelte figure.

After five years with Needham, Harper & Steers, I joined the Chicago office of Young & Rubicam. It was time for God to do a new thing in my life. The honeymoon was over. At Y&R, I would be immersed in massive amounts of work and be required to work at an insane pace just to keep my head above water. Although My Defender was still present, He would now move into the shadows while I learned some valuable lessons.

Y&R may have been the largest advertising agency in the world when I joined its ranks in 1982. My annual salary jumped $10,000 to roughly $50,000. Two years later, I was making more than $60,000 a year.

I was assigned to Del Monte Canned Food. Del Monte was based in San Francisco, so I spent a lot of time on the West Coast during those years. My weight ballooned from the stress. Some nights, I never went home. My boss could leave me at my desk in the evening and find me there the next morning in the same clothes.

After about a year with Y&R, I was asked to work on a new business assignment. We would be competing for the $11 million Tupperware account. I would be responsible for pulling together the business case, from which the marketing and advertising campaigns would be developed. We would be competing with other agencies. I would have to do this work on top of my regular account work. Although I was already working extraordinarily long hours, I agreed.

Finally, the time came to make the pitch. I was invited to participate. We all felt we did well. A few days later, I heard shouts in the corner offices. We won the account. Two days later, I found a set of car keys on my desk after I returned from lunch. I had been given a company car. I was also made Account Supervisor over New Business ... *sans* a raise.

Marrying Mike: God's Jackhammer

My job at Y&R played a significant role in my failed marriage. When I started at Y&R, I had been married only three years. My husband, Mike, resented my career. Looking back, how could I blame him? My career was all-consuming, which left little time for him or our daughter.

I met Mike on a blind date when I worked for Needham. I was 27 years old, and for the first time in my life, I started to feel something was missing. One night, I did one of those half-prayers to God. I asked if He heard me, could He send someone into my lonely world. God always gives us what we need. My life needed a complete demolition. God would use Mike to dismantle every barrier that stood between me and Him.

A day after my prayer for a partner, Carol Moberg, an acquaintance in Needham's Media Department, told me she had a friend she wanted me to meet. Within days, Mike and I met for lunch. He was a handsome, tall, and dark mental health therapist. Neither of us felt sparks on our first date. But we agreed to go out again.

For our next date, he talked me into going roller skating. I had not roller skated since I was a preteen. Mike had the audacity to show up at Needham in a long, raggedy bus from his job with the words, "Newman's Residential Home for the Mentally Ill" emblazoned on both sides. Surprisingly, that was not a turnoff. It showed guts.

He also brought six clients along on our first date, all young Black men—another gutsy move. These men appeared perfectly normal, but Mike assured me they could go nuts under the right circumstances. I boarded the bus and off we went.

They were all expert skaters and skated wild circles around me. They did things on skates I did not know human beings could do. They helped improve my skills that night. By the end of the evening, I looked as if I had skated all my life. I cannot remember having so much fun. I decided

I liked Mike. He made me laugh. In four months, we would marry, and he would make me cry.

I was three months pregnant with Ryan when Mike and I married. (After that breast tumor episode, I vowed never to touch birth control pills again!) I attempted to go through with an abortion at a local clinic. I sat in long line on a long sofa with several long-faced women. Mike did not say a word. The decision was solely mine. I was given a set of papers to read and sign. I could not bring myself to sign the papers.

One by one, the women were summoned behind the closed door. Every time it was my turn, I would go to the end of the line. After a few hours of this, Mike took the clipboard from my hand and handed it back to the lady behind the desk. "We're going to have this baby," he announced to both of us simultaneously.

He gathered up my things and escorted me out of the clinic. The level of relief I received from that decision stunned me. I had not eaten in days. We walked to a nearby Burger King, and I ate two Whoppers.

The next few months flew by. Mike made all the marriage arrangements because I was too depressed to make any decisions. I did not want to get married, but it seemed the right thing to do. It never occurred to me that I could be a single mom.

A native of Chicago, Mike knew his way around town. His friend Ilene Barber arranged for us to be married by Reverend George Ed Riddick in the small chapel of Operation PUSH. Sadly, neither Mike nor I was affiliated with a church.

Mike's best friend and his wife, who later divorced, served as our two witnesses. My mother and father and Mike's mother and aunt were also present. None of my siblings attended the wedding, neither did Mike's two sisters, who lived in Chicago. Mike's mother would die within two years of our union. He never knew his dad.

Decades after our marriage, I saw a photograph on Ryan's kitchen counter of Mike and me cutting our wedding cake. Above the scene, she had added a caption in a thought cloud. It read: "Houston, we have a problem."

Three weeks into our marriage, I felt I had made the biggest mistake of my life. While Mike and I agreed from the outset that we would not discuss religion or politics in our home, we found so many other things to fight about. I believe I cried more during our four years of marriage than when I was a baby. Our personalities and upbringings were so different.

Every time I heard Mike's key in the lock, I would start to tremble. He was like Dr. Jekyll/Mr. Hyde. I never knew what would tick him off. He had a hair-trigger temper. He would fly into rages, and I would not know why. It was nothing for Mike to curse at me nonstop—up, down, and around.

Before our marriage, only my grade school tormentor Lessie had ever cursed me. Mike's profanity-laced tirades drove me crazy. Growing up, my father would not even let us say "dang" in our house. Mike was verbally abusive and sometimes physically abusive. Never one to run or cower, I fought back.

As dysfunctional as our relationship turned out to be, I was always struck by something I did in my childhood that portended my marriage to Mike and underscored my propensity toward the prophetic. In my fifth-grade music class at Angel Elementary School, I used to practice writing my name on the back of my notebook covers. But I did not write Rachelle Hood—my name at the time. I wrote Rachelle Phillips. This was not a childhood crush. I did not know a soul named Phillips.

In my young mind, no other last name went as well with Rachelle than Phillips. So, I decorated the back cover of my notebooks with the name Rachelle Phillips. I drew little hearts around every place I wrote the name. This was from a little girl, who would grow up without a single romantic bone in her whole body. Interestingly, Michael's last name was Phillips!

After we married, I learned his real name was Wiley Renee Phillips. He named himself Michael, from the Hebrew name Mikha′el, which means, "who is like God?" But Michael turned out to be more like God's wily nemesis.

One morning, after wrestling on the foyer floor over something foolish, I decided physically fighting back was not the answer. I can still see the terror on Ryan's little face, standing there, watching; and she was just two years old! In desperation, I finally turned to God.

I started attending a little neighborhood church within the Church of God in Christ (COGIC) denomination. I took Ryan every Sunday. We always sat in the last pew at the back of the church in case I needed to bolt. I never found a reason to flee. Instead, I found solace I could not find anywhere else. This would mark the true beginning of my search for Christ.

Mike and I divorced after four years of marriage. One day, in the heat of an argument, he threw a telephone book at me, just missing my head. He yelled something about a divorce. For years, I had wanted to broach the subject to him, but was too afraid. This was my chance. I jumped on the idea.

I found a lawyer, who, for a small fee, would draw up divorce papers for us. We could be free of each other within 24 hours from filing! We had nothing to split because we were deep in debt from the purchase of a large three-bedroom, three-bathroom condo in Hyde Park. It was a 3,000-square foot money pit and another source of many of our arguments. Every dime I invested in its renovation, I lost. But I did not care. I only wanted two things—Ryan and my freedom. I got both.

As God's Providence would have it, the week Mike and I agreed to divorce, Don Dempsey called from Miami to offer me a job. He was now the executive vice president of marketing for Burger King Corporation. He needed a third marketing director to help manage the chain's $270 million marketing budget. He would divide the chain's annual marketing calendar between the three directors. Would I be interested in the job?

I turned him down at first, because I felt I needed to stay in Chicago for Ryan's sake. She needed to be close to her father. Mike talked me into accepting the offer. The day we left, he wept at the kitchen counter. The only other time I had seen him cry was at his mother's funeral.

I joined Burger King in 1984. During my first month, I finally cried out to God to save me—to come into my life and clean up the mess I had made of it. When I arrived in Miami, I was at my lowest point in life ever.

Following is an excerpt from a speech I gave at a women's workshop in Greer, South Carolina years later. I shared my salvation testimony with the 100 attendees:

April 23, 1996

My Salvation Testimony

When I arrived in Miami to accept a job offer from Burger King, I had been officially divorced all of 24 hours. I had a two-year-old baby in tow and two suitcases to my name. I had no family or friends in Miami. I had never even visited the city before. By the time I arrived, I was bankrupt emotionally, physically, spiritually, and financially. I was drowning in despair, depression, and debt. I best described myself as holding onto life's edge by my fingertips ... and I was losing my grip.

One day, I dropped Ryan off at the sitter's house. The woman was a virtual stranger. She had been referred to me by the real estate agent Burger King assigned to me when I first arrived. The agent was responsible for helping us find a place to live. She knew someone who knew of a woman who watched children in her home in Coral Gables. I was not comfortable with this arrangement, but I had no other option.

While driving to work, I decided I just could not take life the way it was anymore. I pulled my car to the side of Bird Road. I cried, "This Jesus I have heard so much about, if You are real, please help me now. I can't hold on much longer! I am losing my grip!"

From that prayer to this day, my life has never been the same. When Jesus came in, He came in like a whirlwind. Within hours of that prayer, the Lord removed my despair! My depression immediately lifted! In less than a year, He wiped away my debt.

That day, right after I returned to the office, I experienced my first surprise in a long series of surprises.

"Don Dempsey would like to see you," my secretary Maria told me before I even had a chance to put down my purse.

"What does he want?" I asked, grabbing a pad and pen. She shrugged.

I took the elevator to the seventh floor, where all the executive vice presidents were tucked away. I tapped on Don's door.

"Oh, come in. Shut the door," he said. His office seemed to go on forever. I took a seat in front of his oversized desk. "I hear you don't have any money?"

I just looked at him. Was it that obvious? I did not know what to say. Was it because I rotated the same three dresses every week? I never found out where or how Don got his information.

"Look, I tell you what I'm going to do. I'm going to put you and Ryan in King's Court in one of the Company's condos. Just stay there. Save your money, and we'll pay all your expenses."

Don never gave me a chance to speak. Not a single word.

"Here's the key."

I could not believe my eyes when I opened the door to the condo that evening. It was a spacious, fully furnished, three-bed, two-bathroom townhouse. With no rent or expenses, I banked five months of paychecks.

At $80,000 a year, I quickly pulled out of debt. Someone told me that Burger King had never done that for an executive at my level. By year-

end, I could afford to purchase a lovely three-bedroom, two-bathroom house with a large swimming pool.

In time, I ascended the corporate ladder at Burger King—gradually at first. Then, I soared. I started as one of three marketing directors, but ended as Vice President of Corporate Human Resources, Training, Development and Diversity Worldwide. Burger King operated in 56 different countries, so my job was global.

As my compensation rose, so did our standard of living. After three years, we moved to a bigger house. Renovating it became my hobby, my beloved passion. In time, our home resembled the photographs I had seen in magazines while growing up.

God also grew my faith in Him. He stretched it in ways that genuinely challenged me. Within a year of moving to Miami, I became deeply convicted about my divorce.

When I began to explore this conviction with the Lord, I had an acute sense that I had squirmed out of an important test. God had a purpose for Mike being in my life. Through Mike, He had drawn me to Himself like nothing else had. He had only begun this work when I found a way to escape.

In God's economy, broken vessels are the most usable. Broken vessels cast aside all self-sufficiency for the All-Sufficient One. At the time of our divorce, I was a long way from understanding this. I thought my life was my own to do with as I pleased. Mike had been God's instrument of choice to teach me differently, to get me to that blessed state of spiritual brokenness.

Thus, three years later, to everyone's complete and utter amazement, Mike and I quietly remarried at the local courthouse in Miami. I had diligently searched the Scriptures and inquired of the Lord for over a year on the matter. Believing reconciliation is what God desired, I resolved to obey. I knew I was in for a difficult time.

I waited two years before taking the plunge. God needed time to build my faith in Him or we would just repeat the old life we had together in Chicago. I had to learn how to fight differently, using spiritual weapons.

Chapter 9
The Best Thing That Ever Happened to Me

During the early days of our relationship, the Lord wanted me to know He truly existed and that He was powerful and always present. He showed up in my life in ways that would stun (even scare) the average American Christian. I sought to journal the wonders He performed in, through, and for me to help me understand that He was no myth, no legend. He was the Real Deal.

In 1984, when I first arrived in Miami to work for Burger King, I joined Wayside Baptist Church. At the time, it could be best described as a Bible-believing, Bible-teaching, praying church. A member church of the Southern Baptist Convention, it was comprised mostly of good ole', down-home White folks. But I saw no color. I was "blinded" by Jesus. My eyes could see only Him. At Wayside, I became solidly grounded in my faith.

In less than two years, I became a Sunday school teacher. Within three years, I became the director of the Singles Department. Those were rare responsibilities for a new believer. I devoured the Bible and grew like a weed. The Lord demolished decades of misconceptions and wrong patterns of thinking. I hung on to His every truth. He was the Lifter of my head, my Way Maker in a crooked, upside down world.

The Lord made it clear to me that He delighted in my company, so my quiet times with Him became the cornerstone of my life. My daily devotions with God were sacrosanct in my home. It was understood by everyone that until I emerged from my bedroom, I was not to be disturbed.

If I left the house without spending time with the Lord, I felt naked and discombobulated. It became my habit to start my mornings with Him and end my days with divine debriefings. Whatever it took, I made time for Him, even if it meant not sleeping. He became my peace, my joy, my wisdom—all my reasons for being. He became my Beginning, my End, my Everything.

As part of God's plan for my life, I was apportioned a large measure of faith. In the early years, that faith attracted a man named Charles Fant. He was the minister of education at Wayside. Charles, a gentle, Spirit-filled believer, was a devoted husband and father. But Christ was His first love.

Charles believed that God called His followers to pour their lives into a small number of others during their lifetime, just as Christ poured His life into 12 men. He saw something in my walk with Christ that told him I would be a solid investment of his time, energy, and resources. He became a rich source of Biblical knowledge for me. He helped me understand and apply spiritual truths far beyond my years.

But one thing Charles, nor anybody else at Wayside Baptist Church could not teach me, was spiritual warfare. God Himself taught me. And He started my lessons early.

Chapter 10

Learning to War in Christ

I remember well my first two forays into this veiled side of Christianity—veiled at least within Western culture. Driving home after work one day, I was suddenly blinded by a migraine headache. It came out of nowhere. It was so severe that, without thinking, I grabbed my head with both hands. I felt as though my skull was in a vise. I can remember having only one migraine headache in my entire life. It was a few weeks after Ryan was born. It lasted two hours. I rested my head on a pillow until it was over.

For the life of me, I could not figure out what triggered the throbbing headache. I was not stressed or under any pressure at work or home. If I had had aspirin, I would have taken it right there in the car.

Suddenly, without ever hearing these words uttered before by another human being, a rebuke flew out of my mouth: "Spirit of pain, I rebuke you in the name of Jesus! Loose me!"

In an instant, the headache was gone! Where had those words come from? I certainly had not learned them at Wayside. I was just a babe in Christ, not yet a year old. The Spirit of the Lord was teaching me a new thing. I could not wait to tell Suzanne, our live-in housekeeper.

The next incident happened a year later. I was home alone. I needed to put something in Suzanne's room. The house was built in such a way that we had to walk through Ryan's room to get to Suzanne's. Ryan was still a little girl. The minute I entered Ryan's doorway, a terrible stench overpowered me. It smelled like feces. I was livid. I was certain Ryan had carelessly tracked excrement into the house from her shoes. We had white carpet throughout the house. I examined every inch of carpet in her room. I searched every dresser drawer for soiled panties. I found nothing.

Perplexed, I left her room. That is when I heard a Voice clearly say to me: *"Go back and rebuke it."* The Voice was not audible; it came from inside me.

"Go back and rebuke it?" I said to an empty living room. I hesitated for a moment.

"Go back and rebuke it." There! I heard it again! I was sure of it!

I went back into Ryan's room. The odor was still overwhelming. I hesitated for a moment, then I put my hands on my hips and shouted: "Spirit of ... spirit of ... STENCH, I rebuke you in the name of Jesus. Get outta here!"

The unpleasant smell was gone before I could finish the sentence! Oh my, what had I signed up for? They had not told me anything about this kind of stuff in Sunday school!

God used these and other events to gradually mold me into a prayer warrior. Years later, He would call me "Blackbird" and "Black Star" when I warred in prayer. Once in a dream, He showed me pummeling demonic forces in prayer, and I heard Him roaring in the background, "Go, Blackbird, go!"

By the time Mike and I reconciled, God had prepared me for battle. Mike decided to move to Miami and commute, by car, back and forth to Chicago for work. He had just embarked on a career in television and movie production and needed to spend large amounts of time there. This pulled him away from home for weeks, sometimes months at a time. We welcomed his long absences because they gave the household a respite from all the warfare.

When Mike was in Chicago, peace reigned in our home. When he returned, all hell broke loose. God used Mike to show me how to war in the Spirit on an intensely personal level and how to respond in love to every kind of offense.

"Come, get calm in My presence," was the Lord's oft-repeated admonition to me after an argument with Mike. He would speak peace to my heart. Then, He would impart wisdom on what I should do next. Usually, I was instructed to perform some demonstrative act of love for Mike. Time and again, I witnessed the power of these acts in changing Mike's attitude toward me or the matter at hand.

The Lord also taught me how to take authority over demonic spirits and arrest the mayhem in our home and lives. No amount of crying, pouting, cajoling, arguing, or complaining worked because the battle was spiritual; it required spiritual weapons.

Instead, I learned how to trust God's Word and wield it like a sword. I lived on my knees in prayer and discovered, firsthand, the power of fasting in agreement with other warriors. This would become my way of life for the next 11 years, while living with Mike.

I had no idea how valuable the lessons I learned during our marriage would be to my future. I will be forever grateful for what God taught me during that period of my life. I was in training for bigger battles to come.

After Mike and I divorced a second time, not an ill word was ever spoken between us again. In time, we became good friends. And, to my amazement and delight, he turned out to be a wonderful father to Ryan.

Chapter 11
My November Prayer—A Consecration

I had been working at Burger King for six years and faithfully attending church at Wayside Baptist when God decided to fit a piece of my destiny into place. The Lord's Spirit led me to pray a powerful prayer one November evening that would chart the next course of my life.

By this time, people knew me as a prayer warrior and would frequently ask for prayer. I loved to pray because I cherished being in God's presence and seeing his answers thrilled me to no end. However, that November prayer stood out above all the others because its effect was dramatically life-altering. I never prayed so desperately, so passionately about anything before that prayer.

I was planning to stop at the grocery store to pick up a few items on my way to Wednesday night Bible study at Wayside. I was listening to the radio when the Holy Spirit began to move. I never made it to the store. Below is a journal excerpt that captured the event as it unfolded that evening:

November 18, 1990

My November Prayer

Nothing happens by chance. Rarely am I on the road to church at 6 o'clock. But that Sunday evening I was. I had planned to go to the grocery store before heading to church. I was listening to WMCU, a Christian radio station. The topic was about hell. The guy being interviewed was a theologian.

He spoke from Matthew 7:13-14: "Enter by the narrow gate; for wide is the gate and broad is the way that leads to destruction, and there are many who go in by it. Because narrow is the gate and difficult is the way which leads to life, and there are few who find it."

The gentleman conducting the interview could have been me. He asked all the questions I would have asked if I were in his chair. Everything rang true.

However, the thing that gripped my heart, although I had heard it countless times before, was most people will try to enter God's Kingdom through a myriad of ways—other than through Christ— and will end up in hell. This is what is meant by: "... for wide is the gate and broad is the way that leads to destruction, and there are many who go in by it." Jesus Christ is the Way, the Truth, and the Life that leads to eternal life and only a few find it.

The impact of that truth on my heart was immediate and powerful. I never made it to the grocery store. Something suddenly came over me. I had to talk to God ... URGENTLY!

I bypassed the store, sped to church, half-parked in two parking spaces, burst through the double entry doors, ran up three flights of stairs, found an empty room, turned out the light, slammed the door, collapsed on the floor, and sobbed. I sobbed until my eyes hurt.

Why me? Why me? Why me? I did not choose God. He chose me. From among billions of people, I am chosen to be His child. It is by His grace alone that I am chosen. Upon realizing I was one among an untold number being saved, I cried out with unrestrained gratitude, "Thanks for this precious, precious, rare gift!"

Then, my thoughts turned to those closest to me. My whole family was born again—father, mother, sisters, and brothers! One by one God had led each of them into His Kingdom. And my young daughter knew and loved the Lord. We all also enjoyed good physical health.

Not only am I and my loved ones born again, I walk in the Light of God's Word; not all Christians do. Many believers stumble through life just as much as nonbelievers because their relationship with Christ is undeveloped or underdeveloped. God fills me daily with His wisdom and authority. I live a fruit-filled life in Him.

In addition to every spiritual blessing, the Lord has also given me great material wealth. Many Christians in the world are poor. I want for nothing. He gave me a career that provided far more than we needed as a family. My cup overflowed while others' cups were empty. Why? I have not done anything to earn or merit these blessings. My Creator decided I should have them. This thought makes me weep for I am not ignorant to the fact that without God, I can do nothing, I have nothing, and I am nothing! I can take credit for zilch!

Then I MUST ask the question: "Am I doing as much as I can do with the opportunities God has given me?" I was not sure. God says, "To whom much is given, much is required."

Barely able to contain my tears enough to speak, I pleaded with God between sobs to help me fulfill my spiritual destiny and to let me not waste anything He had given me—energy, opportunity, talent, gifts, money, connections—whatever. I told Him I did not want to come before His throne at the end of time to discover I had only done a fraction of what I was supposed to do.

He had entrusted me with much. I asked Him to make me a wise steward. Do not let me waste my life or the resources He had bestowed. I sobbed and prayed for one solid hour. I knew God heard my prayer.

God of heaven orchestrated that prayer. He needed it to help craft my destiny. Countless times after November 1990, when I got caught up in something wild and crazy, orchestrated by heaven above, I had to remind myself, "This is my November Prayer. Be still. Do not panic. It will all work out. He's just answering my November Prayer."

Chapter 12
A Woman of Great Faith

Finally, the time came for God to demonstrate the great work He had wrought in me during my nine years of walking with Him. During my last year at Burger King, He showed me how much He had grown my faith. He chose to do it in a most unusual way. His route took me halfway around the world to Russia and back. It also took nearly three years to evolve.

It was 1993. Our house had been destroyed by Hurricane Andrew and so had Burger King's headquarters. While our home was being rebuilt, Ryan and I lived with Suzanne in her two-bedroom, two-bathroom condo. Mike, for the most part, remained in Chicago.

All of us at Burger King worked out of temporary, makeshift offices while contractors labored around the clock to rebuild Burger King's headquarters. Under these conditions, I was first introduced to a little Russian girl named Polina Suvorova.

November 7, 1993

Polina Suvorova

I slowly refolded the letter and slipped it back into the dark pink envelope. She cannot be serious! I inspected the envelope closely. There was something unusual about it, but exactly what eluded me. The letter had traveled across the country—from California to Florida and found me in a place where I had lived for less than a month. This was no small feat since we had moved three times after losing our home to Hurricane Andrew.

Now my daughter and I lived with our housekeeper Suzanne in a small two-bedroom apartment I helped her win in an auction the year before. Mike worked in Chicago.

The stationery on which the letter was written was distinctly Russian. I remember the fragile, delicate texture of the paper from when I visited the country two years earlier. But the envelope was from a U.S. West

Coast engineering firm. Still that is not what puzzled me. Then, it hit me.

The letter was addressed to our home, which had been destroyed, but delivered to Suzanne's house. Unlike all our other mail, the envelope had not been plastered with forwarding labels as it found its way to us from our previous addresses. How strange!

I turned the envelope over and over in my hand. I wondered if God had something to do with it. I opened the envelope and read the letter again. A woman in Russia was asking for $47,000. Her baby girl was dying of a heart defect, and she needed money for surgery. Nah, $47,000 is a lot of money! I thought God knows I don't have that kind of money to give away.

I looked at the letter again. "Lord, I'm not sure what you want me to do with this," I said. "But the letter found me. If this is from You, then show me how I can help." I waited a few seconds. A thought came. Call.

"Do you know how hard it is to get through to Russia?" I asked the Lord. "Besides, what time is it there anyway? Not to mention, I can't speak Russian! If I do reach her, who will interpret?"

Call! The urge was stronger. I grabbed the telephone and dialed, thinking I would never get through, and the matter would be settled.

A woman answered in Russian. Startled, I babbled something about the United States and not knowing what time it was there.

"Hello?" now a man's voice. He sounded young, congenial—and he spoke English! I composed myself. I told him about the letter I had received regarding Polina.

"Yes, yes!" He became very excited.

"I understand ..." I hesitated. "She's... she's dying?"

"Yes. She needs surgery, but Russian doctors cannot help her," he explained. "She has a heart defect." Despite being born with a heart defect, Polina had lived three years.

"Is she your child?" I asked.

"No. I'm a friend, but her mother is here." He broke away to interpret for Natalia, the mother.

I interrupted, "How did she get my name?" His answer still baffles me.

"From a Russian magazine for Christians," he answered.

Natalia, using names from the magazine, sent six letters to the United States requesting funds for cardiac surgery for Polina. The surgery needed to be performed in the United States because Russian doctors lacked the necessary skills and medical equipment. The letters were a mother's desperate attempt to save her daughter's life. Natalia sent her appeal to what she thought were North American Christian organizations.

My mind raced. In 1991, a few months prior to my trip to Russia, I sent Bibles to 50 evangelical pastors who had been imprisoned by the Russian government for their faith. After years of imprisonment, they had all been released to start life over again. Taken aback by how little they had and how much I owned, I decided to gift them each with a Bible. Bibles were difficult to find in Russia.

Perhaps the Russian Christian community is small, I reasoned. "My Russian Project," as I had dubbed it, may have taken on a life of its own after I sent the packages. Maybe this is where Natalia found my name. I explained without much success that I was an individual citizen of the United States, who happened to be a Christian. I was not a Christian organization.

"How many of the organizations have you heard from?" I asked.

"You are the only one," he said.

"How much money have you raised so far?" I felt myself being drawn in.

"Two thousand American dollars," he said. This was a substantial sum by Russian standards. I learned these funds were the result of an appeal for Polina's life on Russian television the month before.

"Ask Natalia if she believes in Jesus?" I instructed the man. Even as I asked the question, I had no idea where I was going with the conversation.

"Yes," he returned to the phone.

"Ask if she believes in prayer."

"Yes."

"That's all we need!" My words astonished me even as I spoke them. "Ask her to pray that Jesus will heal Polina or allow her to come to America for the operation. Tell her not to stop praying. We'll see what God will do."

Natalia grabbed the telephone. She began thanking me profusely in her native language. I wondered as I hung up the telephone, if she had any idea what a long shot this was.

I put Polina's request on the prayer chain at work the next day. Oddly, a diversity training session I had set up at Burger King gave birth to the Christian Fellowship Network. We started out as six persons but quickly grew to 85 strong. I also asked my church to pray for Polina the following Wednesday. In my provisional rough and ready workspace, I began to make telephone calls, extremely bold ones.

I started with Dr. John Mayer, the senior associate of cardiac surgery and associate professor of surgery in the Department of Surgery at Harvard Medical School in Boston. Dr. Mayer had already agreed with the family to waive his surgical fee and the fees of other medical personnel, totaling $50,000. However, Ms. Suvorova would have to pay for Polina's hospitalization, their travel expenses as well as room and board for herself for an undetermined length of time.

The hospital costs alone would be at least $47,000 for the kind of surgery the doctors thought Polina needed. Since they had not seen Polina—only conversed with Russian doctors about her disorder—no one knew exactly what was required. A series of operations might be necessary, and they wondered if her tiny body was fit enough to survive the surgery. How long would her convalescence be? A six-month recovery was not uncommon after such an extensive surgery. It was all a big gamble.

Natalia was told to deposit $12,000 in an escrow account at a local Boston bank and to bring the remaining $35,000 with her when Polina was admitted to the hospital. Natalia, a single mother, worked as an engineer in Moscow. Her wages, alimony support, and government assistance totaled 23,108 rubles, the equivalent of $193. This was her annual income!

The only option was to get the hospital fees waived. Encouraged by Dr. Mayer's willingness to waive his fees, I called the hospital's business office that same day.

"You will need to speak to Lillian Hughes," the woman advised. "She's not available right now."

No problem. The call was really to confirm the facsimile number I had gleaned from Dr. Mayer's office. "Just let her know I called. I'll be writing her."

I hung up the telephone, whispered a quick prayer, and began drafting a letter. An hour later I had a version I thought might work. I faxed it and waited. Two days passed ... nothing. I resolved on the third day to call.

"Lillian Hughes, please." I held my breath.

"She's not available. Can I help you?"

"Yes, I'm Ray Hood-Phillips, Vice President of HR Development and Diversity for Burger King Corporation." I tried to use all the influence I had. "I'm calling about a fax I sent Ms. Hughes earlier this week."

"Oh, yes. She received it. She wants to speak to you, but she's not here right now." This is a good sign, I thought. "Can she return your call?"

"Absolutely, I'd like to speak to her today if I could. I will be expecting her call," I pushed. The day came and went. No call.

Several days later, she called. Lillian said she would have to take the issue to the hospital Board. The directors would discuss the matter and vote on it. I asked for the name of the chairman and other Board members. She faxed them to me. I circulated their names on the prayer network at work and within my prayer group at church. That was the last week of January 1993.

Days turned into weeks. I struggled not to make a pest of myself. One day in the office, thinking of Polina, I asked, "Lord, will she ever come?"

"She will come," He said clearly. I reminded everybody to keep the matter in prayer.

The Board finally met. I was informed after the board meeting that they would need proof of family hardship. Lillian sent me a Free Care Application that needed to be completed by Natalia. I faxed it to her. Within two weeks, she gathered all the necessary information and faxed the completed application and backup documentation. On March 8, 1993, I sent the application and documentation to the hospital, along with a letter of my own.

On March 15, my office received a fax from Boston Children's Hospital. My secretary was first to see it. Suddenly, I heard screaming in the adjacent room. The hospital had approved the request! My staff went crazy. All medical and hospital expenses would be covered!

We sent a dozen red roses to Lillian. We faxed the hospital's letter to Natalia in Russia. She called immediately with an interpreter. The news was so shocking she simply could not believe it—literally. Choking back tears, she begged us not to joke. I took the telephone.

"It's true, it's true! This is NO joke! They said, 'YES!'"

Now the only thing left to do was to get mother and daughter to the United States. "How will we do this?" I wondered aloud.

"Delta Airlines flies to Russia," one of the office secretaries yelled.

I immediately started making telephone calls to Delta. I was looking for names. Who at Delta could approve two free, round-trip airline tickets from Moscow to Boston? I found him, Mr. A.J. Cantin, district director of marketing for South Florida. One call was all it took.

Now it was a matter of waiting for two free seats to open up. It took a while, but they did. I charged the tickets to my American Express with the understanding I would be reimbursed by the airline. The Burger King Travel Department cut the tickets. How would I get them to Natalia?

The very day I asked that question, I received a call from an American family—friends of Natalia—I did not know existed. They would be traveling to Moscow later that week and could hand-deliver the tickets to Natalia. (What were the chances of that? God was really showing off!) I overnighted the tickets to the family on a Tuesday. They left for Moscow that Thursday.

Polina and her mother flew free of charge from Moscow, Russia to Boston, Massachusetts, compliments of Delta Airlines, on July 13, 1993. An interpreter met mother and child at Boston Logan Airport. The interpreter delivered them safely to Boston Children's Hospital that same day.

Three days later, Polina underwent open heart surgery. She remained in the hospital's care for nearly three months. The surgeons and medical personnel waived all surgical and medical fees. The hospital's board of directors also agreed to waive three months of hospital fees. The hospital provided an interpreter to assist in the communication between Natalia and the hospital staff over the next few months.

As Polina recuperated from the delicate surgery, a wealthy family who had learned of Natalia's plight provided her a home—free of charge. The family would be traveling in Europe for the summer, and they needed someone to house sit. They offered Natalia the job. Before this family appeared on the scene, I had planned to put Natalia in a hotel.

Now, I only had to pay for her food and other incidentals, like cab fare to and from the hospital.

After several weeks of observation, the doctors gave Polina a prognosis for a great life. She also received free dental surgery while at the hospital to salvage and strengthen her rotten teeth. Polina and her mother received more than $200,000 in free medical care and other benefits during their stay. This was overwhelming for a single mom from Russia with an annual income of only $193!

Before Polina and her mother returned to Moscow, I had the pleasure of meeting them. I was on a business trip in Boston when I decided to swing by the hospital. There, I met Natalia and her gorgeous child for the first time. I surprised them; they were not expecting me. A nurse told me the hospital staff had fallen in love with Polina and had "adopted" her. That was when I first heard of the dental surgery. Natalia gave me a picture of Polina. I still treasure it. Words cannot capture the joy I felt leaving that hospital.

Months later, sipping coffee at my best friend's kitchen table, a revelation struck me. Jeri and I had been talking about Polina and her mother. More thrilling and wondrous to me than Polina's free surgery was the faith of her mother. I said to Jeri, "This woman has an enormous faith ...." Then, I caught my words. I burst into tears. I was so stunned that I could hardly speak. Only at that moment did I finally realize that Natalia Suvorova was an answer to prayer—a sweet answer.

Before I went to Russia in 1991, I asked God to allow me to meet a woman, a Russian woman, who had a faith like mine. I knew I had the gift of faith, and I simply wanted to meet a Christian on the other side of the world who believed and loved the Lord as I did. I thought it would be special to meet someone very different from myself, but with whom I had so much in common in the Spirit.

Every day in Russia, I kept my eyes peeled for such a woman. I never met her. Flying home, I was really perplexed because I knew God answered prayer, but this one had not been answered. In time, I totally forgot about my prayer until that moment at Jeri's house.

Ms. Suvorova had sent six letters to the United States, believing with all her heart that God would move one of the six "organizations" to help her—even though it all seemed impossible. That was like believing one could find a needle in a haystack. Despite the odds, she believed. She never gave up. Her faith saved her daughter's life.

Ms. Suvorova wrote me a year later to tell me Polina was doing well and taking gymnastics to strengthen her heart. Seeing myself through Natalia Suvorova's walk, I came to realize I had been given an extraordinary gift of faith. God had taken pains to demonstrate this to me.

Polina was just the beginning. I knew the Lord would continue to challenge and stretch my faith in Him, and because He is a God of purpose, I suspected one day He would ask me to push outside my comfort zone, to do something I never dreamt I could do. I was right. Within two years, I would start my own company. But to do that, I had to be debt free.

Chapter 13
Set Free for Ministry

Only God knows how many times I asked Him to make me "debt free for ministry." If I did not have any debt, I reasoned, I could serve Him more freely, more directly. I could make significant investments of time and money into His Kingdom. But debt had me bound. "Lord, If You make me debt free, I will go into ministry," I vowed.

One quiet morning in 1990, after a poignant time of worship, the Lord informed me I would be debt free in three years. I was quite excited by the prospect. I created a slogan: "Debt free in '93!" I told anybody who would listen—family, neighbors, colleagues, and strangers.

Then quite unintentionally, over the course of a year, I more than doubled our debt! I got entangled in what became known at our house as "The Home Renovation Project from Hell." We started out renovating one thing that led to another thing and then to another until the whole house was nearly redone. Because of my faithlessness, I assumed I had blown the deal.

On August 23, 1992, I was in the Marriott Hotel in Orlando, Florida. Our family fled South Miami to Central Florida to escape Hurricane Andrew. I woke early that morning as I always did to have my quiet time with the Lord. I fluffed my pillow. Everyone else was still asleep.

"Well, Lord, what do you want to talk about today?" I whispered.

"You have a covetous spirit," I heard as clear as a bell. I sat upright in the bed. I looked around. *Who was that? Was it the devil? But ... why would the devil tell me I had a covetous spirit? He would be working against himself.*

I waited. I heard only quiet snoring in the adjacent room. I opened my Bible. I spotted a folded piece of paper in the inside pocket of my Bible cover. I pulled it out. That piece of paper listed every Old and New

Testament Scripture on covetousness! I had not the faintest clue how it got there.

God had spoken earlier, and now He was speaking to me again through the Scriptures. I was instantly convicted. I wept with each verse I read. I repented that morning and ask God to free me, once and for all, from this terrible bondage.

Two days later, we returned home to Miami. We discovered Hurricane Andrew had destroyed our home. It was a powerful symbol of God demolishing my covetous life. The teardown of my life, at that point, was the most wonderful, bittersweet experience. One day we had too much, and the next day we had nothing.

God used the hurricane to reorder all my priorities. Possessions dimmed in importance as we grew closer as a family. Suddenly, I did not have any real financial obligations. All our things had been blown away or ruined. Ryan—11 years old at the time—remarked after an impromptu game of racquetball one afternoon, "Mom, I like being poor!"

Two weeks after the epic hurricane, the City of Miami condemned our house. All my previous renovations lay as rubble on the ground. The City plastered orange signs all over the remaining structure: "Unfit for Human Habitation." I tried to give the property away; no one would take it.

Five weeks after the storm, State Farm finally came. The insurance company saw the signs, agreed with the City, and paid the limits on what turned out to be a "Cadillac" policy. The premium-plus policy, coupled with the fact that I had receipts and photographs of every major item in the house, facilitated State Farm awarding us the policy limits. The insurance payout allowed us to eliminate all debt except for the house mortgage.

For the next eight months, while we sought to have our house rebuilt, we were forced to live in two rooms in a seedy hotel among drug addicts, pimps, and prostitutes in North Miami. The hurricane had wiped out nearly all available housing in South Miami where we had lived. We battled cockroaches, urine-stained hallways, and backed-up toilets.

One day, brown, feces-filled water flowed from the toilet into my bedroom, where I had laid my only surviving Oriental rug. It was a prized possession that I managed to salvage from the hurricane. There was no place else to put it but on the floor.

In the middle of the night, we pulled up stakes. Our third move since we lost our home. I left the rug. We gathered our few belongings in boxes and garbage bags and moved to Suzanne's two-bedroom condo on the other side of town.

Just days after the State Farm adjuster came out, God sent a Christian contractor to us from Orlando. One day, he showed up asking for me at Burger King's temporary offices. He saw the house and found the owner through county records. He offered to rebuild our home. He had gone through the rubble of our condemned house and was confident he could rebuild it. We would be his first client.

His bid was a full one-third less than the other two I had. He promised he could do it if I let his workers sleep in the house while they rebuilt it. I agreed.

When I received the State Farm check to rebuild our house, I sent it to our mortgage company, along with the contractor's bid. Upon receipt of the bid, the mortgage company released the contractor's portion in one lump sum. The contractor managed the money well. This was an act of faith since some contractors ran off with the money they were given.

Faithful to his word, our contractor completely rebuilt our home on time and on budget. Our house was stronger, better, and more beautiful than before. He finished in April 1993.

As the Lord would have it, I did not remember until mid-January 1993—three months after the mortgage company had released the contractor's fee—there had been a surplus of funds. Where was that money? I called the mortgage company.

"Well, let me see," said the woman on the other end of the line. I heard clicking as she pulled up our account. I will never, *ever* forget her words: "It says 'mortgage satisfaction was December 31, 1992.'"

She explained the amount left remaining from the insurance check—after paying the contractor— was exactly the amount left on the mortgage, to the dollar. What were the chances of that? Then, what this meant suddenly hit me.

"Do you mean that on January 1, I didn't have a mortgage?"

"Mortgage satisfaction was December 31, 1992," she repeated.

A feather could have knocked me over. On January 1, 1993, I was totally debt-free! (My slogan "Debt-free in'93!" had come to pass!) In the face of my faithlessness, God had been faithful. He kept His promise. He had made me debt-free for ministry. The message was clear. He had come to collect a vow.

Chapter 14

The Birth of Inclusive Business Strategies—Transferring Wealth

Striking out on my own would not be easy. Not only had I grown quite comfortable with my large salary, I prized the bonuses and perks that came with being an officer of the Company. I would have to kiss it all goodbye.

At the same time, I ached to do more for God's Kingdom. On the heels of Burger King's successful diversity intervention, companies had begun calling me for advice. I realized there was a great need for assistance in this area.

After toying a few months with the idea of starting a wealth-transfer ministry, I took the idea to God. I proposed that He help me start a diversity consulting firm. I would use my skills and work experience to help Fortune 500 companies become more racially diverse and show them how to manage that diversity to benefit the bottom line. They would pay my firm, and I, in turn, would invest significant portions of its revenues into Christ-centered ministries, thereby transferring the world's wealth into His Kingdom for His purposes.

God honored my request. He even gave me the name. He called it Inclusive Business Strategies, Inc. or IBS. I was President and CEO. He was Chairman of the Board.

The possibilities of what we could do were too wondrous to ponder. But as I began to wind down my old life, I started to get cold feet. A big stumbling block for me was health insurance. I always had health insurance. Growing up, I was insured under my parents until I finished college. After that, the companies I worked for covered me. Starting my own company meant I would have to give up this coverage.

Mike, a heavy smoker and drinker, suffered from high blood pressure. And his love of pork and fast food heightened my concerns. What if something happened to him? How would we pay?

One night the Lord woke me up to talk about horses and chariots. He likened health insurance to these ancient war machines. Early Israel desired to own a fleet like the pagan nations around it. The nations relied on their horses and chariots because they gave them a superior advantage in battle. But God wanted Israel to rely on Him alone.

It was also an undisputed fact that God could render horses and chariots useless in battle. He could make them fail as He did when Pharaoh's army pursued the Israelites. While trying to cross the parted Red Sea, the chariot wheels became stuck in the seabed and fell off. Perhaps, the horses' hooves also became stuck. But the Israelites made it safely across.

God then reminded me of a wealthy woman I knew. That very night she lay in her bed, dying of cancer. The doctors could do nothing more for her. It did not matter that she had premium health insurance. She would be dead within a few weeks.

Last of all, He presented Suzanne's case. She was 60 years old and could still climb trees and outrace me! Except for an occasional cold and laser surgery on one eye, she had never been sick a day in her life. His point was that my health was in His hands. He was my health insurance.

"I am with you always! Move out in faith!" He commanded.

With much trepidation, I resigned from Burger King in January 1994. However, the burger chain was not willing to let me go entirely, so the Company asked to become my first client. I agreed.

At the end of our contract negotiations, the CFO offered—completely unsolicited—to cover the cost of my health insurance for a year! I was instructed to build the cost into my fee. This was God's way of saying, "See, I got your back!" However, not once that year did I ever use it. After it expired, I never had health insurance again.

IBS started off small at first, but God steadily grew our revenues until they exceeded what I had been making as a Burger King executive. I started pouring what we made (after expenses) into Christ-centered ministries around the world. We had been operating one year when I received the call from Jim Adamson.

Adamson, the former President and CEO of Burger King had now become the board chairman of Flagstar Companies. He asked if I would help him "fix Denny's." He had been impressed with my diversity work at Burger King and thought I could help transform the beleaguered restaurant chain and help Flagstar's other five chains improve as well.

Denny's was one of six major restaurant chains run by Flagstar Companies. It was America's largest family dining restaurant chain with $2.3 billion in annual sales and 1,500 restaurants. It employed more than 70,000 workers.

Per Adamson, I could write my own ticket. Denny's was embroiled in a national crisis. Two class action lawsuits, totaling $54 million, had been filed against Denny's by African Americans. The group claimed widespread, systemic discrimination.

I agreed to take on Flagstar as a client. I knew my decision to ally with Denny's was God's will for my life. A year before I was asked to join Flagstar, I had gone to visit Mary Browning, a member of my Sunday school class. While there, I was introduced to a visiting couple.

We all talked for about 20 minutes when, out of nowhere, the man and woman asked if they could pray for me. I saw no harm in it, so I consented. But what came next surprised me.

They sat me in a chair in the middle of the room, laid hands on me, and began to foretell my future! They prophesied I would work for a company involved with the federal government, entangled in a legal matter. The company would become a client.

I found the whole idea of someone predicting another's future disconcerting, although Scripture is sated with such acts. Still, it was foreign to me. I dismissed the couple as kooks and sought the chance to make a polite exit.

A year later, during our first meeting, Adamson informed me the two class action lawsuits, brought by two law firms on behalf of African Americans nationwide, had resulted in Denny's being under a federal consent decree. That meant the company's business practices would be monitored by the federal government for seven years.

The consent decree spelled out the terms of compliance. It delineated in detail the diversity objectives Denny's would have to achieve throughout all aspects of its business during that seven-year period. Failure to achieve these objectives could result in penalties and fines and an extension of the decree. The prophecy had come to pass!

In a second meeting with Flagstar, the Executive Vice President of Human Resources joined Adamson and me. He created the title, chief diversity officer (CDO). Years later, the CDO designation would become an industry standard for people who performed similar services for corporations.

I officially began working with Flagstar on April 10, 1995, two years after the lawsuits. What a big mess! By that time, the Company was being battered on all sides.

Hostile media derided the chain daily, lampooning it in newspapers, magazines, editorial cartoons, television newscasts, and radio talk shows. Denny's was the butt of jokes for all the late-night talk show hosts. Customers left the chain in droves. Some who patronized Denny's came with bad attitudes, just to test the wait staff.

Denny's had tens of thousands of demoralized employees on its hands, and it was hard to attract new workers to the troubled chain. Hate mail poured in from around the country from every racial and special interest group. Finally, the parent company Flagstar became the "Pariah of Wall Street." Its stock, trading at $23 a share before the lawsuits, plummeted to under $3. It was eventually kicked off NASDAQ.

Initially, I thought I could commute between Florida and South Carolina, but I soon realized the job was much too demanding for that. I needed to relocate. Flagstar moved our family and my budding consulting firm nearer to its headquarters.

My tenure at Denny's was a Cinderella story. In just three years, the family restaurant chain was named the *second*-best company in America for African Americans, Hispanic Americans, and Asian Americans by *Fortune* magazine! The distinction stunned the corporate world. Just five years earlier, the media had labeled Denny's the "poster child for corporate discrimination."

Corporate America would be even more astonished when *Fortune* ranked Denny's the "Best Company in America for Minorities" in 1999. And, we were distinguished as the best again in 2000. The magazine surveyed the top 1,200 U.S. companies on 16 different measures, seeking the Top 50. Both years, Denny's excelled in 15 of the 16 measures.

Denny's also conducted its own research. In 1993, nearly half of all African Americans nationwide stated they did not feel welcome at Denny's. By 2000, that percentage had dropped to less than 10 percent. Nearly 80 percent said they would recommend the chain to a friend.

Also by this time, Denny's had exceeded all the goals outlined in the federal consent decree—after twice voluntarily revising the goals upward! Satisfied that Denny's was a transformed Company, the folks in Washington D.C. released the chain from the consent decree a year early.

Overnight, I became a national expert on diversity. Not surprisingly, my phone began to ring off the hook. Corporations, colleges and universities, government agencies, nonprofit organizations, public municipalities, even two state penal systems wanted to know the secret. How had it been done?

God did it when I started to apply His biblical principles to my work. It was my common practice, for example, to assemble a prayer team to fast and pray over every claim of discrimination that made its way to court.

The Lord's Word shaped all my business decisions. He guided my every move. Inside Denny's corporate headquarters, this was common knowledge, because I wore Christ on my forehead.

But how could I explain all this to the outside secular business world? I could not. So, the public relations director and I devised a politically-correct answer. It is chronicled in Jim Adamson's book, *"The Denny's Story: How A Company in Crisis Resurrected Its Good Name,"* published in January 2000.

But again, the honest answer is, God flipped Denny's right-side up, choreographing its supernatural ascent from worst to first. How and why He did it are addressed in my book, *Demolishing Racism in America—Secret Key to Worldwide, Last Days' Harvest.* God longed to demonstrate to His body how His Biblical principles worked in the marketplace. But more importantly, He offered a blueprint on how to demolish racial divisions within His body, the church.

Denny's compensated me handsomely for my services. My initial annual fee of $350,000 soon jumped to $375,000. Every month, the Company direct deposited $31,250 into my bank account.

I also received annual bonuses and stock options that rivaled my annual fee. It was nothing to bring home between $500,000 and $700,000 a year. One year, I earned nearly $1 million. Of course, this allowed us to move into our dream house on a hill.

The high compensation also allowed me to make investments in God's Kingdom all over the world. Not only did the Lord set me up to do this with IBS' funds, after my first week at Denny's, I was put in charge of all philanthropic giving for the company—a position I also held at Burger King.

During my tenure at both companies, I seized the opportunity to direct millions of dollars into a myriad of Christ-centered ministries and causes within the U.S. Each company had an annual philanthropic budget of at least $1 million, and during my last four years at Denny's, I oversaw fundraising campaigns that netted an additional $12 million for the selected charities.

During the combined 22-year period at both companies, I invested a conservative estimate of $30 million into programs and projects close to the Lord's heart. He was fulfilling my dream, allowing me to transfer the world's wealth into His Kingdom.

Chapter 15
Failing the Test of Prosperity

Early in my walk, the Lord warned me the enemy would tempt me in an area that could thwart His call on my life. It would be in the same manner Satan tempted Christ in the desert. The Lord, called to be the Savior of the world, was offered the nations of the world. I would be offered a shortcut to glory in the same way He was offered one. He warned me, "Ray, don't take the bait!"

The initial warning came during my days at Burger King. The Lord spoke to me while I was at a business conference in the Bahamas. He warned that riches would be used to test me. "You are about to enter the test of prosperity," He informed me one morning during our time alone.

The best description I can share for what the "test of prosperity" meant to my life is taken from a message I gave to the congregation at the First Baptist Church of Greer. By this time, I was knee-deep in the test. I had been working for Denny's for three years.

The testimony I gave that night came on the eve of having to leave our beautiful dream home in Greer, South Carolina. I would have to say goodbye to our big white house on a hill.

May 31, 1998

The Test of Prosperity

The testimony you're about to hear, I've never shared before. People may have heard bits and pieces, but not the whole story. I share it with you tonight because I suspect many of you are struggling in the same area I find myself struggling.

My tussle with prosperity has been an intense battle, one I did not recognize for the first nine years of my Christian walk. I want to share with you how God dealt with me in this area, the changes He wrought in me, and how these changes impacted His Kingdom.

In January 1986, on a business trip in Nassau, Bahamas, the Lord told me that I was about to enter the test of prosperity. I worked for Burger King Corporation at the time, and I had been born again nearly two years.

"The Test of Prosperity? Lord, what is that?" I asked. Now, being poor most of my life, I secretly thought this could be nice.

The Lord warned it was a sharp test that many failed. "The test of prosperity is more difficult than the test of adversity," He cautioned. He told me that it is more challenging to be Christ-centered—content, at peace, joy-filled, caring, and compassionate—in times of prosperity than to remain so in times of adversity.

I grabbed hotel stationery and began recording His counsel. He gave me 10 pitfalls to watch for as He prospered me in the coming years:

The Test of Prosperity: Eight Pitfalls

1. *Don't become proud. Be on your guard against pride. Endeavor to be humble and maintain a teachable spirit.*
2. *Don't become greedy. Be content with having your needs met.*
3. *Don't trust in things. Rely on Me for everything.*
4. *Don't let your heart grow cold, callous, or indifferent. Be kind and gentle, caring, and compassionate. Help them.*
5. *Don't become undisciplined or self-indulgent. Be disciplined in all your ways.*
6. *Don't grow lazy. Be industrious but with right motives.*
7. *Don't worry or grow anxious about possessions. Stay in peace.*
8. *Don't let riches steal your joy and render you empty. Be joyful always.*

Then He gave four biblical accounts to support what He was conveying to me:

- *David went from being a humble shepherd to king of Judah and later, king over all of Israel. It was at this height—the leader of a prosperous, thriving nation—that David made his most notable stumble.*

- *Solomon, the wisest man who ever lived, had too much of everything. Led astray by his many wives, he fell into idolatry.*
- *Ancient Israel and Judah grew fat, proud, and prosperous as kingdoms and strayed far from God into idolatry.*
- *Satan, as Lucifer, had been given everything, but it made him proud, and he mutinied against God. One-third of the angelic hosts followed him in rebellion.*

I started to think this test was not going to be the piece of cake I initially thought it was. Truly, it is easier for God to get our attention in times of lack than in times of plenty. Riches can be a major hindrance. Then, I remembered Scripture teaches, "It is more difficult for a rich man to enter the Kingdom of heaven, than for a camel to enter the eye of a needle." How shall I ever pass this test?

"It is difficult," the Lord said, "... but not impossible. I had it all, and I gave it all up." (But You're GOD!) Then, He reminded me of four others who passed the test:

- *Abraham was a man of tremendous wealth. He was also a man of tremendous faith. God used his wealth to establish the Patriarchs.*
- *Moses forsook the trappings and treasures of Egypt.*
- *Paul hailed from a family of means and status, but he called it all dung in the end.*
- *Barnabas had riches, but he also had a wonderful generous spirit.*

True to His Word, I started to climb the corporate ladder; it was a supernatural ascent. My responsibilities kept growing, expanding. Every year or 18 months, I was moved or promoted. Soon I became an officer of the company, traveling the world.

With the promotions came the high six-figure salaries, annual five-figure bonuses, stock options, a new luxury company car every other year, an annual wardrobe allowance, a home computer, premium health insurance, free annual physical, free tax and financial planning, free membership into all kinds of exclusive clubs. The perks and benefits were astounding.

"No wonder the rich get richer. They never pay for anything! It's given to them!" I joked with my parents.

During that time, my tithes and offerings kept pace with my increases. I would give God His off the top. Ten percent of my gross was the floor. My tithes and offerings ranged between 15 and 25 percent of my gross income. I felt I gave generously to God's work. I tried to increase it every year. I got a kick out of giving. While I was pleased with myself, God was not. Without ever realizing it, I became undisciplined in my spending, self-indulgent, and covetous.

The Lord sent me to a five-day, nightly seminar, How to Find Abundance in Your Budget *at our church. It opened my eyes. The seminar leader told us nearly one-third of the Scriptures dealt with the topic of money. I did not know God's Word had so much to say about money management. It is the best finance book ever written.*

I quickly discovered the only thing I had straight was the tithe. God was not pleased with how I was managing the other 85 to 75 percent of what He had given me. Our savings account never rose above $5,000. All those years, I either spent the money or gave it away to God and others.

I was undisciplined in managing what God had entrusted to me. We had two car loans, a large home mortgage, and moderate-to-heavy credit card debt. Sounds like we were living the American Dream, right? We were. And therein, was the problem. As Christians, we were never called to live the American Dream.

Our family was wasteful in our use of things—everything from not using all the lotion, shampoo, or ketchup at the bottom of the container to regularly throwing away perfectly good leftovers to getting only a single bid on major house renovations.

I wasted a lot of money, making hasty decisions. If I did not like the wallpaper, a built-in bookcase, or tile floor, I would rip it up and do it again. I would do it a third time if I had to.

I grew to be extremely self-indulgent. I did not want for anything. If I liked it, I bought it. I thought this was okay since God received His portion first. And His part was hefty enough. But I did not realize that what I gave the Lord was not sacrificial. I felt no pain. King David said, "I will not give to the Lord that which costs me nothing."

Soon I had a house full of beautiful antiques and expensive Oriental rugs. It was nothing to pay $3,000 for a table chest. In my spare time, I managed to make it to this and that auction. I was extremely impulsive in my purchases. I could go out for a loaf of bread and come back with a bed.

We ate out two, three, and four times a week at moderate to pricey restaurants. We ate whatever we had a taste for and never took home "doggie bags." We ate out so much, sometimes food spoiled in our refrigerator.

I did not know the prices of things in grocery stores. This drove my mother crazy. She is an avid coupon clipper. She will go to two and three stores every week to get the absolute best deals. You could charge me $10 for a head of lettuce, and I would not know the difference.

After the seminar, I became so convicted of my sin. The scales fell off my eyes. I wept for hours. I had been warned! And still I failed!

I asked God to forgive me and to show me how to manage His money because it was all His. He owned it all. The last night of the financial seminar, I destroyed all my credit cards except the one I had to pay off every month. We had bought a charming home in Miami, a step up from our first one. We were in the midst of some major home renovations. I stopped what I could.

We promptly paid off our car loans and have never had a car loan since. We established a family budget, and I monitored all expenses to see where the money was going. For the first time, I saw in black and white how I was blowing God's money. We started diligently saving and investing. The Bible warns that a fool spends all he gets (Proverbs 21:20, NLT).

I learned to pray before I made a purchase, which helped me distinguish between needs and wants. There were so many things I could do without. And when I truly needed something, I cannot tell you how often God led me to an absolute "steal." Sometimes I saved hundreds of dollars.

I started doing things myself instead of hiring people. I can still remember the thrill of installing track lighting in my bedroom office all by myself—just me and the Lord. I giggled with delight when I flipped the switch and the lights came on ... and the house didn't blow up or burn down!

I started comparison shopping, and my mother fell in love with me all over again. I discovered thrift stores. To this day, I rarely visit regular retail stores.

I learned to shop with a purpose and a list. Forget hanging out at the malls or browsing store windows. If I had spare time, I planned walks in the park and other activities.

I learned to take a razor blade and cut open every plastic container to get to the contents at the bottom. I was surprised how much I saved by using things to the last drop.

My biggest blind spot was covetousness. What an insidious sin! Many American Christians have been taken captive by this spirit and do not know it. It is Satan's chief tactic against us because it has a powerful and direct impact on evangelism.

A study by Campus Crusade for Christ shows that 80 percent of all the wealth needed to finish evangelizing the world concentrates in the United States of America. Satan has lulled us to sleep with riches. But we do not even realize we are rich. We do not feel rich. But we are.

The United States constitutes less than 5 percent of the world's people, but we consume more than 30 percent of the world's resources. There's something desperately wrong with this picture. Church, we have been duped by the enemy!

I told the congregation how God had gently nudged and prodded me about my covetousness for years, but I could not see. Even after attending the seminar, I explained how God had to do more to rock my world, to get my attention. He had to blow away my house—literally!

The sin of covetousness for me manifested itself primarily in the renovation and decoration of my house. I had dozens of home decorating magazines that fed my desire to change this or renovate that. I rationalized this as an outlet for my creativity. This was money I could have invested directly into the Kingdom of God.

Why spend $25,000 remodeling a kitchen when I could finance the translation of the *JESUS* film for a tribe in Africa or India, leading hundreds of souls into God's Kingdom? Why spend $10,000 updating a spare bathroom when I could sponsor the annual fundraiser for a local crisis pregnancy center that led 100 women to the Lord every year and saved the lives of many unborn babies? (As a former board chairman of a Miami-based pregnancy center, I knew this was easily achievable.)

What is more, think of the time and energy I wasted doing these renovation projects. I could have been doing something more useful for God's Kingdom. My covetousness competed with God for my resources, time, attention, and affection.

I had been active in church during the entire time I squandered God's money. I had always been active in church and in the community. I thought that if I gave generously to others, it was okay to do "my thing." God told me so clearly one day, "You don't have 'a thing.' I AM your thing."

With the founding of IBS, things changed. I began to invest in God's Kingdom in earnest. Through IBS, we transferred large amounts of money into evangelical, Christ-centered ministries around the world:

- We supported missionary work in Russia, Rwanda, and Bosnia.
- We became supporters of the Underground Church of China, where Christians are martyred daily for their faith. We funded the purchase of motorcycles to help nationals spread the good news of Christ.

- We had the *JESUS* film, based on Luke's Gospel, translated into the language of the Kurds in the Middle East.
- We also had the film translated into the language and dialect of tribes in Nigeria and India—people groups who never heard the Gospel of Jesus Christ.
- We paid the annual rent for a 24-hour prayer house in Ethiopia, where men and women gathered every day after work to pray for their nation.
- We purchased Range Rovers to help missionaries in Uganda take the gospel to the remote regions of the nation.
- We funded the underground production and distribution of evangelical videos for Christians in Egypt.
- We sponsored the airlift of Jewish families from Russia to Israel to escape persecution.
- At home, we became major supporters of the pro-life movement.
- We also supported missionaries and missionary families who were trying to revive American churches.

I finished my talk that evening by telling the congregation how, just that week, God had provided $125,000 to fund five translations of the *JESUS* film for five remote tribes in Africa. Each translation cost $25,000.

What I did not tell them that night was the financing for those five translations came from the equity in our home after I sold it to Denny's. The Company agreed to purchase our home to facilitate my sudden relocation to Detroit.

In a bold, unexpected, unprecedented move, God upended our lives. In the course of just seven days, He split our family. Ryan and I left South Carolina to live with my parents in Detroit. Suzanne was sent to Wichita, Kansas to nurse her dying sister-in-law and best friend, and Mike moved to Chicago permanently.

A chapter had closed in my life. God was about to begin another. Everything up to this point had simply been training, preparation for a mysterious call on my life.

PART TWO: THE CALL

Chapter 16
"Things Are Not as They Seem"

Often God allows His saints to glimpse the end of something He will accomplish in their lives, at the beginning. Joseph was given a prophetic dream in which God showed 11 sheaves of grain, representing his 11 brothers, bowing before him. God gave him a second dream in which his whole family was subject to him. But Joseph would have to wait 22 painful years—after he was made prime minister of Egypt—for his dreams to come to pass.

Such dreams are foundational in nature in that they underpin and reinforce something remarkable God will do in the future. Their fulfillment seems far-fetched, even impossible, so God allows the person to glimpse the end of it at the beginning. He lets the person know upfront what He will do, and He will use the dream in the ensuing years to keep the saint persevering.

God gave me such a dream on April 17, 1997. Upon this dream, He built the irrefutable case that nothing in the earth was as it appeared to be. The world was upside down—flipped inside out. People and things appeared to be one way but, in the light of heaven's reality, they were not. For His call on my life, I needed to be unshakable in this conviction.

I was not who I appeared to be to myself or to others. Only the watching heavens knew who I really was. I had an extraordinary role to play in the coming rapture of the church. Many souls would be affected. I would have to learn who I was in God's eyes, accept it, and then go do what He asked.

Until that point, God had simply been laying the groundwork. It was time for Him to unveil His real plan for my life. The unveiling would take 17 painful years. What God revealed in the ensuing years would challenge my faith like nothing before. Following is the introductory dream that kick-started the wild adventure.

April 19, 1997

A Dream: "Things Are Not as They Seem"

It was Thursday, April 17, 1997. I had just finished my quiet time with the Lord and decided to rest a little longer before preparing for work. We had been engaged in a conversation about my life's call. I told Him I had some idea of what He was trying to do in and through my life, but that everything seemed impossible.

I sensed I was called to help demolish the stronghold of racism within the American Church. But that could take a lifetime—maybe two or three! There appeared to be innumerable facets to the call and, so far, nothing had been accomplished.

I also reminded Him of my many physical and spiritual shortcomings. I was only 5 feet 3 inches tall, stubby, and chubby. Because of hypoglycemia, I shook when I did not eat every four hours. And I trembled when anyone yelled at me. I had no national platform to pull off anything. I was nobody in the eyes of the world.

My point: I was not endowed with extraordinary beauty, brawn, or brains. By choosing me, He surely would be using the "foolish and lowly" to confound the seemingly "wise and mighty" of the world. How could He achieve a movement of any kind through someone so weak and frail? He said, "Things are not as they seem."

As soon as my head touched the pillow, chills began to race up and down my body. I just laid there. I sensed something significant was about to happen. The phenomenon of the "racing chills" first occurred on September 20, 1996. Now they were happening with greater frequency. By this time, the chills occurred two or three times a day, especially when I prayed.

Just prior to falling asleep, I heard the Lord say, "Things are not as they seem." I repeated after Him, "Oh, things are not as they seem." Mine was not a question, just a statement of fact. Suddenly, I was pulled into the most curious dream.

The dream, rich in detail, included an opening segment, followed by three separate scenes of activity. During the first two parts, I simply sat in a chair and watched the action unfold. It was as if I were watching a film or theatrical performance. My participation in the third part, I discovered later, was significant.

The Opening Segment

The dream opened with me sitting in a chair, holding a large CD player. To my left were CDs. As I reached for one, the CD player turned into a desktop computer. I never witnessed the actual transformation. Unperturbed, I repeatedly pressed a button on the computer that activated an elevated television situated to the left of me. I turned to watch.

First Scene

There was a figure on television. It resembled a black crow. As soon as the picture flickered on, the crow reached outside the television set and pushed a button to change its appearance. Like a shade rolling from top to bottom, the crow changed into a cartoon character—a lady duck. The duck appeared mean. It looked tired and angry. Suddenly, another scene to the right of the television set caught my attention.

Second Scene

Three old African American women entered a stage. All three were wearing multiple layers of clothing. All three were bent from age. The trio headed for a single chair in the middle of the stage. One woman was the mother of the other two. They playfully scoffed at one another as they slowly made their way to center stage.

The mother took the seat, flanked by her two daughters. Quite unexpectedly, one daughter ripped off her costume to reveal she was really the mother; the other two were her daughters. She took the seat.

But the matter was not settled. The other daughter suddenly claimed to be the mother. She, then, took the seat. It was like musical chairs. Things became so confused that I did not know who was telling the truth.

They spoke uninhibitedly and with lots of attitude. Finally, I saw one of the women close up. She was dark with short-cropped hair. She had big pretty eyes.

Third Scene

As I sat intently watching the three women, my housekeeper Suzanne appeared and handed me a portrait of a beautiful woman. The three women faded as I focused on the painting in the gold metal frame. The lovely woman was illustrated in soft pastels. Suzanne explained someone had given her the portrait. She wanted me to have it as a gift.

I rose to hang the picture on the wall. As I reached up to place the portrait, I realized it was a lot smaller than I originally thought. I looked closer. It was not the same picture at all! I was now holding a sketch of a stout, stubby ballerina. And the canvas was damaged—ripped. But it had not been torn seconds earlier!

I turned it over. On the flip side of the canvas was a cut-out of another ballerina, tall and dressed in a hot pink tutu. Now the frame was no longer smooth metal, but pine and rough to the touch.

I searched everywhere for the original portrait. It must have fallen out of the frame somewhere, I reasoned. I searched high and low, but it was nowhere to be found. It was gone!

During my search, I noticed debris strewn across the floor. It looked as if someone had just moved and left papers and trash everywhere. Amidst all the debris, I spotted two toy soldiers, framed in a picture, lying on the floor. Seconds before I awoke, I heard the Lord's voice: "Things are not as they seem."

My eyes popped open. I looked at the clock, astonished by the passage of time. I started my quiet time at 6:30 in the morning. It was now 9 o'clock. Where had the time gone? God immediately reminded me of the dream and flooded my being with understanding. In all three scenes, nothing was as it seemed—*nothing*.

The first two scenes involved deception. The crow in the first setting attempted to be a duck. Although it could transform its overall appearance, it could not hide its annoyance or anger. This was a detail that troubled me. One would expect a cartoon character of that type to be engaging and cheery, not irritable.

In the second scene, there was deception of a different kind. The women were actors who continually lied about their identities. Who was telling the truth? I was totally confused when they faded into the background.

In the third scene, there was no deception. The portrait of the beautiful woman just transformed before my eyes. In the end, it was gone.

Never in a million years did I expect God to do what He did next. He was determined to drive home the point that things were not as they seemed until it was embedded in the very fiber of my being. My deep, unwavering comprehension of this truth was crucial to what He intended to accomplish in my life.

April 25, 1997

A Dream Come to Life!

God has blown my mind! He allowed me to live three scenes of a recent dream. It happened over the course of five days, immediately following the dream. The Lord later explained He allowed me to experience these real-life events to reinforce my understanding of the truth that things are not as they seem.

Quacks

Ryan, now 15, has been suffering from depression, and although she has been out of the slump for two weeks, we all thought it would be best to keep her appointment with a psychologist, made weeks earlier. Perhaps, we could learn something from the experience.

On Monday, April 21, 1997, four days after the dream, my daughter and I visited the psychologist. As God would have it, we were late. In my haste, I grabbed the directions to the accountant's office rather than the counselor's. By the time we arrived at the right office and completed the necessary papers, only 15 minutes remained to speak to the psychologist.

The woman invited us into her office. (Ryan and I joked later how her face resembled a duck's!) The counselor started with Ryan, who offered an extremely vague explanation as to why she was there. I stole a quick glance at the therapist. Her irritation was obvious. She sighed and then looked at me with a tired expression on her face. "Mother, what can you add to this story?"

I summed up my perspective in about five minutes. Her diagnosis was swift—Ryan needed immediate psychiatric help. She even named the four-syllable malady. I was taken aback. She never probed Ryan, and I had only expressed a few thoughts. On what basis had she so quickly formed her opinion?

Earlier, she told us their team of doctors staffed the local psychiatric hospital. She recommended Ryan be evaluated at the hospital that day. It would take only an hour. An evaluation sounded reasonable, so we went. She called ahead to let them know we were coming.

It turned out to be a long, three-hour process that consisted mostly of waiting. A woman finally talked to Ryan alone for about an hour. She then talked to me privately for 10 minutes. We waited while she went to "consult with the doctor," whom we never met.

She finally returned, took us to a private room, and informed us the doctor wanted to admit Ryan that afternoon.

"What?" Why does everybody think she's about to jump off the nearest building? Is there something I'm not seeing? The evaluator pushed hard. I was unsure. "How long would she stay? What exactly would they do?" I asked.

She said they would evaluate her and prescribe medications. The whole process would take about three days. By the way she responded to my questions, I suspected she was not telling me the whole story. I thought about Ryan falling behind in her classes.

Finally, I expressed my concern that things were moving too fast. Not only did Ryan and I need time to talk, I certainly was not going to make such a decision without consulting her father. He was in Chicago on a production shoot. The woman suggested I page him right away.

In the meantime, she would check my insurance coverage. She brought a telephone in from another room. I hesitated.

"Your child's well-being is the most important thing," she admonished.

"Maybe, we should return tomorrow?" I suggested.

She informed me the entire evaluation process would have to be repeated if I tried to leave and come back. Why? Everything we shared had been historical. What could change so drastically in a day? She left.

I picked up the telephone to page Mike. No dial tone. The line was dead. I immediately thought—a sign from God! I decided we would not be rushed into something we might regret later. Satan always rushes people. They were disappointed with my decision. I left utterly bewildered. I drove Ryan to school, so she could pick up her car.

"Mom, I don't know what to do either," she said tiredly. "Just pray, okay?" She exited the car and closed the door.

The fact is I had been praying throughout the whole ordeal. As I drove home, I poured out my heart to God. I told Him I trusted Him only. If Ryan were on the brink of hurting herself—although there were no signs of that—He alone would have to protect her. He was the only one who knew her secret thoughts or could watch her around the clock. I put all my trust in Him.

Right after that prayer, the Holy Spirit began to reveal many inconsistencies in our afternoon odyssey that I could not see before. One by one, the inconsistencies mounted. By the time I pulled the car into the driveway, I had decided. No way! I knew beyond a shadow of a doubt God was not in it. Instantly, peace flooded my heart—a peace that eluded me all day.

I paged Mike and told him all that had happened. He agreed with my decision, and by the time Ryan arrived home, she had come to the same conclusion. I checked the answering machine for telephone messages. I was surprised to find one from the hospital. They wanted me to call right away about my insurance coverage.

Things were truly not as they seemed. I was now utterly certain the psychologist and her cohorts were not at all what they presented themselves to be. They posed as concerned, helpful, mental healthcare professionals. However, they did not have Ryan's best interest at heart.

They were far more interested in making money than helping her. In the end, I felt it was all a deceptive ploy to profit off unsuspecting people. Perhaps, they would have caused more harm in the long run. They never called again after discovering I did not have insurance, although I could have paid cash for anything they prescribed.

Musical Chairs

The event involving the musical chairs began with a protracted investigation two weeks prior to the dream. Two days before I had the dream, I flew out to Oakland, California to investigate a claim of discrimination against a Denny's restaurant by an African American woman. I prayed for wisdom before, during, and after the meeting, which occurred on Tuesday, April 15, 1997.

Someone had stolen $2,800 from the restaurant safe. It was an inside job. Members of our Asset Protection Department were convinced the woman claiming discrimination did it.

After reading the Department's report and interviewing a witness I, too, was convinced the woman was guilty. I flew out to meet her and local NAACP officials, who represented her. Ten minutes into the meeting, I became convinced she did not steal the money.

As the woman took the floor to make her impassioned case, I noticed her dark complexion and her pretty eyes. I liked her short-cropped hairstyle. One thing I did not like was all the bravado she displayed in our meeting. She had a lot of attitude. Inexplicably, the woman brought her mother to the meeting. That surprised me because the daughter was 40 years old! Why did she need her mother?

The woman alleged that during his interrogation, our asset protection investigator had brought up the subject of her dead daughter. Her daughter had been killed three years earlier by a drunk driver. What she claimed he said was tremendously offensive to her and her family. If her accusation was true, his comments would have been grossly inappropriate since her deceased daughter had nothing to do with the missing $2,800.

Unfortunately, the witness I interviewed earlier kept changing his story. At the meeting, I learned things I was not told before. The witness did not refute the new facts. I flew home fully believing the woman was not guilty and that we needed to fire the asset protection investigator, who grievously mishandled the interrogation. Surely, we now had a discrimination lawsuit on our hands. Already operating under a federal consent decree, lawsuits of this kind panicked senior management.

On Tuesday, April 22, 1997—five days after the dream—I flew the investigator in for a meeting at our corporate offices. I wanted to hear his side of the story before deciding to fire him. As it turned out, he was highly credible. I received new and very significant information about the case that reversed my position. Clearly, the woman was guilty. We would fight the case in court.

But while debriefing the case with the Lord on Thursday, April 24, I started to waver a bit in my latest decision not to go through with the dismissal. I said, "Father, I hope I did the right thing by not firing the investigator. It has all been so crazy! She's guilty, she's not guilty, she's guilty. My goodness—it's like musical chairs!" I caught my words. Suddenly, I remembered my dream!

Was the case not just like the dream? In the dream, three Black women—two daughters and a mother—kept changing their story until I was utterly confused. The Oakland case involved an African American family; specifically, two daughters and a mother. The daughter under investigation resembled the woman in my dream—dark with pretty eyes, short-cropped hair, and a lot of attitude. Most importantly, the shifting facts in the case had resulted in my being completely baffled as I had been in my dream.

The Missing Nightgown

On April 24, during this same time alone with the Lord, I also started to make striking connections between the first scene in my "things are not as they seem" dream and the pseudo psychologist. She resembled and behaved just like the tired, irritable duck in my dream. I sat in my bed completely dumbfounded.

Finally, I joked, "Okay, Lord, now I will be on the lookout for something beautiful that really isn't!" I was thinking of the third dream scene in which the portrait of the beautiful woman mysteriously disappeared and morphed into two unattractive ballerinas, one on one side of the canvas and the other on the flip side.

At that very moment, I looked down at my nightgown. I reminded the Lord I wore The White Gown—a difficult feat for me. On March 20, 1996, I wore a white nightgown in a terrifying dream. The dream—the worst of my life—was so upsetting I refused to wear the gown again in real life. It was silly, but whenever I reached for it, I remembered the dream and opted for other nightwear. More than a year had passed since I wore the gown. Last night, for some strange reason, I put it on.

"Wait a minute!" I looked down at the gown again. "This isn't the gown. It's white, but it's not the gown!" I shouted. I jumped out of bed. I ran to my dresser to find the original gown—the REAL white nightgown. I rummaged through all my dresser drawers. I found a set of long, hot pink pajamas, but not the white gown.

The gown had been a gift from my mother. The one I wore must belong to Suzanne. It was tight across my chest and arms. It hit my legs at mid-calf. The sleeves were shorter. And the material was not as fine either. It felt like rough cotton.

My gown was fuller and longer—silky and soft to the touch. How could I have made such a mistake? I was certain I put on my white gown the night before. I'd bet the farm on it! The differences between the two gowns were unmistakable. Where did this one come from and where was mine?

Maybe Suzanne had it. Perhaps, she gave me hers by mistake when she did the laundry. This made no sense because I was confident, I slipped on my gown the night before. Nevertheless, I raced to Suzanne's bedroom to search her dresser drawers and closet. I also checked her dirty clothes hamper. No gown!

Slowly, it dawned on me that the lost gown was like the portrait in my dream! One minute, it was there. The next minute, it was gone. I headed for my bathroom to get ready for work.

I glanced at my image in the large vanity mirror. For the first time, I noticed the gown I wore had a large tear on the underarm. It was torn like the canvas in my dream! But the gown I put on the night before was not torn!

"Could this really be happening?" I whispered.

Suddenly, another possibility occurred to me. Perhaps, Ryan had it. Suzanne could have given my gown to her by mistake. I scurried down the hall to Ryan's bedroom, hoping I would find it and put the matter to rest.

I searched Ryan's closet and dresser, even under the bed. No gown. But I noticed her room, as usual, was a mess. Clothes were thrown everywhere. School papers, books, pencils, pens, candy wrappers, and other things littered the floor. It reminded me of the last scene of my dream—chaotic, debris strewn everywhere. I felt like I had stumbled into Rod Sterling's Twilight Zone. I hardly knew what to think.

Finally, I gave up looking for the gown. It was gone. Like the portrait in my dream, it had disappeared. With all the searching, I was now running late for work. I went to get dressed.

While eating a quick breakfast, I read only one article in the morning newspaper. The hostage situation in Peru was over. Seventy-one of the 72 hostages were freed, but all 14 rebels were killed, along with two soldiers.

"Like the two soldiers in my dream," I muttered.

Five days before the Lord allowed me to connect my dream to actual events unfolding in my personal life, He explained what He meant by the expression, "things are not as they seem." He presented to me two panorama perspectives—heaven's and mankind's. He explained what was frequently seen as reality by earth's inhabitants was not the reality of heaven's inhabitants.

April 20, 1997

A Cosmic Stage Play

The whole world is a theater, a stage, and every human being plays a part—wittingly or unwittingly. Everything in the world, from the tiniest sparrow to the highest mountain, is a prop. This includes Microsoft, Walmart, Wall Street, Main Street, the World Bank, the West Bank, the Westside Mall, the neighborhood laundry mat, the local barbershop, the middle school down the street, every park, house, school, dog, cat, ant—all props. Anything the eye can see, the hand can touch, or a human being can engage, has been placed here to support the unfolding drama.

There is no hiding place on this stage. Most people have no idea their present life is a dress rehearsal for an eternal role. Everything that is done under the sun is observed from above.

Earth's residents are being watched from different heavenly sectors. The celestial audience divides into two theaters. One arena houses a heavenly gathering of angels, saints who have crossed over into eternity, and God Himself. Members of this sector are kind, caring, and compassionate.

Not all spectators of the world's events are benevolent. Some are quite malevolent. The Word of God refers to these other spectators as "authorities, powers, and spiritual forces of evil in heavenly realms." Satan, whom the Bible refers to as the "prince of the air" and his minions (fallen angels) comprise the menacing assembly. They are housed in the other theater.

On this stage, there is both a war and a race unfolding. The war is as old as mankind. It is between two kingdoms—between good and evil, light and darkness, life and death, God and Satan. The two kingdoms are not equal.

Although God alone is the Victor in any contest, two-thirds of all the angelic hosts stand ready to do His bidding. They are His messengers, sent to aid earth's inhabitants. Everything they do undergirds God's redemptive plan for mankind.

The devil and his cohorts are vastly outnumbered and outclassed. Since God is not on their side, their power over human beings must come from another source. They rely largely on deception to accomplish their goals. God never succumbs to deception. In fact, He uses their evil tactics to accomplish His righteous plans and purposes in human history.

The spoils of this war are priceless—human souls. The war is about where human souls will spend eternity—in heaven or hell. It is God's desire that no human should perish, but all would come to everlasting life through His Son, Jesus Christ. However, all will not.

It is the devil's desire to destroy as many souls as he can, to take them with him to eternal damnation. Satan hates God and mankind made in His image. He hates God, for his greatest desire is to be God and to be worshipped as God.

There is also a race being run on this stage. It is a race of life. The race is an individual marathon as well as a team pursuit. It is not a race of speed. The winner's crown does not go to the fastest runner. Success is measured by how well one fulfills his or her potential in Christ—to help build His Kingdom—given the life he or she has been dealt.

Potential or capacity varies by individual. Different people have distinctive capacities. All of them have unique life circumstances. God apportions each person a capacity—a set of abilities, talents, gifts, and resources. He also establishes the circumstances under which each is born. Some people have every imaginable privilege and, others, every unimaginable obstacle. God knows intimately each person's special circumstances.

Not everyone runs the same distance. Some run a few hours, some a few months or years, others run a whole lifetime. Each generation of runners passes the baton to the next.

Only God can judge rightly how well a person runs life's race for His glory. Only He knows a person's true God-given potential, his or her unique gifts, talents, or resources. He is the only one who can judge how high the odds are stacked against a person's life. Only He knows the amount of spiritual light a person has been given in Christ. Regardless of the difficulties facing an individual, God knows what seems impossible is possible with Him. There is no obstacle that cannot be overcome through Him.

Interestingly, most human beings are not even in the race. Nonbelievers never make it to the starting block. ("The road to life is narrow and few people find it.") Only those who have accepted Jesus Christ—the Author of Life—as their Lord and Savior are in the race. Others represent the "living dead." They have the appearance of life, but they do not have His Spirit inside of them—teaching, guiding, equipping, and changing them. They are breathing and animated, but they are not living the existence God intended for His highest creation—a life abundant in grace and mercy that is free and eternal.

Many of the living dead appear successful and productive, but they are not. Any human achievement, apart from Christ, profits nothing in heaven's economy. Earthly achievements apart from Christ turn to "wood, hay, and stubble" in eternity. They are reduced to ashes at the Judgment Seat, where all human works will be judged by His fire. He warns those who do run the race: "to whom much is given, much is required."

All spectators of this war and race are not equally knowledgeable. Only God is all-knowing. The angels, God's messengers, who stand poised to help those running the race of life, do not know all things. The saints, who have completed their leg of the race for God's glory and await the final laps to be run by the rest of us, do not know all things. The devil and his minions who fight God's runners at every turn, do not know all things. While all have a panoramic view of world events, they cannot read the hearts and minds of men, nor do they know the future. Only God knows all things.

While the knowledge of the angelic hosts and others is limited in scope, their perspective is greater than man's. Man's view of himself and the world around him is severely restricted. His point-of-view is equivalent to that of an ant on a railroad track. The ant has no clue where it is, and, sooner or later, it will be destroyed by a train if it does not get off the track. A human being has only one hope of knowing what is truly going on in life and in the world around him or her. The person must seek God.

God knows everything and is pleased to share with His runners His will, plan, and purpose for their lives. Each person has been strategically placed in his or her generation. Each person's contribution to God's Kingdom is significant to Him.

It is not God's will that His people run in darkness. He desires they run to His Light so that He can show them the way. He can make the path smooth and straight or grant the runners the "feet of deer" with which to traipse the rough, treacherous places.

Light and Truth can be found in God's "Rule Book," the Holy Bible. The Rule Book contains everything runners need to know to run a successful race. Light and Truth can be wielded to combat Satan's deceptions. They are a tremendous aid to the runners. The Rule Book shows the runners the best paths to take and how to sidestep pitfalls and landmines.

Unfortunately, most runners do not read the Rule Book. Even fewer use it. Those who run by the Rule Book are the most powerful runners. Obedience to the commands found in the Rule Book—not speed—determines the success of a runner.

While a war rages in the heavenly places between God and the devil, human beings try to run the race on earth. It is the devil's intent to hurt, maim, and destroy as many runners (and non-runners) as possible. He will stop at nothing to keep the runners from successfully completing the race and to keep those on the sidelines from entering it.

He employs countless distractions—pleasures, burdens, and cares—to hinder the runners and to keep new runners from joining the race. He does whatever it takes to keep people preoccupied with the things of life in this present world, blinding them to their spiritual destiny in the next.

Since the devil is not all-knowing and cannot read human minds, he attempts to speak deceptions to them. This is his greatest weapon. He must deduce from his observations of a person's life the kind of deceptions that work best.

He masterminds plans of destruction against the person's soul. The devil makes sure that unsuspecting people receive whatever their corrupt hearts crave if what they desire has the potential to distract and destroy them. The nonbeliever is especially susceptible to his ploys.

To lead people to destruction, the devil exalts certain people (e.g., entertainers, sports celebrities, heads of state, corporate titans), using popular media such as music, the Internet, television, and movies. (God's use of a CD player, computer, and television in my dream was not random.) Satan is the "prince of this world" and has the power to make ordinary people the world's superstars.

Many famous, rich, powerful, achieved people are simply pawns or puppets of the devil. He inspires their every thought and uses them to distract or lead the masses astray. Eventually, they are destroyed—leaders and followers—if they fail to heed God's warnings to receive Jesus as their Lord and Savior.

Some of the world's most powerful, accomplished people think they have it all. They think they have it made. But in reality, they have nothing. They are deceived. They are traveling that broad road to destruction. Sometimes they leave useful legacies to the world that the Lord employs for His own good purposes.

Conversely, there are many obscure, unassuming people to whom the world pays no attention. They are earth's real power brokers. These people are believers who quietly change human history without anyone in the world knowing it. They use their God-given gifts, talents, and resources to serve mankind as Christ served mankind. Our service to others, in light of our God-given ability and resources, determines our ultimate success as a runner.

While the world may be blind to their existence, achievements, and pursuits, all the heavenly spectators know these are the ones to watch. The angels help them. The saints are rooting for them. The devil plots their demise. He can only hurt them if they are disobedient to God's commands. Even if physically killed, they are promoted into glory at their deaths. Nonetheless, they are the people who are truly making a difference in the eternal scheme of things.

The most powerful of these nobodies are those who are most obedient to the Lord's commands. They know the Rule Book and use it. They are warriors of prayer. They know there is a spiritual war going on in heavenly places that profoundly impacts human events. They partner with God and His angelic hosts to achieve God's righteous purposes. They know how to use their spiritual weapons—Word of God, prayer, faith, fasting—to fight wicked spiritual forces in high places. They are strategic runners and achieve considerably more for God's glory than others during their lifetimes. These warriors have written off the world. They live not for the present world, but for the next.

They have God's view of what is really going on. They are soldiers in His army, not distracted by civilian affairs—worldly matters of no eternal value. They know the present world is passing away, and they are just passing through. They know what matters most is their eternal destiny and how well they run their leg of the race for God's glory.

The institutionalization of evil—structural evil throughout the world and across the ages based on a system of mammon-chasing—suggests Satan's deceptions have been extremely successful. However, he has done nothing the Lord has not allowed him to do. The Lord is Sovereign over all things, including the war and the race. He uses both to sift earth's inhabitants—sheep from goats, wheat from chaff. The dress rehearsal decides who is fit for the Kingdom of God, who will rule and reign with Him in eternity as well as each saint's eternal role and assignment.

God was laying a foundation with the "things are not as they seem" dream and this subsequent revelation. In a few short weeks, through several other disclosures, He would fully persuade me that I was not who I appeared to be—even to myself. I was a living sign and symbol of His corporate bride! She was not whom she appeared to be either. She appeared weak to the world, but she would prove to be strong. Further, the rapture of His church was not an event that would happen one day, far off in the future. It would happen in my lifetime. And finally, He convinced me I would go first as a sign to His corporate bride! My translation into eternity would serve as a sign to the Church that her departure was imminent!

Chapter 17
Symbolizing the Bride of Christ

"Your life will be a sign for her," the Holy Spirit gently counseled. Finally, that absolutely, utterly, completely "impossible" thing I always suspected God would bring to my doorstep and then command me to believe, had arrived. I never suspected the half of it. What God revealed to me during the spring and summer of 1997 was inconceivable. It was downright mind-blowing.

The following journal excerpt reveals how the Lord first introduced me to the idea that my transition from this world to the next would be like Enoch's and Elijah's translation and how His corporate body would follow in the same way.

May 4, 1997

Am I the Missing Portrait/Gown?

I discovered a new route home from church. I was amazed to learn for nearly two years we had driven many miles out of the way! The new route cut our traveling time in half. I could not wait to show Suzanne, who traveled back and forth to church three, four, and sometimes five times every week to serve in the nursery. She, too, was astounded.

On the way back to the house, I said, "How could we have been so stupid?" She said we were not stupid; we just did not know. I wondered what the aerial (heavenly) view looked like of us driving to church. We made one gigantic circle since our points of origin and destination were practically next door to each other.

I queried Suzanne, "Why would God allow us to waste so much time, energy, and gas for so long?" It was my strong conviction that some unusual events happen in our lives because God is trying to drive home a point or teach a lesson. I mused, "Things are not as they seem." In this case, what appeared far away was actually near. Suzanne and I drove home in silence.

During my evening walk, I asked God if my new route discovery was an object lesson of some kind. He confirmed it was! During our walk, He reminded me that the first two scenes in my "things are not as they seem" dream involved deception. They demonstrate how Satan deceives many in the world. Referring to the cosmic stage play revelation, often those who appear weak in the world, such as Spirit-filled saints, are strong. And those who often seem strong and powerful in the world, such as popular entertainers or heads of state and corporations, are weak.

"What appears far away, indeed, may be very near," He continued. For example, the church seemed far when all the time it was quite near. "Likewise," He said. "The culmination of My will for your life seems impossible because time is short, and many things appear undone. It's nearer than you realize, closer than you think."

"Okay, what seems weak is really strong." I tried to summarize what the Lord was saying to me. In the first two scenes of my dream, deception cloaked the truth as many truths in the world are masked. Further, "what seems far is really near." The newly discovered route to church demonstrated that.

I questioned the Lord about the third scene. It was quite different from the first two. It did not involve deception; I was not a spectator; I was an active participant. What was its message?

"What is ... is no more," the Holy Spirit counseled.

Incredible as it seemed, I suddenly realized I was the missing portrait in the dream! In real life, I represented the missing gown! God had already revealed that I would be coming home sooner than I thought. Last fall, He began telling me, "Get your house in order. You will be coming home soon."

I have had many indications since that time (too many to record here) that my crossing over may not be a "typical" transition into eternity, but a departure like Enoch's or Elijah's. I have been fighting these revelations for nearly eight months. It all seems so impossible. But God is telling me to believe it. I suspect, as with the missing gown, people will search for me as they searched for Enoch and Elijah, but I will not be found.

As I struggled with God's revelations about my rapture to heaven, God interrupted my thoughts with a series of direct questions. Studying the list, I saw His point. If I could accept the following things and events as true, what made my situation so impossible to believe?

"Do you believe ...

- *In Heaven? (Yes.)*
- *Noah built the ark? (Yes.)*
- *I took Enoch and Elijah? (Yes.)*
- *David slew Goliath? (Yes.)*
- *Noah was ridiculed for obeying Me? (Yes.)*
- *Joseph enraged his brothers with his dreams? (Yes.)*
- *Joseph interpreted dreams of the Pharaoh? (Yes.)*
- *I spoke through My prophets across the ages? (Yes.)*
- *I was ridiculed for obeying My Father? (Yes.)*
- *Mary had Me through the Holy Spirit? (Yes.)*
- *Mary and Joseph were ridiculed?" (I bet!)*

"The righteous shall live by faith," He said. "Look around you. Look at the evil in the world. Evil is real. The spirit realm is real."

Then I remembered faith was being sure of what I hoped for and certain of what I did not see. Nothing—absolutely nothing—was impossible with God.

"Do you believe that when you sing it in church?" He interrupted my thoughts.

"Yes!"

"Have I not prepared the hearts of those with whom you've already shared?"

"Yes, You have," I admitted. "Lord, how shall I behave? How shall act?" I finally asked.

"Act like you believe!"

The Lord revealed that before any one of my days came to be, He ordained me to serve as a symbol of His corporate bride, a sign to her. He established my call before the foundations of the earth. The first thing He did was demonstrate to me through Scripture that my situation was not unique.

Scripture brims with examples of how God used signs and symbols to reveal truth to His people. He used everyday things in the lives of people or their *very lives* to reveal His divine plans to a generation. For example, using signs and symbols, through Ezekiel, God delivered prophecy after prophecy to the nation of Judah regarding His coming judgment:

God Instructed Ezekiel to:	*Represented/Symbolized:*
Draw the siege of Jerusalem on a clay tablet.	Siege of Jerusalem to the people of Israel.
Lay on his left side while prophesying for 390 days, then lay on right for 40 days.	Duration of Israel and Judah's punishment, respectively; a day equaled one year.
Ration his bread and water for 390 days.	Scarcity of food and water during the siege against Israel.
Shave his head and beard; divide the shavings into three parts and save a few strands.	Approximately one-third of the people to be killed in the city, one-third to be killed in battle, one-third to go into exile, a tiny remnant saved.
Pack his belongings as if he were going somewhere.	One-third of the people to be sent into exile.
Tremble when eating his food.	People eating in anxiety and fear during the siege.

Likewise, God told the Prophet Jeremiah to wear a yoke on his neck to demonstrate to the nations how He would use Babylon to punish and enslave them for their wickedness (Jeremiah 27). The prophet was also told to visit the potter's house, buy a clay jar, and smash it to pieces to demonstrate how God would shatter Judah (Jeremiah 19). When the country was under siege, God instructed Jeremiah to buy a field to demonstrate to His people that they would one day be restored to the land (Jeremiah 32).

God used Hosea's *life,* commanding a grievous marriage to Gomer, to demonstrate His grievous relationship with Israel His wife with whom He held a covenant love (Hosea 1:3-8). Is it then, so unusual that the *same* God, described in Scripture as the "same yesterday, today and tomorrow," could be doing a same or similar thing in our generation?

The journal excerpt below discloses how God revealed to me that I had been called to be a symbol and sign of His corporate bride. At this juncture, it felt like a fairy tale, a Cinderella story. Later, He would reveal His Cinderella was a mess. I was ... she was... we were covered with shameful, inglorious blemishes.

June 27, 1997

Glimpsing Eternity

My entire day yesterday was spent with God. My morning quiet time was extended by an eight-hour road trip. We talked as I drove. Upon my return, the Lord and I took our usual evening walk. I showered, dressed for bed, ate dinner, and then I spent another hour debriefing the day with Him.

Afterward, Suzanne and I finished a wonderful movie on the life of Joseph (of Egypt) that we had begun the night before. Then, I turned out the lights and talked with God some more. Our discussion was quite unusual.

Earlier in the day, I asked the Lord to confirm conclusively for me whether all the unusual revelations I had received since fall 1996 were from Him or the enemy. He always cautions believers to test the spirits since the human heart is deceitful above all things, and the enemy is cleverly deceptive.

Specifically, I asked Him to speak to me about symbolizing His bride. I wanted to review His communication to me on the subject, using three filters—His written Word, the Holy Spirit, and my unfolding providential circumstances. (In my experience, if an impression passes this three-pronged litmus test, then the thought, idea, or impression is from God.) He started right away, that morning, during our time together.

Later, on the road trip, we talked about life on earth being a dress rehearsal for eternal roles and assignments. The analogy was most appropriate—more than I had originally thought. As I remembered the life of Christ, just after His resurrection, He resembled His pre-resurrected self, although at times His disciples had difficulty recognizing Him.

God explained while we will resemble the physical beings we were on earth, each of us will be made new, whole, and complete in heaven. So, there will be some changes to our physical heavenly image.

I inquired about our personalities and temperaments. These will remain, basically, the same as well, but all that does not glorify God or express Christ will be removed. Building godly character was a chief part of the sanctification process on earth.

I asked, "Could it be also that our earthly calls, roles, and functions—the things we enjoy doing, and the areas in which we are gifted—have something to do with our eternal assignments?" God confirmed there was a connection. This was exciting to ponder.

Next, I thought about myself—beyond what I do on earth. I thought about my love for Christ. I have had a crush on the Lord for a long time. (According to the Webster Dictionary, a crush is an "extravagant admiration or love for someone.") If this was wrong, I asked God to forgive me and, by His Holy Spirit, lead me to think rightly about my relationship with Christ. (I had been asking this for months!)

Then the thought hit me: to know Christ is to love Him. Period. If anyone knew Him—really knew Him—they could not resist falling madly, deeply, head-over-heels, hopelessly in love with Him. He was irresistible. Even the hopelessly rebellious at heart would fall hard for Him, if they truly knew Him.

I boldly challenged Him. How could He expect a vessel not to fall deeply in love with the Potter when the vessel finally realized what the Potter was doing? He was making the vessel into a beautiful, one-of-a-kind masterpiece, to be loved and treasured by the Potter for all eternity. What else was a vessel to do, but fall in love when it discovered the Potter, Himself, to be the Origin of all that was exquisite, majestic, and good? It was impossible not to fall in love! There was no way not to!

It occurred to me that although I have an earthly husband who I am fully convinced was ordained to be my spouse from the beginning, Christ is my Prince Charming. I pondered this idea for a while.

I started to mourn the fact that I had picked my Savior as my Prince Charming. What was wrong with me? My earthly husband was not my soul's mate. God was. God offered this comfort: no one should lament not being swept off her feet by a human Prince Charming. There was no such person.

Our human relationships were designed to teach us about our true relationship with Him. For example, our children allow us to understand and experience the joys and pains of being a parent, a loving authority figure in their lives. God wants us to know that He often experiences us as we experience our children.

In the end, I concluded Christ was Prince Charming to every believer—male or female, happily or unhappily married, widowed or single. Unlike all other human beings, He is perfect.

When I returned from my road trip, the Lord and I talked further about His love for me and mine for Him. Later, I asked the Holy Spirit to help me record my feelings toward the Lord. There was much in my heart and head that I wanted to put on paper, to help sort it all out. He led me to write the following exposé.

A Perfect Love

There was a child who matured into a young girl ... a teenager ... and then a woman. She was not especially beautiful. There was nothing about her that would make a young man look twice. She had no illusions about herself. She was simple and plain and knew it. Through the years, she had learned to be comfortable and content with who she was. She knew some things could not be changed, so she decided to make the best of who she was.

There was an extraordinary, attractive gentleman who had observed her from afar for many years, since she was a child. He had loved her forever. He had watched over her and helped her in ways she did not know. She was unaware. For many years, she did not know he even existed.

This was incredible since he was the catch of a lifetime. He was perfect in every way. He was kind, sweet, generous, funny, gentle, tender, powerful, and exceedingly wealthy. He had no equal; no, not one.

Slowly he began to make himself known to her. He moved very slowly so as not to overwhelm her. Time and again, he demonstrated his love for her in unique and special ways.

Gradually, she noticed his favor toward her. She was grateful for the help and humbled by the attention. She mainly thought he was just being nice, thoughtful. That was his way. He had a reputation for being charitable and kind to everyone. Then one day, she realized she meant something more to him than she had originally thought. She was stunned. Surely, I am misreading his messages, *she reasoned.* It cannot be possible! *But it was possible.*

He saw something in her that no one else saw. She did not even see it. She had grown and changed much through the years. He had chronicled her growth and loved her for the person she had become inside, not for what she looked like on the outside. He also saw all she would become in time. He loved her passionately.

She tentatively broached the subject about his passion for her, not wanting to humiliate herself or him. He gave her no indication she had misunderstood his actions. He was someone whom she had quietly admired for years. She was in awe of him and adored him more as a protector and caregiver than as a beau. Who was she to catch the eye of such an extraordinary person? She was amazed at her good fortune.

When it finally dawned on her that she was being courted by him, she fell hard. Lavished in his boundless love and attention, she realized she also had a crush on him too. He had stolen her heart. She realized she was in love with him and had been for a long time. He was pleased that she returned his passion, for it was God's will that she become his eternal companion.

In fact, God had been preparing her for His Son for a long time—before establishing the foundations of the earth. She was the bride of Christ. This was God's plan all along, to create a masterpiece for Himself, a perfect love ... a holy people for His Son. She was the Son's inheritance, and He was hers.

After writing the exposé, I finally had a much-needed, frank discussion with the Lord about our relationship. It led to the breakthrough revelation that I was a symbol of His glorious bride. I recorded it in the same journal excerpt:

A Glorious Revelation: Symbolizing the Bride of Christ

A stray thought. Countless times, this stray thought occurred to me, but I diligently beat it back. Even now I am trying to ignore it. It just seemed too extraordinary to contemplate, especially at the end of a long, tiring day. But I could not sleep.

The Father knew all my thoughts—even the stray ones. Everything about me, about everyone, was laid bare before Him. He had seen me at my worst. He had seen me participate in things that would have destroyed my mother, had she known.

"Why not be transparent so the Lord can deal with it?" I asked myself. The risk seemed too great. What risk? Did the Lord not know everything about me? Nothing was hidden from Him. Finally, I sat straight up in my bed in pitch darkness.

"Lord, I need to get this out." I began to spill my heart. "Father, the relationship between Hosea and Gomer is the best example I can give in Scripture about what I have been thinking. You used them to demonstrate your unconditional, boundless love for your chosen people, Israel. Gomer was a prostitute, who despised all that was good. Yet You commanded Your dear servant Hosea to redeem her, to take her into his home as his wife—very much against her will! They had three insufferable children from their union. While that did not seem fair to Hosea, You ordained him to take Gomer as his own. Their union was a demonstration to his generation and generations to come of Your covenant love for Your faithless wife, Israel. In another instance, You used the relationship between Ruth and Boaz to demonstrate Your covenant love for Israel and Christ's love for the Church. It was the same with Solomon and the Shulammite woman. Scripture is filled with such examples." I stopped.

"I have waited a long time to have this discussion with you," the Lord said. "Come." He wanted me to continue.

I hesitated for a moment, but then I decided to lay all my cards on the table, to put it all out there. There was no point in hiding the secrets of my heart.

"Lord, because of the extraordinary revelations and dreams You have given me—and You know exactly what they are— I am beginning to feel as though I am being prepared to marry Christ Himself! As in a REAL marriage, which we know cannot be true! But You have done nothing to make me think differently. In fact, the evidence continues to mount. What's going on here? Are You using my life as You used Hosea's? Are You using me to symbolize something—Your covenant love for Your bride?" By this time, I was crying.

Weeping before the Lord, I began to recount many of the events and revelations that had led me to this incredible conclusion:

1. He had observed and tracked my growth from a little child. He had confirmed this fact in countless, extraordinary ways.
2. He had been refining me from the beginning—first with a jackhammer; next, with a hammer and chisel; and finally, with

sandpaper. In the later years, He lavished me daily with tender, unending mercies, from sunup to sundown.

3. All my life, He had poured His favor on me. This truth was so undeniably obvious that even a blind man could see it.
4. He had given me so many spiritual gifts that I was too embarrassed to discuss the subject with anyone anymore.
5. He had revealed Himself to me in so many extraordinary, supernatural ways through the years that I stopped long ago trying to record them all.
6. He had revealed the enemy to me in ways that would have terrified the average Western believer. Nonbelievers simply could not have received it. And He started this process early in my Christian life. For so many years, I could not understand why.
7. He always protected me. I can recall numerous instances of His divine intervention. Like during my college days when that man I did not know tried to rape me. Soon after, he was the lone victim of a fatal automobile accident.
8. He had given me several remarkable prophetic visions and dreams, all of which came true.
9. He told me that I had been chosen as a vessel for noble use and that He foreknew me and ordained my journey from the beginning. In a 1993 vision, He said He would make me like a tree, rooted and established in Him, and He promised I would bear much fruit because of it.
10. He had entrusted me with His delegated power and authority on earth. He had anointed me to do battle in His name.
11. He revealed that I would be caught up to heaven like Enoch and Elijah in a kind of pre-rapture event and that I should "get my house in order" for the occasion.
12. He told me my transition into eternity would serve as a sign to His church that she would soon follow.

At this point, I could not help but recall the dream scene of the missing portrait of the radiant woman. In the blink of an eye, the portrait—His

Masterpiece—was gone! I searched for her everywhere, but I could not find her.

The vanishing portrait paralleled my missing gown in real life. Just like that, it was gone forever, and a counterfeit replaced it! Is this not how it will be at the Church's rapture? In an instant, Christ's bride will disappear and be replaced with a counterfeit.

The debris I saw in my search for her reflected disorder—the chaos and confusion after the church disappeared. And what about the two toy soldiers lying on the floor amidst the debris in my dream, and the two real soldiers killed during the Peruvian hostage standoff? I now knew those scenes represented the terrorism, anarchy, and war that would follow the Church's rapture.

Finishing my list, I told the Lord I was consumed with thoughts of Him. I thought of nothing but His Second Coming and when I will join Him in His Father's house. I confessed I was thrilled at the idea of being betrothed to Him. Clearly, He was aware that I had experienced every thought and emotion a bride experiences at the prospect of finally marrying the beau of her dreams.

Now, it was out. Everything had been said. I was relieved to get the matter off my chest. The Lord invited me to rest. I quickly fell into a deep, peaceful sleep.

I was up bright and early the next morning. I had predicted that in the light of a new day, with a rested mind, I would be completely ashamed of myself for having such a discussion with the Lord. I was not.

"Lord, couldn't any Spirit-filled believer make the same assertion? That he or she is being prepared to symbolize the bride of Christ?"

"I have chosen you," He said. After that, I rose from bed to record our discussion.

Against all rational thought, I resolved to agree with Him. I decided to live each moment as God brought it to me, to ponder what He had unveiled while I waited for more to be revealed. Whenever I wavered in this resolution, a terrible sense of uneasiness overtook me. My spirit became disquieted.

God patiently unveiled things that encouraged me to respond in faith. I admit to resisting some; nevertheless, He persisted. In every instance, my acceptance dispelled inner tumult and quieted my spirit. Any doubt led to inner turmoil; belief always led to peace.

Right after the revelation that I was a symbol of His bride, the Lord started referring to me as "a sign of the bride-to-come." For the life of me, I could not figure out the "to come" part. Did it mean I would be "coming to" heaven? Of course, I would. All of us in the body of Christ would. Why would that make me a sign? What would I point to?

A physical sign points to something. It shows the way. A spiritual sign reveals something, a hidden truth. God would use my life to point to something—to show the way and to reveal hidden truth. But what exactly would that be? Everything would be unveiled in time.

One day, sitting in my office at Denny's, the meaning of the phrase came to me. It meant just what it said. I was a sign to the "bride to come"—the Lord's corporate bride, who would eventually "come to" heaven in the rapture!

Suddenly, it made sense why He said I would go first. I would point the way. I would go first as a sign to her that she was, indeed, coming ... *and* soon! The world would have so unraveled by then, terrifying even the most stout-hearted; she would need the reassurance when the time came.

Further, I would symbolize her *before* I was taken. I reflected her. She reflected me. We were a mess in heaven's eyes! I... she... often became entangled in Satan's web of structural evil, particularly when it came to mammon (money). We were caught up in the world's systems in ways we could not see. The consequences of the entanglements were vast.

Most of us manage God's resources, in fact, our very lives, as though they were our own and there was no eternity. We behave as though we will never be required to give an account of how we invested our lives and His resources. We are woefully mistaken.

There will be a reckoning of accounts in eternity. Mismanagement of what God entrusted to us is one of our big spots, one of our big blemishes. Christ is returning for a bride without spot or blemish. He must remove our spots before His return. The body must match the Head!

I wholly confess that I struggled with everything the Lord was showing me and doing in my life during this period. The idea of being a symbol of the body of Christ was hard to believe. But so was the idea of God coming to humankind in the form of a baby—through the womb of a virgin, mortal woman—to, then, be crucified by His own creation to save their souls. That I fully accepted. Why could I not accept this without wavering?

Finally, I hit upon an idea.

"If it is Your will that I symbolize Your spotted bride, then I want to embrace it fully. But I need to believe it like I believe in my salvation," I proposed to the Lord. Nothing could dissuade me from believing that I had been saved by grace through Christ's atoning sacrifice on the cross.

God had shown me too much in Scripture and had done too much in my life and in the lives of others for me to believe otherwise. I was entirely convinced of this truth. I needed to believe this "new thing" like I believed in my salvation. He would have to convince me, starting with the Word of God.

That very day, the Lord began to unveil Scriptures to me on the matter. He began with Psalm 45. It is the only passage in the entire Bible that indicates Christ will have an individual companion as well a corporate bride.

Psalm 45 is a Messianic Psalm, describing a royal wedding of the Son to an individual, who is described in verses 9-15. It is a perplexing passage of Scripture since Christ says, *"At the resurrection, people will neither marry nor be given in marriage; they will be like the angels in heaven" (Matthew 22:30, NIV).* Some commentators believe Psalm 45 refers to an ancient, royal, secular wedding, used as a backdrop for the Messiah's wedding.

The New Testament refers to Psalm 45 in Hebrews 1:8-9 and applies it specifically to Christ. In addition, Christ says, *"Everything must be fulfilled that is written about Me in the Law of Moses, the Prophets and the Psalms" (Luke 24:44b).*

After careful study of the Psalm, I still had my doubts. Doubt is a very slippery slope. I wavered and hesitated. Finally, I dismissed the Psalm completely. The idea was just too foreign. In due course, the Lord grew weary of my doubts and forced the issue in a way I will never forget.

July 12, 1997

> *"Pejorative!"*
>
> *I awoke at 6 a.m. with the word "pejorative" echoing in my mind. I did not know what the word meant. I thought it might be a legal term. Half asleep, I grabbed my Webster dictionary off the bookshelf. I could not find the word. (At the time, I was spelling it "perjorative.")*
>
> *I began my quiet time with a Bible study. What did the Scriptures say about the bride of Christ? Everything I read pointed to the church being the bride of Christ—a congregation of holy people being prepared and fitted to marry the Lamb of Christ. These saints will dwell in the New Jerusalem with their Lord. "Married" in this case meant a people redeemed, kept, and protected by the Bridegroom. These people shall be like Him. They shall have His character.*

Perhaps, the Lord's reference to the Sadducees about no marriage in heaven meant the institution of marriage will be unnecessary in eternity because people, like angels, will not procreate. A set number of saints will have been saved forever, and they will never die. In this case, there would be no need for procreation.

The kind of marriage associated with Christ throughout Scripture, including Psalm 45, refers to a divine, pure, passionate love Christ has for saved souls and they for Him. After all, He is the Lover of our souls.

As I pondered this, I was joyous that Christ had a bride, and I was a part of her. However, I was still doubtful I was a symbol that pre-figured her and, therefore, disappointed. Scriptures weigh heavier on the side of Christ marrying a congregation only.

Suddenly, the word "pejorative" came to my mind again. What does that word mean? Who could I call to ask? Finally, I asked the Holy Spirit: "If the definition exists anywhere in the house, let me find it."

I ate breakfast, read the newspaper, and began to prepare my Sunday school lesson for the week. As I sat down to write, I heard the word again. It had to be the tenth time that morning!

"Check it on the computer!" I heard in my spirit. Why had I not thought of that earlier? I ran upstairs to my office.

This time, I spelled the word correctly. I clicked on the thesaurus. I was more than horrified by the word's synonyms: belittling, degrading, and derisive (i.e., mocking, scornful); derogatory, negative, dubious, doubtful, skeptical, uncertain, irresolute, and ambivalent.

The last string of words was especially upsetting since it aptly described my secret heart attitude about being a symbol of the "bride to come"—despite my earlier study on the subject. According to the thesaurus, the antonyms of these faithless words were "trusting," "sure," and "certain." They were key words in one of my favorite Scriptures on faith: "Faith is being sure of what we hope for and certain of what we do not see" (Hebrews 11:1).

At this point, the Lord was saying to me, "I have shown you enough to believe, as much as necessary to start the journey. It is an issue of your faith." He also reminded that which is not from faith is sin.

"I feel trapped," I whispered to myself.

"God does not trap!" the Holy Spirit responded.

Hadn't I experienced numerous wonders related to the matter? Hadn't He begun to show me scripturally what all this meant? Never once had He lied to me. He cannot. I concluded what God revealed to me was true. Now, by faith, I must choose to accept or reject it. I made up my mind to freefall into His providence for my life.

Chapter 18

The Unveiling of a Mystery

Just as the Lord was reconstructing Denny's from the inside out during this time, He was reconstructing me and everything I ever thought about Him. The reconstruction began in spring 1997 and culminated in a divine visit on October 31 of that year. That visitation would forever alter my life.

November 1, 1997

A Visitation from the Lord

After wrestling with a request from the Lord for several days and spending time on my knees at the altar last Sunday, I finally said, "Yes."

Five days later, He acknowledged my acceptance of His request with a special visit. It all had a dreamlike quality in the end, but not in the beginning. I was wide awake when it began, lying in the bed in my dark room.

We were in the middle of a conversation when the Lord said, "I want to come to you."

"Then come, Lord, come," I said. I fully expected a spate of running chills—a sign of His presence that I had experienced many times before.

But this time I heard a soft thump in the room. It sounded like a pillow fell from the bed to the floor. Then I heard a louder noise. My eyes popped open. My mind screamed, "He's here! He's in the room!"

A split second later, I experienced something that felt like a continuous electrical sensation enveloping my entire being. I felt no pain. I was facing my bedroom window. I never lifted my head. Instinctively, I knew I could not lift my head even if I wanted to.

Everything in my line of sight had a bright white glow to it. It was difficult to gage how long I was enveloped in this electrical state and light. It could have been two, five, or 10 minutes. It could have been even longer.

Next, I felt a laser of light go straight through the very center of my being. It started at the top of my head and exited between my legs. I prayed through the entire episode.

Then, two big hands enveloped mine. I felt I was going to be pulled up and out of bed by my hands, but I was not. Perhaps, it was because I started shouting in my spirit, "I don't want to see Your face! I don't want to see Your face!" I thought no human being could see the Lord's face and live.

I did, however, see a bright white shadow of a Figure hovering above me—the head and torso only. I saw the image in my spirit since my head never left the pillow and my eyes were tightly closed by this time.

I knew the Figure was Father God. I felt Him gently kiss the very top of my head. Then, He disappeared. His visit came between 4:00 and 4:49 a.m. on October 31, 1997.

Four months after that October visit, stepping out of the shower, I caught a glimpse of my image in the bathroom mirror. My mouth fell open. I saw something strange, new—a circular, protruding mound in the middle of my stomach! I had not noticed it before because my bathroom was the only room in the house, where I could see my full figure. I had not used my bathroom to take a shower since my parents came for an extended visit to escape the brutal Michigan winter. During their four-month stay, I slept on an air mattress in my home office and used Michael's bathroom, where I could see myself only from the chest up.

I knew the little mound in the middle of my belly was a result of the Lord's visit in October. I stood in the middle of my bathroom floor, looking in the mirror, rubbing my tummy and repeating, "*This* is a BIG IDEA! *This* is a BIG IDEA!" (I felt these words were not really my own, but the Holy Spirit's.)

Two weeks later, I had an ultrasound that revealed an empty womb. Pressing with the tips of his fingers all along my abdominal area, the gynecologist acknowledged I appeared to be four months pregnant. But there was no child. During the ensuing years, the "baby bump" would remain whether I gained or lost weight.

For days, I lied awake at night wondering what was happening to me. How could I explain it to anybody—especially Michael, a nonbeliever? Soon I would have to, I thought.

Hesitantly, I told my best friend Jeri. She had no doubt I was telling the truth. Next to the Lord, she knows me best. We are like sisters. Emboldened by Jeri's response, I told Suzanne. She examined my stomach and was satisfied when she saw me unclothed and could trace with her finger a dark vertical line running from navel to pubis; the line had not been there previously.

In due course, I told Ryan, whom the Lord eventually convinced through dreams. Later, I told my parents, sobbing throughout the entire affair. Both were quiet. Finally, my mother broke the awkward silence. "Nothing is impossible with God," she softly proclaimed to my father and me. That was it. We never spoke of it again.

Mike never knew about the Lord's visit. After the negative ultrasound, he jokingly informed me I had dodged a bullet since we both knew he had a vasectomy 16 years earlier—three weeks after Ryan was born. (My severe postpartum depression drove him to that decision.)

I never broached the subject with Mike again. I did not have to. The Lord orchestrated a surprise split between us four weeks after I discovered the bump. Ryan and I moved to Detroit, and Suzanne moved to Wichita. Mike relocated permanently to Chicago after Denny's purchased our house.

Jeri was the only person with whom I could dissect the wild encounter. Unfortunately, she told a woman at Wayside Baptist Church, whom she thought was a friend. That woman told several others.

The devil had a field day. All hell broke loose in Jeri's life because of her association with me. As the Lord would have it, during the tumult, her husband was looking for work and found it in South Carolina. The Lord moved her family to Simpsonville, South Carolina, only 30 minutes away from where I lived at the time.

As for me, I had already left Wayside. Nevertheless, I heard the reports. I was labeled a deranged nut by many who once knew me as a gifted Sunday school teacher and director. It was one of the most hurtful experiences of my life. That period marked the beginning of the Lord freeing me from the opinions of others.

In another painful incident, a friend of mine from Wayside, who had already relocated her family to Spartanburg, South Carolina a year before the church scandal, inadvertently learned of the Lord's visit while editing one of my prayer journals.

At first, she believed. But when I did not give birth nine months after the October visit, she turned antagonistic, incited by a woman from her church. That woman did not know me. Together, they wrote a disparaging letter to six of my closest friends. Although they copied me on the letter, the Lord commanded me not to read it. I destroyed it. So, to this day, I don't know exactly what the letter said.

All I knew was Jeri crafted a loving reply, defending me. Jeri copied the other women on her letter. She proposed we all wait on God before rushing to judgment. None of the other women ever questioned me about the visit or changed their behavior toward me.

Despite the big split that would come between us two months later, God graciously gave my doubting friend a dream about me giving birth to a child. Her dream occurred a month before Ryan and I relocated to Detroit.

In her dream, I gave birth to an unusual baby boy. Right after his birth, the two of us disappeared. We were taken to heaven by two angels. Her dream fueled my eager expectation of being called home to heaven that year. But that was not the Lord's plan.

April 18, 1998

A Friend's Dream: A Special Baby Boy is Born

My friend called today to tell me of an extraordinary dream she had on April 17. When she awoke from her dream, she asked God to wipe the dream from her memory if it was not from Him, to let her not remember it in the morning. But when morning came, she remembered every detail.

In the dream, she and I, and our two husbands, were having dinner at a restaurant. I was pregnant, but I did not look pregnant. Unexpectedly, my water broke. She and I excused ourselves from the table. The men had no idea what was happening. We gathered up some cloth napkins and made our way to the bathroom.

Suddenly, I went into labor—a painless labor. I experienced no discomfort. She prayed fervently to God to allow her to see the baby about to be born. If it fell to her to deliver the child, she wanted the baby to be visible. She also prayed that if she was not to touch the baby, to let her know. She feared she might be struck dead.

Out of nowhere, two angels appeared and calmly told her they would take over. She explained that I quietly delivered a radiant, translucent baby boy with shocking white hair and blue eyes. She put a cloth over the top of his head and kissed it. Then, together—the baby, angels, and I—disappeared.

She exited the bathroom alone. Her husband was stunned when he saw her.

"What happened to you?" he asked. Her hair, naturally blonde, was now snow white, and her face glowed brilliantly!

"I was in the presence of God," she answered.

After my friend's dream, the Lord kept bringing Revelation 12 to my attention. It seemed every book or article I read pointed to that specific book and chapter. Prior to that time, I may have read the passage twice in my entire life.

At first, I could not understand why the Lord kept bringing it to my awareness. It never occurred to me the upheaval that had suddenly seized my home life was directly related to those Scripture passages. Initially, I made no personal connection.

April 19, 1998

Revelation 12

God keeps bringing Revelation 12 to my attention. I suspect He is trying to teach me a fundamental truth. Little by little, my perspective about who the woman is in this chapter has shifted. At first, I thought the woman was Mary, His mother. Now, I believe the woman represents something larger than an individual. She is symbolic of a corporate body.

Since the Apostle John is referring to what is to come, how can this be Mary? Moreover, verse 3 refers to the Antichrist and the revived Roman Empire: "And another sign appeared in heaven: behold, a great fiery red dragon having seven heads and 10 horns, and seven diadems on his heads."

This period is more than 2,000 years after Mary's time. I believe the woman represents Israel. However, I know Apostle John's end-time message is intended for Christ's body as well. But what about the baby? Who is this child? Jesus?

History Repeats

I believe the Holy Spirit is also showing me through Revelation 12 that history repeats itself—not precisely in the same manner—but enough to know what happened in the past can recur in the future. Satan tried to dispose of Moses and Jesus at their births, for he knew they represented threats to his reign as prince of this world. He slaughtered many innocent children in the process. It seems something similar will occur at the end of the age.

The fact that history repeats is evident, not only in biblical times, but also modern times. A careful examination of the amazing parallels between the lives and assassinations of U.S. presidents Lincoln and

Kennedy strongly points to the existence of an Almighty God, whose sovereignty orchestrates the events of human history in conjunction with man's freewill:

- *Lincoln was elected President in 1860, Kennedy in 1960.*
- *Both were concerned with Civil Rights.*
- *Both were assassinated on a Friday in the presence of their wives.*
- *Both of their wives lost children to death while in the White House.*
- *Both men died of gunshot wounds to the head, shot from behind.*
- *Both of their successors were southern Democrats from the Senate.*
- *Both successors were born exactly 100 years apart.*
- *Both successors were named Johnson.*
- *Both of their assassins were southerners, born exactly 100 years apart.*
- *Both of their assassins were known by three names.*
- *Both of their assassins were killed before they were brought to trial.*
- *Lincoln's secretary was named Kennedy. Kennedy's secretary was named Lincoln.*
- *Lincoln's secretary advised him not to go to the theater that night. Kennedy's secretary advised him not to go to Dallas.*
- *John Wilkes Booth shot Lincoln in a theater and was captured in a warehouse. Assassin Lee Harvey Oswald shot Kennedy from a warehouse and was captured in a theater.*
- *Lincoln was shot in a theater owned by a man named Ford. Kennedy was shot in a Lincoln built by the Ford Motor Company.*
- *After the Lincoln assassination, Secretary of War Stanton sent for the N.Y. Chief of Police to help search for Booth. The chief's name was John Kennedy.*

These were not coincidences. The Lord's Providence was at work. Our Creator often communicates through patterns, shadows, and types.

Take the fascinating similarities between the lives of Moses and Christ, for example. Moses delivered God's people from the bondage of Egypt and brought them God's Law—the Old Covenant. Christ delivered mankind from the bondage of sin and death and ushered in a New

Covenant. Christ fulfilled the Law of Moses through His sacrifice on the cross. What happened in Moses' day foreshadowed what was to come in Christ's.

Events thousands of years apart were repeated by God's sovereign hand:

1. Moses' birth opened the way for the Old Covenant. Christ's birth opened the way for the New Covenant. In God's dealing with mankind, both ushered in new epochs.
2. The little Hebrew boys of Moses' generation were a threat to the reigning Pharaoh, so Pharaoh had them murdered. Only Moses survived the slaughter. Jesus was a threat to King Herod, so Herod had all the little Hebrew boys, two years old and younger, murdered. Only Jesus survived the slaughter.
3. An Egyptian palace became Moses' refuge as a little child; he was sent there by God to escape Pharaoh's massacre. Egypt became Jesus' refuge as a little child, after Mary and Joseph fled there to escape Herod's bloodbath.
4. Moses was raised in the royal splendor of a prince, but he forsook it all to fulfill God's call to deliver His people. Jesus abdicated His royal and splendid throne in heaven to fulfill God's call to deliver mankind.
5. Moses dwelled in the desert wilderness for 40 years in preparation to deliver God's people from the bonds of slavery. Jesus spent 40 days and 40 nights in the desert wilderness before embarking on His ministry to free mankind from the bonds of sin and death.
6. Darkness fell over Egypt for three days, just before the Angel of Death passed over the land and killed the firstborn male of every household that did not have the blood of an unblemished, male lamb over its doorpost. When Jesus, God's only begotten Son—who was without blemish and sin—became our Passover Lamb on the cross, the land was plunged into darkness for three hours.
7. Scripture identified Moses as the humblest man on earth in his generation. Surely, Jesus was the humblest Man who ever

walked the earth: "… *who being in the form of God, did not consider it robbery to be equal with God, but made Himself of no reputation, taking the form of a bondservant, and coming in the likeness of men, He humbled Himself and became obedient to the point of death, even death on the cross" (Philippians 2:6-8).*

8. God gave His people manna (bread) through Moses. God gave us His Son, Jesus, who Scripture calls the "Living Manna" and "Bread of Life."
9. Moses mediated the Old Covenant between God and His people. Jesus mediated the New Covenant between God and mankind.
10. Moses instituted the system of sacrificial offerings to reconcile Israel to God. Jesus abolished the old sacrificial system when He became the final and ultimate sacrifice. He reconciled the elect to God.
11. Moses led God's people out of Egypt, through the wilderness, to the Promised Land, Canaan. Jesus is the Truth, the Light, and the Way. He leads His people through the wilderness, and out of the world—a type of Egypt—to the ultimate Promised Land, heaven.

How did this all speak to me about my personal life? It didn't. I recorded what God revealed to me with a great sense of personal detachment. At the time, I did not see how it pertained to my life in any significant way. But God was about to open my eyes.

Chapter 19
"Wake Up! I Come to Divide!"

The time soon came when I could no longer bury my head in the sand. After the Lord's visit, I suddenly became a target in the spiritual underworld. Unworldly warfare erupted all around me—at work and at home. It intensified to an unimaginable level, though I never understood why or what was happening.

God gave me a dream in which an assassin's infrared target followed me everywhere I went, but the bullets missed me and hit other people. In real life, people started dying around me! Some were killed in car accidents. One was killed in a robbery assault. Another had a massive heart attack right in the middle of a business presentation. Some were family members, others were friends. One was a colleague.

"Ray, Jesus has the keys to Life and Death," Jeri told me one afternoon after I poured my heart out to her. That truth calmed me down enough to function. Then, I prayed a protection prayer for everyone I knew.

I was in my fourth year at Denny's when the onslaught began. Without warning, the Company suddenly became a lightning rod for every kind of malcontent in the marketplace. Lawsuits poured in ... and death threats.

We received at least one lawsuit per day. Complainants would hold national press conferences to announce their lawsuits. We often learned about the litigation when the media called for our response. There was no forewarning. Some complaints were pure extortion.

As Denny's Chief Diversity Officer, I was at the forefront of these unrelenting attacks. I traveled the country putting out fires. At this point, my career became one of crisis intervention and management. How God catapulted Denny's to the top of the heap in the face of all this mayhem is a powerful testament to His supremacy and might.

At home, my entire life was about to be upended in a way I never imagined. If someone had told me, "In seven days, you and Michael will be separated; you and Ryan will move to Detroit; Suzanne will move to Wichita; and your house will be sold in less than one hour," I would have laughed. I would have *never* believed it. Yet, that is exactly what happened. I never saw it coming, despite numerous warnings from the Lord.

Six months before the split, God warned He was about to make a move. I sensed something was coming, but exactly what, I did not know. The two journal excerpts below reveal how the Lord tried to ease me into the coming upheaval.

April 5, 1998

"I Come to Divide!"

God allowed me to experience a very private spiritual event last Sunday. Mike announced on Saturday that he and Ryan would be joining me and Suzanne at church. I was glad he told me, so I could prepare spiritually. Ryan and her father frequently joked and talked throughout the church service. They could be extremely distracting. Sometimes, I wondered why they even bothered to go, since they rarely listened.

Ryan had not attended in a month, and Mike had not gone in several months. On the other hand, Suzanne and I never missed a Sunday, and we always went early for Sunday school. It was often a feat saving seats for Mike and Ryan when they came to church together because they were frequently late.

Suzanne and I preferred to sit upfront, where space was limited and difficult to get. Sometimes, we would have to gather our things and move to the balcony, so we could sit together as a family when Michael and Ryan finally arrived. So, on that day, rather than concern myself with how to reserve two seats on a crowded pew for Mike and Ryan, I simply prayed on my way to church for God to work out the seating.

"Lord, it's always a challenge when those two come to church together. I'm not going to worry about how to save seats for everyone. I'll leave that to You. I trust You will work out our seating exactly the way You want it. If we must sit in the balcony, so be it." I drove to church without giving it another thought.

As I walked into church after Sunday school, I saw Suzanne seated in the second pew from the front. She had just enough seats around her for the family. Great! I took the seat beside her and placed my Bible next to me to reserve a seat for Mike. She placed her Bible next to her to save a seat for Ryan.

Suddenly, Holly, the pastor's daughter, who is a member of my Sunday school class, came up to our pew and asked, "Can I sit with you?" She had never sat with us before. A college student, Holly is an extraordinary, young Christian woman, in whom God moves powerfully. She has a beautiful, intimate relationship with the Lord. God knows how much I admire her walk with Him.

Just as Holly slid into the seat next to me, the sanctuary door opened, and Mike and Ryan walked in. Mike did not ask Holly to switch places with him, nor did she offer. It never occurred to Holly, as gracious as she is, to offer Mike her seat. Ryan sat next to Holly, to my right, and Mike sat next to Ryan. Suzanne was on my immediate left.

Because I had made our seating a matter of prayer that morning, the arrangement caught my attention. I knew there was something unusual about it. Holly, Suzanne and I—the three who adored God—seemed more like a unit than did our family. I thought nothing more about it until the pastor began to preach the sermon.

"Do you think I came to bring peace on earth?" Jesus inquired of His disciples. "No, I tell you, but division. From now on there will be five in one family divided against each other, three against two and two against three. They will be divided, father against son and son against father, mother against daughter and daughter against mother, and daughter-in-law against mother-in-law" (Luke 12:51-53, NIV).

Pastor Nelson continued, "Although Jesus is called the Prince of Peace, often the proclamation of the gospel brings division among family members. His truth and light often divide families, where both believer and nonbeliever reside under one roof." He had my full attention.

"When Jesus asked, 'Who is my mother, who are my brothers?' And then answered '... whoever does the will of My Father in heaven is my brother and sister and mother' (Matthew 12:49, NIV), He was saying

His Spirit, between believers through His shed blood, was stronger than the blood between relatives."

How can I explain what I felt at that moment, listening to those words and then pondering our unusual seating arrangement? After the service, I did not say a word to anyone, not even Suzanne. I just recorded my thoughts in my journal. It was abundantly clear to me that God had arranged our seating exactly as He desired—to make a powerful, symbolic point. I was flanked by two strong Christians and separated from Mike. A month later, the separation became real.

May 20, 1998

An Extraordinary, Unexpected Move

If someone had told me, "Next week, at this time, your house will be sold, and your family will be split," I would not have believed it. Mike and I had no plans to separate. That was the furthest thing from either of our minds. There had been no discussion. However, that is precisely what happened. It took just seven days for God to flip our lives.

A family crisis—clearly heaven-orchestrated—caused Ryan and me to flee our home in South Carolina. After 15 years of faithful service, Suzanne will be going her own way. Ryan and I will miss her. By the end of this week, all the necessary arrangements will be made to relocate the four of us to three different cities.

God orchestrated and financed everything—the packing, the moving, even the shipment of three family cars. I could not have conceived or carried out something so large and extraordinary in a week's time. Still, I should not be surprised since the move fulfills three dreams God gave me—one through Suzanne and two of my own.

First Dream: "It's Time for Ray and Ryan to Come Home."

In a dream I had on March 20, 1996, Ryan and I were fleeing our home in South Carolina. I feared for our safety. We were headed to Detroit to live with my parents. Suzanne and Mike were not with us. In the dream, we were trying to escape a hideous demon spirit that had Mike's voice. We were carried home, supernaturally, to Detroit.

In November 1997, my sister, who lives in Detroit, heard God's audible voice while in church. He told her twice, "It's time for Ray and Ryan to come home." She was clear when she shared the message with me that it was not for a visit. We were to move back home to Detroit.

What she heard dovetailed with the dream I had on March 20. At the end of that dream, a heavenly voice said it was time for Ryan and me to go home. After the dream, I immediately made plans to visit my family in Detroit. At the time, I could not imagine moving there.

Second Dream: An Angry Mother

In November 1997, God also gave Suzanne a dream portending the family split. She came to me deeply disturbed after her dream. She dreamt I was highly agitated about a matter; she had never seen me so mad. Everyone around me was also angry, but I was the angriest—about what, she did not know. I should have guessed, then, that if I was as angry as she described, Ryan's well-being must have been involved.

Suzanne also explained that I was naked from the waist up in her dream. When she told me that, I knew something previously hidden would be brought to light, exposed. At the time, I did not know what.

After 16 years of remarriage, Mike forced my hand with his angry, explosive temper. He threatened Ryan in a way he had never done before. In the past, I rarely argued with Mike. God taught me to take all my issues with Mike to Him and leave them. This time, He wanted me to do more.

I was in Detroit on a business trip when everything fell apart at home. I was scheduled to speak on a local television program in two hours. Suzanne and Ryan were in South Carolina and Mike was in Chicago.

Mike called me for my credit card number. He needed to catch a flight home right away. I could not give it to him. After a speech, the day before, I had stopped to buy gasoline. While pumping gas, I slipped the card into my suit jacket and forgot it. I did not discover it missing until I tried to rent a car the next day in Detroit. I had only my driver's license.

"You have a friendly face," the rental car agent told me. He then gave me the car after making a copy of my license! At the time, the unlikeliness of our exchange did not dawn on me. Now, trying to convince Mike of it, I sounded like a big, fat liar. He flew into a rage and hung up the phone.

Immediately, I called home to find out what was going on. Suzanne told me Mike and Ryan had a vicious exchange that morning about her not being in school. But she had a good reason. She explained to me the night before. Mike refused to listen. He kept cutting her off, and when he began cursing her, for the first time in her life, she cursed him back. That threw him into a fury.

Ryan, frightened out of her mind, packed a few things and ran away. I tracked her down at her friend's house. She vowed never to return.

"Mom, I have to go. You don't understand. He's going to kill me."

I tried to assure her that would not happen. Then she spoke 12 words that caused the hair on the back of my neck to rise: "Mom, you can't protect yourself. How are you going to protect me?"

Is that how she saw me—saw us? It unleashed the lioness in me. "Then, I will die trying." I called my boss, Jim Adamson. I explained everything that happened.

His executive assistant, Dory Djerf, called me back 15 minutes later. "Can you get to Signature Airport? A private jet is waiting for you there. It will bring you home."

On the way to the airport, I was stopped by a cop for speeding. He gave me a ticket and took my driver's license. Afterward, he let me go. Alone on the jet with just the two pilots, I sobbed a thousand tears. I repeatedly asked God for wisdom. The flight took one hour.

As soon as I walked through the door, the phone rang. It was Mike. He was driving from Chicago to South Carolina. God had blocked him from purchasing an airline ticket. I tried to reason with him. I attempted to explain Ryan's struggle with repressed anger against him.

Ryan had been in therapy for several weeks. While those sessions were between Ryan and her doctor, she chose regularly to share her progress with me. Up until then, she had turned the anger in on herself, frequently swallowing cough medicine to numb her pain. But that day, exhausted from lack of sleep and no longer able to contain her anger, she lambasted him. I tried to explain all this to him.

Mike's response sent me through the roof. I snapped. I blasted him in a way I had never done before and ripped the cord to the land line out of the kitchen wall. I called Ryan and coaxed her into coming home.

By the time she arrived, I had our bags packed. Adamson's office had arranged for two, first-class Northwest airline tickets to Detroit. I used my passport for identification.

The dream was unfolding before my very eyes! Ryan and I were headed home to Detroit to live! A few days later, our house was empty and sold.

The sudden move threw everybody for a loop. Specific people had to be told what happened, so they could help, and from there, the news spread. By the time the dust settled, everyone at my job, Ryan's school, and our church knew about our family's crisis.

Before the split, we looked like the perfect family in the big white house on the hill. But God knew that was a farce. Now everyone else knew too. Everything was laid bare, exposed.

Third Dream: He Fell from a High Place

In late autumn 1997, I had a strange, disconcerting dream. In the dream, I was in a room sitting by a window, singing. I was dressed in all white. A tall man, dressed in all black with headphones on his head, was looking for me. He kept calling, "Where are you?"

"I'm here," I responded. He searched for me, but he could not find me. I had disappeared.

In the next scene, the entire room where we both had been, started to hum and pulsate. The walls and floorboards pulsed faster and faster until there was a huge explosion. Suddenly, my view changed.

Now I was outside the room—far off. I saw the window where I had been sitting and singing. I realized the room where the explosion had occurred was in a high structure.

The man was now lying flat on his back, covered in debris. Groggily, he started to move. He stood and shook off the debris. As he did, he moved slightly to the right and fell out of the window. It was a long fall.

For months, I did not know who the man was in my dream. Then, one day as I headed out the backdoor to take my evening walk, I turned to look at Mike standing in our sunlit family room. His back was to me. He was a tall, dark silhouette with headphones on his head. (He records music as a hobby.) I gasped, taken aback by the sight. The scene was the exact one from my dream. From that day on, I knew Mike would fall from a high place. But I did not know how, when, or under what circumstances.

A day after Ryan and I arrived in Detroit, we drove to Canada. We spent a week at my brother-in-law's cabin by the lake. I needed time to reflect and decompress. Mike searched everywhere for us, but he could not find us.

Denny's purchased our house over the telephone during a 30-minute telephone conversation. Once our house was sold, I knew Mike and I would never reunite. Mike would have to start his life over again without me. That dream, too, had now come to pass.

Thus, in May 1998, God permanently separated Mike and me. Five years later, we divorced as friends. God had retired His jackhammer. That did not mean He was done refining me, not by a long shot. For what was needed next, He would employ other tools.

Chapter 20
Discovering My Jewish Lineage

Shocked, amazed, and dumbfounded, I was back where I started. I returned to Detroit, to my parents' home. When the movers pulled up to their house with just a smattering of our things from South Carolina, they marveled. (Denny's had stored the rest of our furniture.) We had left a spectacular home in South Carolina's exquisite Barrington Park subdivision to come to this humble home on the outskirts of Detroit's inner city.

I returned to the tiny bedroom I slept in when I was 16 years old. Ryan, two weeks shy of 16, took the even tinier bedroom next to mine. I commuted by plane to my South Carolina job for 3½ years, to the day. In Scripture, 3½ years or 42 months is the number for a trial or test. I certainly was in the midst of a big one.

I became convinced my life was over. Surely, God would be calling me home soon. In time, I gave away all my earthly possessions. Except for $80,000, I emptied all my accounts—including my retirement savings account—and invested the money in an elementary school in Uganda.

One day, I sat next to a Ugandan woman on a plane ride home. We talked the entire trip about the school she ran with her husband. I was so moved by their sacrificial work. The school was also a farm. They grew food to feed their 600 students daily. For most of the children, it was their only meal of the day. Without her knowing it at the time, I resolved to help them.

I purchased a shipping container and filled it with all manner of goods for the students—notebooks, pencils, pens, paper, scissors, coloring books, crayons, paste, tape, staplers, and so much more. I tried to supply 600 sets of everything. I also provided toiletries—facial soap, toothbrushes, toothpaste, deodorant, and face cloths for each student. Lastly, I included many toys for the school, like soccer balls, basketballs, and blowing bubbles.

I put the $80,000 aside for Ryan. When the Lord took me home, she would have money to finish high school and maybe even start college, if she managed it well. Until He called me home, I would do battle at Denny's.

While I had returned home to Detroit, God wanted me to know the city was not my ancestral home. There, He began to reveal to me the truth about my family's ancient origins.

First, He told me I was Ethiopian. Shortly thereafter, He sent me on a trip to the ancient nation to confirm it. I saw myself everywhere in Ethiopia! (Three years later, DNA tests confirmed that truth.) After the Lord opened my eyes, it was not difficult to believe I was Ethiopian since I looked just like one.

I traveled a great deal to New York and Washington D.C. on business. Both cities have large Ethiopian populations. For many years, Ethiopian cabdrivers told me, "You look just like the women from my homeland." Before the Lord's revelation, it never occurred to me that I came from Ethiopia. A year after the Lord told me my origins were Ethiopian, He dropped another bombshell on me.

"You are also Jewish." My first reaction was disbelief. How can I be both Ethiopian and Jewish? I had never heard of such a thing! I had come to accept His first assertion that I was Ethiopian, even without the DNA tests. But I was reluctant to embrace His latest one. The new revelation, however, explained a dream He gave me that year.

December 24, 1999

A Dream: A Woman in Purple

Earlier this week, I had a brief, but elaborate dream. I saw a woman walking down a long residential street. I had a distant view of her from the back. Although I saw only her dark silhouette from behind, I could see she was naked.

As she walked, the woman was suddenly attired in a black skirt and a deep purple, round-neck sweater. Next, I saw her close. She wore large, stunning gold earrings. She continued walking.

At this point, I noticed her dark complexion. Her medium-length, crinkly black hair bounced gently in the wind as she walked. Suddenly, my view of her changed again.

Now I was looking straight down at her from above as if I were a hovering bird. From that angle, I saw she had large round breasts. While I could not see her face, I knew she was unusual by the way everyone else looked at her as they passed. Men and women driving by gazed at her as she walked. While the woman was not a celebrity, people acted as though she were someone they had heard about.

Suddenly, I was no longer observing the woman. I was the woman! As I glanced to the left, I saw a large, worn brick house with a storm door. The house, surrounded by similar houses, sat somewhat elevated on its site. I recognized the houses from my parents' neighborhood! Snow covered the front yard. I kept walking.

Finally, I saw three men walking toward me in the distance. As they drew nearer, I realized they looked out of place. They were dressed in black suits and white shirts. But each man wore a white keffiyeh on his head—the traditional headdress for Arab men.

As we approached, I could see admiration on their faces. Just as I was about to pass, the tall man in the middle asked, "Where are you from?"

"Do you mean my original country?" I asked. The three nodded.

"Yes, where are you from?"

"Israel."

At first, I did not understand the dream. However, the very morning God gave me the dream, He took me to Ezekiel 16. The woman in my dream eerily resembled the woman in Ezekiel 16!

According to the passage, God rescued the woman as a child. When she became a woman and ready for love, He covered her naked, exposed body with His wing—a metaphor for marriage. She became His wife. She was nothing until He claimed her as His own (vv. 4-8).

As an attentive, adoring Husband, God clothed her in the finest garments (vv. 8, 10 and 13). He adorned her in fine jewelry (vv. 11, 13). He gave her the best food (v. 13). He made her beautiful to gaze upon, and her beauty spread among the nations (vv. 13-14).

However, she became a harlot. Israel was not faithful to Him. She chased after other "husbands." Her idolatry was akin to adultery in His eyes (vv. 15-34).

Until this day, Israel has not returned to her Sovereign Lord. But He has not forsaken her. He has loved her with an everlasting love. God has a plan to bring His wife—scattered and abused among the nations—back to Himself and her original homeland.

During Christ's millennial reign, even Israel's centuries-old enemies, the Arab nations, will find her alluring, beautiful (Isaiah 2:1-4, Micah 4:1-5). As the prophets foretold, Israel will once again be a jewel among the nations as God always intended.

I pondered the dream often, and each time I did, I warmed to the idea more and more. Who really knows their ancient roots? But we can be sure God knows.

My second reaction to the Lord's claim that I was Jewish was, "Let's just keep this our little secret." Since I could not bring myself to believe Him right away, I did not think anyone else would either. I was both Ethiopian *and* Jewish? Nah! Whoever heard of such a thing?

A few years later, I would be digging water wells for Black Jews living in villages in and around Gondar, Ethiopia. Many, isolated for generations in remote mountains, thought all Jews were Black like themselves, which I found quite amusing. They had never seen or heard of a White Jew!

As I grew in the knowledge of my Ethiopian *and* Jewish heritage, I began to call Jesus by His Hebrew name, Yeshua. I also began attending a Messianic synagogue, Shema Yisrael, on the Sabbath. On Sundays, I attended Highland Park Baptist Church. Both were in Southfield, Michigan, in the same building.

I found it highly symbolic (and amusing) that the Lord pulled me into both congregations, and that I took great pleasure in both forms of worship. Why not? I was a mixture of both—half Jew and half Gentile—a modern-day Samaritan woman! Around this time, I also began taking Hebrew classes in preparation for my Bat Mitzvah. I would take classes for 30 weeks to prepare for this special day.

May 5, 2001

My Bat Mitzvah

After 30 weeks of preparation, I had my Bat mitzvah today! Only three people attended. Two were Messianic Jews—Rickki and Ryan—and one Gentile believer.

While I spoke to a nearly empty room, I knew the event was highly symbolic. I knew all of heaven was watching! I also knew Yeshua was there, front and center. He promised He would be.

I was so nervous! I had spoken before thousands of people, as many as 300,000 at a Southern Baptist Convention once. But I had never been this wired! I rehearsed every spare moment I had in preparation for today.

I opened with the reading of the Shema in Hebrew. Then, I gave the English translation. Next, I read in Hebrew, The Blessing Before the Reading of the Torah. Then, I translated it into English. Then, I read one of the most meaningful passages of Scripture to me, Philippians 2:4-10, in Hebrew. After the reading, I gave the English translation.

After I read the English version of Philippians 2:4-10, I read The Blessing After the Reading of the Torah in Hebrew and gave its English interpretation.

I received high praise from my tiny audience. I knew the Lord was pleased. According to Jewish tradition, I was now ready to assume my spiritual duties and responsibilities as a Jewish believer and follower of Messiah. This occurs for most Jews at age 13!

Although I had been serving Yeshua for nearly 17 years, I believe He was telling me that my Bat Mitzvah was a significant step in assuming my new role in His eternal plan. When I returned home, I had the most beautiful bouquet of flowers awaiting me from my office staff at Denny's, congratulating me on this important milestone.

Chapter 21
The Woman in Revelation 12

The Lord *never* stopped bringing Revelation 12 to my attention. Slowly, tentatively, apprehensively, I embraced the idea that I might be the woman in Revelation 12, who gave birth to a male child just before the Great Tribulation.

The woman is "clothed with the sun," symbolic of being clothed in the righteousness of the Son. Thus, she is a believer in Jesus Christ. So am I. At the same time, she represents Israel. This is indicated by the garland of 12 stars on her head. According to the Lord, my ancestral roots trace all the way back to Israel. Surely, the extraordinary revelations and wonders that had occurred in my life up to that point gave some credence to the idea that I just might be the woman. It would also explain why I had been suddenly and fiercely caught between two battling forces in the spirit realm.

But if I was the woman in Revelation 12 and God was using my friend's dream of giving birth to a male child to bolster my understanding of that, I had two problems. First, in her dream, I experience no pain during delivery. In Revelation 12:2, the woman "cried out in labor and in pain to give birth."

Second, in the dream, both the mother and child are taken to heaven. That did not match the surface text of Revelation 12:5b in which the baby alone is snatched up to God's throne. In verse 6, after the baby is taken, the woman flees into the wilderness to a place prepared by God to be nourished for 1,260 days or 3½ years.

After living in Detroit for nearly a year, the Lord solved the two mysteries for me. First, He revealed Revelation 12:1-6 is layered. Like many Scripture passages, it points to more than one fulfillment. The passage involves two women in labor giving birth to two male children more than two thousand years apart. Both women symbolize Israel at two different points in history. Mary, the mother of our Lord and Savior, Jesus Christ, fulfilled the first layer at His First Advent. No doubt, she suffered labor pains. While I had not yet given birth, I was surely crying out to Him in pain, laboring to fulfill the second layer.

Second, the Lord helped me see that parts of the Revelation passage refer to yet "another woman." She, too, represents Israel. And, like Mary and me, she is laboring to give birth to earth's Messiah. And, ultimately, she will.

She is a remnant of Jews that finds refuge in the wilderness during the Great Tribulation. She is the one who flees into the desert after the child and I are caught up to His throne. In her desert hideout, she is protected and nurtured by God. She will cry out in repentance at the end of the 1,260 days. Her cry will "deliver" Messiah to the scene of a nearly decimated world. At that point, He will end the planet's mayhem.

July 22, 1999

Who is the Woman in Revelation 12?

Many Biblicists believe the woman described in Revelation 12:1-6 is a symbol of Israel. She is "clothed with the sun, with the moon under her feet." On her head is a garland of 12 stars. The garland of 12 stars represents Israel's 12 tribes.

However, the description also indicates the woman is a believer in Jesus Christ. She is "clothed with the sun," which signifies she is covered in His righteousness. Also, Malachi 4:2 refers to Christ—the Light of the World—as the Sun of Righteousness*: "But to you who fear My name the Sun of Righteousness shall arise with healing in His wings; and you shall go out and grow fat like stall-fed calves."*

The expression "under her feet" connotes "controlled by" or "subject to." Since the Hebrews used the moon to establish their times and seasons, the phrase "moon under her feet" suggests the Lord has fixed or established the times and seasons of the last days around the woman and the birth of her child.

What most people do not realize is that the passage refers to two separate women, symbolic of Israel, more than 2,000 years apart. One is Mary, the mother of Jesus. The other is a woman, symbolic of Israel at the end of the Church Age.

The woman, symbolic of Israel at the end of the age, will be caught up to heaven along with her child. The "woman" who flees into the desert to a place prepared for her by God, where she will be taken care of for 1,260 days or 3½ years, is a surviving remnant of Jews during the Great Tribulation. She also symbolizes Israel.

Isaiah 66:7-8 (NIV) is a perfect example of God using the symbol of a woman in labor interchangeably with that of the nation of Israel—all within the same passage:

> *"Before she goes into labor, she gives birth; before the pains come upon her, she delivers a son. Who has ever heard of such a thing? Who has ever seen such things? Can a country be born in a day or a nation be brought forth in a moment?"*

The passage in Isaiah points to the creation of Israel as a state in 1948, after being lost within the Gentile nations for 1,900 years. It reveals before Israel "goes into labor" during the Great Tribulation, she will give birth to a country, a nation, as she has already done. Before the pains of this unprecedented travailing come upon her, she delivers a Son. That is, Mary gives birth to Christ, the Son of God. Thus, Isaiah spoke of a woman, symbolic of Israel and the actual nation of Israel, interchangeably, within the same passage:

"Before she goes into labor"	Refers to Israel
"She gives birth"	Refers to the woman
"Before the pains come upon her"	Refers to Israel
"She delivers a son"	Refers to the woman

By this time, I knew the passage had another layer of meaning. Just before unspeakable horrors unfold on earth during the 3½-year reign of the Antichrist, the time of "Jacob's Trouble," the second woman in

Revelation 12 will give birth to a male child. She and the child will be taken.

Afterward, the Antichrist will rage against Israel and her offspring (i.e., believers of Christ) during the Great Tribulation, which will affect the entire world. During these years of horror, Israel will go into labor; pain will come upon her. But in the end, a Jewish remnant in the desert will come to know and embrace Christ Yeshua as her long-promised, long-awaited Messiah whom she rejected during His First Coming. In a manner of speaking, she "delivers" Messiah (God's Son) to a scene of near desolation to overthrow her enemies brought forth by her long-awaited repentance.

In the Isaiah passage, a woman is symbolic of Israel and Israel is symbolic of a woman. Once more, God's use of a person as a spiritual symbol to convey messages to a particular generation should not be foreign to serious students of the Bible. As discussed previously, the prophet Hosea's relationship with Gomer, a prostitute, was symbolic of God's relationship with faithless Israel. Boaz' loving relationship with Ruth was symbolic of God's relationship with restored Israel and Christ's relationship with His bride, the Church. God used the prophet Ezekiel's life as a sign and symbol to warn the people of his day.

Chapter 22
The Child in Revelation 12

Four months after discovering Revelation 12 is layered, God started to reveal the identity of the child. Only a single verse in the passage refers to Christ, Rev. 12: 5a: "She bore a male Child who was to rule all nations with a rod of iron." The other three mentions of a male child—verses 2, 4, and 5b, refer to another child who is caught up to God's throne.

According to Revelation 12:4, the dragon will try to devour the woman's child just as he is born. Satan tried to devour Christ at least two years after He was born. King Herod's mass slaughter of all male children two years of age and younger residing in Bethlehem during the time of Christ, validates this. Other Scriptures teach that after His resurrection, Christ was not snatched up to God's throne as a baby. He *ascended* into heaven more than 2,000 years earlier as God-Man. There, He remains, seated at the right hand of God the Father, serving as our Mediator and High Priest, until His Second Coming.

The figurative description of the dragon (i.e., seven heads and 10 horns and seven diadems on its seven heads) points to the dominion of six past worldly kingdoms (i.e., Egypt, Assyria, Babylon, Medo-Persia, Greece, Rome) as well as the Revived Roman Empire (i.e., seventh head) *and* a future, short-lived, 10-nation confederacy (i.e., eighth head). The first six of these earthly kingdoms oppressed Israel at some point in history. The seventh and eighth empires will do the same in the future. All of them were (or will be) under Satan's sway. The seventh and eighth heads in the description help us understand the Apostle John is speaking of a woman and child of the latter days.

In 1998, the Lord told me the child's name. It is Joshua. He is named after Him, his Father. (In Hebrew, the names Yeshua and Joshua are synonymous.) At that time, the Lord began giving me and others dreams about him. But where was he in Scripture?

In 1997, a year earlier, near the beginning of our strange odyssey, the Lord showed me Scriptures that indicated He would have children of His own. At the time, the revelation stunned me. Isaiah 53:10 foretold of Christ, the Suffering Servant, having offspring: *"Yet it pleased the Lord to bruise Him; He has put Him to grief. When You make His soul an offering for sin, He shall see His seed, He shall prolong His days, and the pleasure of the Lord shall prosper in His hand."*

Some Biblicists generalize the word "seed" in this passage to apply to future generations of believers. However, the Hebrew interpretation of seed (zera, zeh'-rah) refers figuratively to a fruit or plant for sowing *and* carnally to a child or one's posterity.[1] It is the same word God used in Genesis 3:15 when He spoke judgment against the serpent: *"And I will put enmity between you and the woman and between your seed and her Seed."* It is the identical word used in Genesis 21:12-13: *"But God said to Abraham, 'Do not let it be displeasing in your sight because of the lad or because of your bondwoman. Whatever Sarah has said to you, listen to her voice; for in Isaac your seed shall be called. Yet, I will also make a nation of the son of the bondwoman, because he is your seed.'"*

Psalm 22:30 offers another example. The Messianic psalm prophesied of the Savior: *"A posterity shall serve Him...."* Posterity here also refers to the Lord's future progeny or descendants. Isaiah 22:15-25, a layered prophecy, spoke of God's trusted servant Eliakim who lived in the days of Isaiah. But the passage also pointed to Messiah's latter-day fulfillment of these Scriptures. Eliakim foreshadowed Messiah who, according to verse 24, would have offspring and posterity: *"They will hang on Him all the glory of His Father's house, the offspring and the posterity ...."* Lastly, in verses 16 and 17 of Psalm 45, another Messianic psalm, the psalmist wished for the King, who was also God, according to verses 6 and 7, to have many children from His marriage union. Before His ascension, Christ

---

[1]James Strong, *Strong's Exhaustive Concordance of the Bible, Hebrew and Chaldee Dictionary*, Hendrickson Publishers, 2009.

told His disciples: *"Everything must be fulfilled that is written about Me in the Law of Moses, the Prophets and the Psalms" (Luke 24:44b).*

Now, the time had come to learn more about this mysterious child, the Lord's firstborn. I did not want to learn about him just through my dreams or through the dreams of others. I wanted the Lord to show me more about this child in Scripture.

November 28, 1999

The Prince

"Yes."
"No, say it so I can really hear it," I pleaded.
"Yes, yes, yes!" The Lord responded with a hearty laugh.

My mind spun with wonder. Joshua is the Prince in Ezekiel! Another mystery unfolding! What am I to make of all this?

Last night, I asked Yeshua if Joshua represented an offering to God the Father. The Holy Spirit counseled, according to Law of Moses, the firstborn child always belongs to the Lord. Exodus 34:19, 20b reads: "The first offspring of every womb belongs to Me, including all the firstborn males of your livestock, whether from herd or flock ... Redeem all your firstborn sons." *That indicated to me our Savior's firstborn would also belong to the Father.*

This morning, the thought of Joshua being an offering to the Father hit me with great force. I asked again. The Lord confirmed the child was a gift to God the Father. Suddenly, my vague sense that Joshua was the Prince in Ezekiel 44-46 strengthened into a conviction.

Ezekiel 44-48 describes a restored Israel during Christ's millennial reign. In these chapters, the prophet speaks of a mysterious man who will minister before the Lord and the people. He is referred to as "the Prince."

Weeks earlier, the Lord took me to these obscure passages, and I wondered, then, if they pertained to Joshua. I was not confident. Might a resurrected King David be the Prince? Of him, was it said, "My servant David shall be their prince forever" (Ezekiel 37:25)? *However, deeper study revealed 19 additional Scripture references that the "Lord's servant David" referred to Christ—The Davidic Prince.*

In several dreams, God had already revealed Joshua would be an exceptional child, and he would grow up to be an extraordinary servant of the people. The Prince in Ezekiel is such a person. He is a special minister to God, his Father. Only the Prince can sit inside the temple gateway and eat in the presence of the Lord (Ezekiel 44:1-3).

His purpose seems to be to lead the people in worship (Ezekiel 45:17). We know he is not Christ the Messiah because he makes a sin offering for himself and for all the people in the land (Ezekiel 45:22). This is a symbolic or memorial offering in memory of what was accomplished for us on the cross since Christ abolished the old system of sacrifices. Interestingly, the Prince will have sons of his own (Ezekiel 46:16-18).

Finally, today, I mustered the courage to ask the Lord if Joshua was the Prince in Ezekiel. I wanted to hear His answer clearly in my spirit so I would have no doubt. His response was conclusive: "Yes, yes, yes!"

A year after informing to me that Joshua is the Prince in Ezekiel and a special gift to God the Father, the Holy Spirit took me back to Revelation 12:1-6 to show me actual references to him as a child! This is when I first discovered the passage spoke of two male babies, born more than 2,000 years apart. It was Jeri, not I, who discovered it.

December 17, 2000

The Child in Revelation 12:1-6

Jeri could not wait to show me what new things she found in Scripture. First, though, she gave me two lovely birthday gifts and a card featuring a big lion. The cover read, "You shall go out with joy!"—Isaiah 55:12. Assigning a double meaning to the expression, we both laughed.

Afterward, she started a fire in the fireplace. I popped a big bowl of popcorn, put on my pajamas, and we were off and running with the Scriptures. She showed me a nugget of a discovery about the male child in Revelation 12:1-6. I wondered why we had not discovered this before or why no other commentary mentioned it. She and I had researched this passage for two years. Jeri was convinced that it was God's will for it to remain a mystery to us until now.

The passage read:

> *A woman clothed with the sun, with the moon under her feet, and on her head a garland of 12 stars. Then being with child, she cried out in labor and in pain to give birth. And another sign appeared in heaven: behold, a great, fiery red dragon having seven heads and 10 horns, and seven diadems on his heads. His tail drew a third of the stars of heaven and threw them to the earth. And the dragon stood before the woman who was ready to give birth, to devour her child as soon as it was born. She bore a male Child who was to rule all nations with a rod of iron. And her child was caught up to God and His throne.*

Jeri made two curious discoveries in the text. First, the original Greek rendering of the word "woman" in the first verse refers to a "wife." This explains why most theologians believe the text refers to the nation of Israel who is considered a wife to God.

Second, there are four mentions of a male child in the passage. However, according to the Greek text, only one refers to Christ Yeshua. The other three refer to a different male child.

The child in verse 2, "Then being with child, she cried out in labor" refers to an ordinary male child ("teknon"), not the holy and divine term used to describe our Lord. The child in verse 4, "And the dragon stood before the woman who was ready to give birth, to devour her child as soon as it was born" also refers to an ordinary male child ("teknon"). However, the male child described in verse 5a, "She bore a male child who was to rule all nations with a rod of iron" refers to a divine being ("huios"). The last mention of a male child in verse 5b, "And her child was caught up to heaven" refers to a regular male baby ("teknon"), not the divine baby ("huios").

Even without discovering the Greek renderings, I never believed the passages about the male child referred solely to Yeshua because He ascended into heaven as a fully-grown adult—the Perfect Man-God. Christ was not snatched up to God's throne as a baby.

Jeri's discovery confirmed what has taken me two years to admit: Joshua is the baby in Revelation 12, and I am the woman, his mother. I am a Christian woman of Jewish Ethiopian ancestry and a symbol of both Israel and the Church!

The birth of the first Child (Christ) ushered in a new epoch in God's dealing with mankind. The first woman, Mary, gave birth to a male Child who, as the Suffering Servant, reconciled mankind to God through His atoning sacrifice on the cross at His First Coming. He shall one day rule all nations with a rod of iron (v. 5a).

The birth of the second child will also usher in a new epoch. His birth is tied to Christ's Second Coming as the Conquering King and Messiah. The second woman gives birth to this child, who will be snatched up to God's throne near the end of the age. His birth and snatching up will signal the beginning of the Great Tribulation, the last 3½ years of the present age. His birth also marks the dawn of the New Millennium or the 1,000-year reign of Christ.

Chapter 23
A Cosmic Coup

At the tail end of 1999, the Lord fit together several other missing puzzle pieces that gave me a greater understanding of what He was doing in my life. I marveled as His plan unfolded before me. No matter how many wrenches the freewill of man throws into His works, He will not be outdone. In the end, He will have His way. He is unstoppable. All He sets out to do from the beginning will be accomplished in the end.

Regarding His bride, the Lord had a plan that no man (or devil) could understand or thwart. Against all odds, He managed to transform His faithless wife, Israel, into a faithful one. It took the shedding of His blood to do it.

December 31, 1999

The Greatest Love Story Ever Told

I sat straight up in my bed and shouted at the top of my spirit to the Lord: "It's a clear day!" He laughed. That phrase is what first hit my spirit when I awoke yesterday morning. He knew exactly what I was referring to. For years, He had lovingly reminded me in song that a day will come when I finally realized who I was in Him and to Him.

How do I begin to tell the story of what the Lord has done and is doing? So much for so long has perplexed me. I have asked time and again over the past three years, "What's the point of this? What's the point of that? Lord, what are You doing with me?"

Now things are starting to make sense. I always believed the Lord was brilliant beyond all human comprehension. (Of course, He is. He's God!) But now that I have witnessed the major spiritual coup that He has executed using my life, His brilliance, in my mind, has catapulted to heights unknown. Who could have guessed His remarkable plan? No one. Not a single soul.

A Faithless Wife

Israel has always been the apple of God's eye. It has always been the Lord's desire that she, His beloved wife, be a jewel among the Gentile nations. God raised Israel up from nothing.

According to Ezekiel 16, God nurtured Israel from an infant. He cared for her through adolescence and brought her into womanhood. When He saw she was ready for love, He covered her nakedness. That is, He married her. The Lord and Israel entered a covenant relationship, analogous to a marriage. As her Husband, He would protect and provide for her. As His wife, she would revere, obey, and worship Him.

As a loving, adoring Husband, the Lord gave His wife Israel everything. He adorned her in jewels, attired her in the finest clothes, and fed her choice foods. She became a queen among the nations of the world. God intended for all the other nations of the world to flock to see her beauty, a beauty given to her by Him.

The nations would so marvel at what the Lord had done with and for His beloved wife that they would know Israel's God was the one true sovereign God of the universe. They would forsake their idols and worship Israel's God.

But Israel failed to keep her part of the covenant. In her prosperity, she grew proud and arrogant. She began to trust, not in God, but in her own beauty. She walked away from the Lord's love and took other lovers. She obeyed and worshipped other gods. The Lord pleaded for her to return to Him, but she would not.

The Lord, who foreknows all things, knew Israel would spurn His affections. He knew before establishing the foundations of the earth that His wife would choose other lovers (gods) and reject Him. The Lord, who grants mankind freewill, would not force His will upon Israel. She would have to choose to obey and love Him in response to His love for her. Thus, it appeared Israel would not be the light to the nations God intended her to be—at least, not at first.

A Faithful Wife

When Israel failed, as God knew she would, He initiated His plan for securing a faithful wife. It was a plan totally, completely hidden from all the prophets—the Church. Oddly, the Church was never mentioned in the Old Testament.

In the New Testament, the Church is referred to as the bride of Christ. The relationship between Christ and His bride is still a great mystery, per the Apostle Paul:

> *For this reason, a man shall leave his father and mother and be joined to his wife, and the two shall become one flesh. This is a great mystery, but I speak concerning Christ and the Church. Nevertheless, let each one of you, in particular, so love his own wife as himself, and let the wife see that she respects her husband (Ephesians 5:31-33).*

Ephesians 5:25-27 reveals Christ's atoning sacrifice would ultimately produce a bride—sanctified and cleansed—whom He could present to Himself. He had to give Himself up to obtain her. He had to shed His blood to redeem her and to secure her as His own.

The Lord is accomplishing in the end what He set out to do in the beginning—to secure for Himself a wife—a chosen companion—who will rule and reign with Him throughout all eternity. She will be a glorious, holy church—a bride without spot, wrinkle, or blemish.

The great mystery of Christ's bride is unfolding in our generation! God's plan for the redemption of His people marvelously follows the ancient Hebrew tradition through which a father secured a bride for his son:

- A son traveled from his father's house to the home of the prospective bride.
- The father negotiated with the bridegroom the price that must be paid.
- When they agreed upon the purchase price, the marriage covenant was established.
- The woman became his betrothed, set apart exclusively for him.

- Groom and bride drank from the same cup to symbolize their covenant relationship.
- The groom left the home of the bride to return to his father's house to prepare a place for her.
- The bride used that time of separation to prepare herself for married life.
- After a period of separation, the groom came back with other male escorts, usually at night, to retrieve his bride.
- While the bride knew the groom would return for her, she did not know the exact time.
- She knew his arrival would be preceded by a shout.
- The groom received the bride with her female attendants.
- The groom and bride entered the bridal chamber and consummated their marriage.

Given this ancient Hebrew marriage tradition, is it any wonder why Christ referred to Himself as the Bridegroom? Is it any wonder why He eluded to His wedding and marriage in so many of His teachings to the Church?

What the world did not know then, and is only finding out now, is that God has used the last 2,000 years—a parenthesis in the history of His dealing with Israel—to achieve two ends. First, He secured a holy congregation of civic rulers called "The Bride of Christ." Second, He secured an individual bride for His Son.

The Church, comprised principally of Gentiles, will help Christ rule the Gentile nations during His millennial reign. How appropriate! During her time on earth, the bride is being prepared and fitted to rule with her Husband in eternity.

Christ said everything written about Him in the Law of Moses, the Prophets, and *the Psalms* must be fulfilled (Luke 24:44). Although some believe Psalm 45 was written against the backdrop of an ancient secular, royal wedding, it is also a Messianic praise song that foretells the marriage of the King of kings to an individual. The reference to this sacred psalm in Hebrews 1:8-9, confirmed its application to Christ.

Christ often interpreted Scripture literally and not always allegorically. He recognized double references and twofold fulfillments within prophecies.[2] According to Psalm 45, interpreting Scripture as Christ did, one can conclude that He will not only marry, but He will also produce children of His own (v. 17).

The world will soon learn that God accomplished exactly what He set out to do from the very beginning—to secure for Himself a wife—an eternal companion from the House of Israel. The woman He has chosen is a daughter of Zion. She is of Ethiopian Jewish descent and, as a believer in Christ, worships and adores Him as her Messiah. She, too, is from the House of David, the tribe of Judah. (But she is also a Gentile and thus, could be considered a modern-day Samaritan!)

The Lord hid her Jewish lineage from the woman, her family, and the world. But most importantly, He hid it from Satan until the end. It took many centuries to accomplish this feat. Satan, familiar with the Scriptures, knew such a woman would be revealed in the last days. Out of hatred and jealousy toward the Lord, Satan made Jews and people of African descent special targets in his quest to annihilate all humankind.

Satan still seeks to destroy the Messiah's line (Revelation 12:4). But he will not find the Lord's chosen mate until the very end of days. Her ancestors were scattered among the nations; as a judgment for their idolatry, some of them were eventually taken captive as slaves and brought to the United States of America. Her people were enslaved for hundreds of years; but through that brutal oppression, many of them came to know, love, and adore Christ as their Lord and Savior.

---

[2]*As an example of how Christ interpreted Scripture, see Luke 4:14-21. At the commencement of His earthly ministry, He read Isaiah 61:1 in a Jewish temple. He split v. 2 of Isaiah 61:1-2, because He knew only vv. 1 and 2a would be fulfilled at His First Coming. Verse 2b would be fulfilled more than 2,000 years later, at His Second Coming.*

Her dispersed people are now among those who are being restored to the land of Israel:

> *It shall come to pass in that day that the Lord shall set His hand again the second time to recover the remnant of His people who are left ... from Assyria and Egypt ... from Pathros and Cush (Ethiopia) .... He will set up a banner for the nations, and will assemble the outcasts of Israel, and gather together the dispersed of Judah from the four corners of the earth (Isaiah 11:11-12).*

In the last days, the daughter of Zion will bring a special gift to the Lord: a son. It is conceivable that the gift the Ethiopian people will bring to the Lord at the end of the age is the child, Joshua:

> *At that time, shall a present be brought to the Lord of hosts from a people tall and polished, from a people terrible from their beginning and feared and dreaded near and far, a nation strong and victorious, whose land the rivers or great channels divide—to the place [of worship] of the Name of the Lord of hosts, to Mount Zion [in Jerusalem] (Isaiah 18:7, Amplified Bible).*

Perhaps, the passage in Zephaniah also points to the time when Joshua will be offered to Lord by His dispersed worshippers:

> *From beyond the rivers of Cush (Ethiopia), those who pray to Me, the daughter of My dispersed people, will bring and present My offering (Zephaniah 3:9-10, Amplified Bible).*

A *spiritual* seed of the child was given to the woman as a guarantee, evidence of a promise of her role as a wife and mother in the Millennial Age. The birth of her child will serve as a trigger for the world. His birth and rapture will signal the beginning of "Jacob's Trouble" and the Great Tribulation (Revelation 12:2-6, Micah 5:3, Isaiah 66:7). The child's removal will also serve as a sign to the Church that the rapture is very near.

Three months after revealing His plan for securing a faithful wife of Hebraic descent, through the creation and building of a corporate body of believers called the Church, the Lord led me to an obscure passage of Scripture in Jeremiah that pertained to this ages-old plan.

Never would I have associated this Old Testament Scripture with His plan for my life had He not given it to me. After sharing the Scripture with Jeri, she did even more digging. What she found undergirded what the Lord revealed to me:

March 27, 2000

More on the Unfolding Mystery of the Bride

Bible commentator John MacArthur called Jeremiah 31:22 one of Jeremiah's most puzzling statements: "How long will you gad about, O you backsliding daughter? For the Lord has created a new thing in the earth—a woman (female) shall encompass (compass) a man."

Many used to think this verse referred to the virgin birth of Christ. Now, most are certain it does not. MacArthur wrote: "The term, 'woman' in the passage means woman, not virgin, and 'encompass' or 'surround' does not suggest conceiving."[3]

The key to the passage lies in the term "encompass" or "compass." According to some scholars, the word "compass" means to woo, win, and protect a man:

> *To compass is to woo and win. That the early translators attached that meaning to it is clear from the fact that Shakespeare, their contemporary, so used it (Charles Ellicott, A Bible Commentary). Probably the implication is that Israel, the erring but deeply penitent wife, instead of going about after other lovers will devote herself to winning back and being worthy of the love of her divine Husband and Lord, who had rejected her (Amplified Bible Commentary, P. 867).*

John MacArthur's commentary on the verse dovetailed with that opinion. MacArthur suggested the passage may refer to "the formerly virgin Israel, now a disgraced, divorced wife, who will one day in the future embrace

---

[3]John MacArthur, *The MacArthur Bible (NKJ),* Word Publishing, 1997, p.1106.

her former Husband, the Lord, and He will receive her back, fully forgiven."[4]

Jeri did an even fuller study on the passage and shared her findings with me. In the commentary of an old Bible, she found the following explanation of the strange turn of phrase:

> *"A woman to encompass a man" means to protect ... to turn a man to herself in terms of fondling and cherishing; to embrace him. It means a weak and tender being shall embrace the strong. And the strong shall once again take the weak into his closest intercourse, under his protection and care.*

God has since shown me the Bible commentaries are correct. Israel was a faithless wife to the Lord. The bride of Christ is His faithful wife, just badly spotted. But she will not be when He finishes with her and presents her to Himself.

He has, indeed, done "a new thing" in the earth. His bride, the Church, chases after Him, seeks to obey Him, and lavishes Him with attention and love. She reveres and worships Him as her Bridegroom.

At the same time, the Lord will also take an individual bride at the end of the age in preparation for His millennial reign. He will woo to Himself the woman who is a virgin in the spiritual sense of the word (not the literal sense). She will woo Him back and win His heart. He will propose marriage, and she will accept.

Why would the Lord do such a thing? The best explanation for what the Lord is doing at the close of the Church Age can be found in the extraordinary book, *The Divine Romance* by Gene Edwards. A woman I do not know asked Jeri to send me her copy of the book. The woman never read it. However, she insists God asked her to give it to me. I suspect it had been sitting on her bookshelf for years ... waiting for me.

---

[4]John MacArthur, *The MacArthur Bible (NKJ)*, Word Publishing, 1997, p.1106.

I read the book, my mouth agape, in almost a single sitting. Much of what the Lord was doing in my life was contained in its pages! I kept asking the Lord, "How does Edwards know?" The Lord assured me that he had been divinely inspired to write the love story.

Edwards had no idea how close he was to the truth when he conjectured the Lord's intent to secure a wife. From the creation of Eve, He sought an eternal companion for Himself; one who would come through the line of Jacob, who would treasure and adore Him, and who would not chase after other lovers (gods). As Eve was flesh of Adam's flesh, His bride would be spirit of His Spirit.

One poignant speculation in Gene Edwards' *Divine Romance* was that the Lord's chosen companion would be a compilation of millions of particles of light. Each particle, representing a portion of Him, was destined in eternity past to be a partaker of His glorious plan of salvation. Although that was pure conjecture on Edwards' part, I recognized the idea had a tinge of applicability to my life.

I have always been considered odd—beyond eccentric—by many people. I have cried to the Lord *for years,* "Why am I so different? Why do I not fit in anywhere?" I realized that could be the cry of every radical believer of Christ in every age. We are not supposed to fit in. But my peculiarity seemed extreme as my daughter astutely pointed out one Christmas Eve.

December 24, 2005

A Compilation of His Bride?

"Mom, I don't know ... you are so strange. It's like you are made up of spare parts. It's like you're made up of the arm of a Cheetah, a leg of a lion, a foot of a bear, the head of ... nothing matches! It's like God made you from spare parts!" I could not understand the point she was trying to make. To her, I was beyond unique, beyond eccentric.

"Eclectic?" I offered.

"I know I'm not making myself clear, but you could be a whole other gender! You've always been weird! I saw it in the pictures Grandma

showed me of you growing up. In every picture, you didn't fit. And your eyes seemed so sad." She offered more examples to help me understand.

"Okay, you're a Black woman, right? But you think like a White male. Do you realize that?" (She meant I related extremely well to White males in business.) "You're a grown woman who loves cartoons and fairy tales. You can be so smart, brilliant even, and so dumb—all at the same time. You're tough as nails, but you can't get through the newspaper without crying. You're extremely cheap, but extravagant when it comes to giving away money. You're rich, but you think like a poor missionary. You have nice clothes but dress like a bum! You have a beautiful home, but you never invite anyone over. You love people, but you prefer to be alone. We have to drag you to social gatherings, but you end up the life of the party. Nothing matches! You're a walking, talking, breathing paradox."

She went on to talk of my work as a consultant at Denny's and all my responsibilities there. Yet, I was also involved in a sizeable project acting as my own oil and gas company, exploring for oil in Michigan.

"Mom, usually people pick a profession. They do one thing, maybe two. You're into everything. You're all over the place." I could not tell if her description of me was good or bad. Finally, I came to my own conclusion.

What Ryan was saying was not too different from what God had been telling me. Years ago, He told me that I had been called to be "a sign of the bride to come." The bride of Christ is made up of all kinds of people—men, women, and children of all ages, from every nationality, race, tribe, and tongue. They are the high and low, spanning all walks of life for more than 2,000 years. I represented a radically mixed body of believers.

It made sense that I would be an oddball. For all I know—and only God could accomplish such a thing—I could be a compilation of millions (or billions) of tiny parts or portions of every believer in the body of Christ, making me a true representative of the bride in His eyes. Yes, making me like a "whole other gender!"

Chapter 24
"Ishi"

Although the Lord had performed many wonders in my life to help me understand who I was to Him, one of the most startling was a simple revelation He gave me the night of November 22, 2004. It took place several years after He revealed that I was both a symbol of His bride and a latter-day symbol of Israel, His wife.

November 23, 2004

My Husband

I experienced one of the biggest shocks of my life last night! Over the course of two days, a fragment of a verse of Scripture kept coming to my mind: "You will call me Husband." It would come out of nowhere. Finally, I could not resist any longer.

I decided to do an Internet search to find out where in the Bible I could find that verse to study it. Although I was already prepared for bed, I went downstairs to my office to do the search.

I typed in the search engine what I heard in my spirit: "You will call me Husband." I perused the list of results. Right near the top was the verse Hosea 2:16. I had read the verse before, but I never thoroughly examined it. Eight versions of the verse, including the King James Version, popped on the screen.

My eyes scrolled down the list. I gasped when I discovered six of the eight versions used the word "Ishi" in place of Husband: "And it shall be in that day, saith the Lord, that thou shalt call Me Ishi; and shalt call Me no more Baali" (Hosea 2:16, KJV).

WHAT ARE THE CHANCES OF THAT? Until that very moment, I thought Ishi was a pet name I made up for the Lord! I HAD BEEN CALLING HIM ISHI FOR YEARS—just to tease Him!

My mind raced back ... trying to remember how and where I had come up with the name Ishi? My Bible did not use the term Ishi. It used Husband. I racked my brain. Slowly, it came back to me.

Years ago, the music director at Wayside Baptist Church was named Ish. At the time, I thought it was odd. Who would name their child Ish? The moniker stuck with me for some reason.

Later, I learned "Ish" in Hebrew means "Man." One day, in the process of preparing my Sunday school lesson, I discovered the word "man" and "husband" in Hebrew were interchangeable. After I taught the lesson, I thought no more about the matter until years later when I moved to Greer, South Carolina.

There, the Lord began to speak to me in extraordinary ways, slowly revealing who I was in Him. As our relationship evolved, the Holy Spirit reminded me the term "Ish" in Hebrew means "man" or "husband." I honestly had forgotten. I also recalled in the book The Divine Romance, *the author, Gene Edwards, referred to Adam's Eve and Christ's Eve (Second Adam's wife) as "Isha." I liked the sound of it.*

One day, putting all the tidbits together, I simply started calling the Lord, "Ishi." I took the term "Ish" and added an "i" on the end to make "Ishi." It matched "Isha." Also, "Ishi" sounded like a more intimate, endearing, and playful term for husband—like "hubby." At the time, I had no active knowledge that Hosea prophesied the Lord's betrothed would one day call Him Ishi.

When I was in an especially playful mood, I called the Lord "Ishi-Man." I would say the last part with a Jamaican accent to make it sound funny. It amused Him, so I did it often. More and more I began to call Him "Ishi" or "Ishi-Man." Sometimes I would slip and use one of those terms in the presence of someone other than my daughter or Jeri. I would quickly correct myself.

It blew my mind to discover a prophecy in Scripture, written thousands of years earlier, that predicted in the latter days, the Lord's betrothed would call Him by the very name I had been calling Him in jest. Considering everything the Lord had shown me about our relationship, I could not dismiss this as coincidence. Ancient prophecy was unfolding in my life. I was fulfilling it! Surely, I was a living representation of Christ's "bride to come" *and* a symbol of a restored Israel.

Finally, the time came for me to live the message I would ultimately bring to Christ's spotted bride. Of course, looking back at what happened, most of it is clear now. But I was just as blind going into this next phase of life as I had been entering the previous one. Everything—absolutely everything—would have to be walked out by faith.

PART THREE:
LIVING THE MESSAGE

Chapter 25
An Unwitting Slave

Like an actor on a stage, I had a role to play in God's master plan of redemption for mankind. For years, the Lord told me I was a "sign of the bride to come." Up until this point, I had no idea how dirty I (she) was, how spotted, blemished, and wrinkled. There was no way we could pass through heaven's gates in our woeful condition. However, before I could give a message, I had to live the message.

One of the most effective ways to make a message heard and credible is to make the messenger identify with the message on a personal, visceral level—to feel the pain. If one is to say, "I know how you feel," one must have lived through a similar experience and felt similar feelings. Otherwise, the person's words are purely academic, without veracity. The grief and sorrow experienced by the messenger render the message more poignant and more tenable. For example, Christ had to become one of us in order to identify with our weaknesses and infirmities. He had to become the sacrificial Lamb to qualify as our High Priest and Mediator.

In this same way, I reflected all the disgraceful spots of His redeemed; and I would have to be cleansed of them. The cleansing process required me to walk out an Old Testament pattern. Like ancient Israel, I would have to escape Egyptian bondage and wander a barren desert as God tested and proved my faith in Him. After that, I would be led to the Promised Land, where God's promises are ultimately seized.

At this juncture in my life, I thought I had been through enough, having been ripped from my home in South Carolina and forced to start over in Detroit. But God was just beginning. I was about to be tested in ways I never experienced before. Fiery trials would burn off the dross in my life that I could not see. God's plan was to cleanse me through difficulty, hardship, and affliction. A year prior to being thrown into the refining fire, the Lord had given me an extraordinary sign pointing to this period of my life. But I did not realize its importance until years later.

April 17, 1998

The Burning Match

It had become my custom to light a scented candle by my bed every evening before retiring. The scent reminded me of the Lord. Late in the night, I always blew it out.

On the night of April 15, 1998, I discovered I had run out of long matchsticks. I searched around until I found a packet of regular paper matches. My candle had burned to about half its original size, which required me to stick my hand, with a lit match, down into the long, cylindrical candle holder.

As I did this, the flames shot up the paper match and almost burned my finger. I dropped the lit match in the melting wax. A fire flared over the little match and consumed it. I tried it again. But this time something strange happened.

The flames engulfed the second paper match, covering it entirely; but the match would not burn! Enveloped in flames, the little match stood, leaned against the glass holder! I watched in complete disbelief. I waited and waited for the flames to devour the match. Were my eyes deceiving me?

I ran to get Suzanne. I needed an eyewitness. No one would believe me if I didn't have a witness. Mike was in Chicago and Ryan was spending the night with girlfriends. Suzanne was watching television in her bedroom, setting her hair.

The hair curlers fell from her lap as I flew into her room and urged her to come see. We both ran back to my bedroom. Sure enough, the little paper match was still engulfed in flames! It would not burn!

Our eyes glued to the glass cylinder, we watched together for another 10 minutes. Neither of us could explain it. Finally, I blew out the match and the wick. (The wick had been lit when I dropped the match into the candle holder to keep from burning my finger.)

I mulled the experience over and over in my mind, but I could not comprehend the meaning of it. I knew it was significant. God was trying to show me something, but what was it?

I thought about how God had used flames in my life to symbolize greed and covetousness. He always said, "The flames will not set you ablaze." But that application simply did not fit this situation. I wondered what the flames symbolized in this case. I fell asleep wondering.

The next day, rummaging through a drawer, I found a pamphlet entitled, "God's Heart-Warming Fire" by Billy Graham. It was published in 1957 and 1998. I had no idea where it came from. However, the little booklet was filled with Old and New Testament examples of fire symbolizing God. The first line read, "Fire has always been the symbol of deity."

The pamphlet gave me a clue that the fire surrounding the little match was God. Then, it slowly dawned on me ... I was the match! God was telling me I would be engulfed in flames—His flames—but I would not be consumed!

God's plan was to have me experience what it was like to be a slave in Egypt. He needed to move me to a whole new setting to make the experience real. Of course, I did not understand any of this at the time.

After living in Detroit for a year, I emptied the warehouse full of my belongings. I gave everything away. Right after I did this, Debbie came to visit me. She came to deliver some news. She asked to talk to me privately. We left the others in the kitchen and went upstairs to my bedroom. I closed the door behind us. She sat on the edge of my bed. I sat in my chair.

"Guess what?" I could not imagine.

"I had a dream about you last night," she smiled.

"Was it good?" I asked studying her face.

"You told me you moved to Memphis, Tennessee. You had that chair." She pointed to the chair I was sitting in. "And you had this throw!" She patted the gold-colored throw lying across my bed. "It was flung over the chair."

"Debbie, there is NO WAY! That, my dear, is not possible." My response was immediate and resolute. "Let me tell you something and listen to me very carefully." I spoke slowly for emphasis, "I am done! I am finished! I'm not moving anywhere. Okay, you're laughing, but I'm telling you, I have just thrown all my stuff to the four winds. I am not buying so much as a broom! DO YOU HEAR ME? I AM DONE!"

On January 2, 2002, Ryan and I moved into our new home in Harbor Town, right off the Mississippi River in Memphis, Tennessee. Up until November 23, 2001, I would not have thought it possible.

But a few days before Thanksgiving, after a long night's sleep, my eyes popped open. I sat straight up in bed and shouted in complete amazement, "Oh, my goodness! We're moving to Memphis, Tennessee!" The revelation came out of nowhere! There had been no thought of it until that moment.

I ran into Ryan's room and shook her awake. "Ryan, Ryan! God just told me we're moving to Memphis, Tennessee!" At first, it made no sense. Just 11 months earlier, I had purchased and furnished a three-story condo in Southfield, Michigan. I saw it in a detailed dream the Lord gave me. Then, He opened the way for me to buy it. At the time, I thought it was for Ryan and her fiancé. But after six weeks of premarital counseling, they both called off the engagement. Now, Ryan and I lived in the condo.

Why would we be moving again? I could not explain why I was so confident it would happen, but I knew it would occur soon. Later that morning, the explanation unfolded in my mind. The move suddenly made all the sense in the world.

Before the 9/11 terrorist attacks, it took me only an hour to commute from Detroit to Greenville-Spartanburg, South Carolina by plane. After

9/11, a connecting flight was added to the route. My commute lengthened to seven hours. I lost a full day just flying! There were, however, several daily direct flights from Memphis. I could get there in an hour. I surmised later that morning, "If God is in this, Ryan, Denny's will pay for the relocation."

President Nelson Marchioli did not blink an eye when I asked him if Denny's would relocate us to Memphis. "Of course, we'll move you."

On the day before Thanksgiving, we flew to Memphis to find a house. God showed me in a dream the exterior of the house we were going to purchase. It was a quaint, sky-blue, two-story house with lots of white trim; and it was gorgeous.

When the real estate agent pulled up in front of the house for the first time, I screamed, "This is the house I saw in my dream!" It was the first house on the agent's list. She showed us several homes during the day, and they were all beautiful; but none of them could rival the sky-blue one with lots of white trim.

It was love at first sight when Ryan and I walked into the house. Floor-to-ceiling wraparound windows graced the living room, dining room, family room, and kitchen. The kitchen overlooked a lush courtyard with a running fountain, all hidden behind a high privacy fence.

Two sets of French doors in the second-floor master suite overlooked a private screened porch and a sun-drenched deck. The living room, dining room, and master bedroom had working fireplaces. Shiny, dark wood floors ran throughout the entire lower level of the house. Even the garage was customized with large floor-to-ceiling storage cubbies.

In the end, we chose the "dream house." Another interesting feature about the residence was that its square footage was equal to that of the Southfield townhouse. Every piece of furniture I had purchased for that condo found a place in our new quarters. God had gone ahead of us.

Before our relocation, God gave me a dream in which I saw myself sliding down soft mattresses. This indicated the move would be smooth and easy. It was. (I did not realize the significance of the *down* direction at the time.) Never had a home purchase been so simple. The move was as effortless as buying a loaf of bread from the store.

I used the $80,000 I had put away for Ryan for the down payment. Ryan's condo in Southfield sold within a few weeks, and I broke even on the sale. Denny's coordinated and paid for the entire move. I just walked out of one place and into the other.

The day after I signed the contract on the new house, Northwest Airlines changed its flights back to their original route! Once again, I could have flown directly from Detroit to Greenville-Spartanburg in one hour. Mortified, I notified Nelson about the change. There was not one hint of regret in his voice. He readily agreed I should go forward with the transfer since I had already signed the contract.

The way everything unfolded—the ease, the pace—it was clear heaven wanted us in Memphis, Tennessee. Yet, I knew there was some other special reason why the Lord orchestrated the move. Shortening my commute to work was just a ploy to spur the move. What was the *real* reason? I could not put my finger on it.

December 29, 2001

Why Memphis?

I lost count of how many times I asked the Lord, "Why Memphis? Why are You moving us to Memphis?" I now knew our move had nothing to do with my plane commute to work. There must have been a spiritual reason.

Slowly, the answer unfolded as I learned more about Memphis, Tennessee. The city was named for, and patterned after, the ancient city of Memphis in Egypt. Around 3050 B.C., Memphis became the capital city of Egypt.

Our heavenly Father called Moses out of Egypt. Forty years later, He called the children of Israel out of Egypt. The Lord also called His Son Yeshua out of Egypt. Mary and Joseph had fled there when Yeshua was just a child to escape Herod's murderous rage. In due course, Christ will call Joshua, His own son, out of "Egypt" and then His church, His bride. That is to say, He will call His own out of the world (the land of bondage) to the ultimate promised land (heaven)!

Interestingly, from our safe, protected inlet in Harbor Town, I can see the enormous pyramid that sits squarely in downtown Memphis, off the Mississippi River. (The pyramid is a stadium where the Grizzlies play.) The Mississippi River runs through Memphis, Tennessee, much like the Nile River ran through the ancient city of Memphis, Egypt. In front of the Pyramid stands a colossal statue of Ramses the Great, the Pharaoh who tangled with Moses and lost.

I did not realize it at the time, but I was to spend seven God-ordained years in the flaming fire. The first 3½ years were spent in Detroit and Southfield, Michigan, and the last 3½ years would be spent in Memphis, Tennessee. In each location, I remained *exactly* 3½ years—*to the day!* I did not orchestrate the moves to coincide with the calendar. They just happened.

In both cases, I discovered the preciseness of the timing *after* the moves had occurred. I knew God arranged things that way, but He did so without my fully understanding why. I later learned that in Scripture seven is the number for spiritual completeness, wholeness, or perfection. Three and a half is the number for trials and testing.

God needed the seven years to burn off the dross—the scum, refuse, and garbage—gumming up my life. There were things in me, about me, and around me that held me captive to the world in ways I could not see. As far as the Lord was concerned, those things represented hindrances. They held me back from being all I could be in Him. They kept me from running the race He knew I could run. All impediments would have to be removed.

Right after we settled into our new home, my days in Memphis became as tumultuous as my days in Detroit. Every other day, there seemed to be some new ordeal to go through, some new hardship that threatened to take me under. I often complained, "It is always two steps forward, three steps backward; three steps forward, five steps backward!" Obstacles were everywhere. I could not catch a break.

It took me a long time to finally put together the puzzle pieces of my difficult life and the difficult lives of my family members. Ryan and I and the rest of my family were symbolically living out something so big, I would not be able to connect all the dots to fully understand until it was well over. More than five years would pass before I realized what God was doing.

In due course, I discovered that burning off the dross was only one aspect of God's refinement plan for me in Memphis. He would also use my stint there to demonstrate two other profound truths about what happens to His people in the land of Egypt.

As residents of "Egypt," we often get caught up and entangled in the world's system of mammon-chasing and debt-creation. They are twin evils that commandeer our attention, strength, and resources. They often work in tandem to pull us away from God. They thwart His plans for our lives and His agenda for mankind in unimaginable ways.

No wonder God warns us that we cannot serve two masters, and He asks us to choose between Him and mammon. If the prince of this world ("Pharaoh") can keep us preoccupied ("making bricks") in Egypt, we will not have the time or the inclination to worship God in the manner He deserves or desires. And His agenda sits idle. Moreover, if the world's prince can entice us to create debt, we eventually become slaves to the lender and to the world. It is all a terrible web of bondage.

During our 3½-year stay in Memphis, I accrued $1.1 million in debt! It was pure, unmitigated bondage. Surely, what happened must have been ordained as part of my destiny! As unbelievable as it may sound, *every* decision that led to that bondage was first taken before the Lord in prayer. Yet, that is where I ended up.

My only explanation is God saw what needed to be worked out of me and what needed to be worked into me, so He allowed (or orchestrated) the circumstances that took me to a place of bondage. There, I would learn some valuable lessons for us all. God also needed my life experiences to speak to a generation of greedy, covetous believers, who did not know the extent of their insatiable avariciousness. I was a perfect image of His spotted bride—in bondage, in Egypt.

My Parent's New Home

The process of creating that staggering debt began innocently enough. My parents came to visit me from Detroit. They loved Memphis' temperate weather. The next thing I knew they were examining the rear of my house to see how they could add a couple of rooms. They had decided they would spend the summers in Detroit and the winters with me in Memphis. They had $40,000 to offer toward the project. I knew living with my parents at that specific juncture of my life was not God's will. What was the alternative? I prayed.

A few days later, I purchased a three-bedroom, three-bathroom house for my parents, about 15 minutes from my house in Harbor Town! It all happened so fast—whirlwind fast! One day we were looking, and the next day we had a house under contract. We received financing approval almost overnight.

For the longest time, I felt purchasing that property was the worst real estate deal I ever made in my life. As God would have it, I discovered the problems with the house, one by one, over time despite a nearly day-long inspection by a supposedly reputable company. I learned too late that the owner of the house was a good friend of the man doing the inspection. Not surprisingly, I received a thick, glowing inspection report.

I did not know when I signed the contract the home had been badly water damaged and had sat unoccupied for years. Mold had taken over the place, hidden within the walls. We ended up practically rebuilding the entire house! We installed new walls, new doors and hardware, new windows, and a new master bathroom. We also overhauled the second and third bathrooms. We sanded and stained the wood floors throughout the living room and dining room and repaired the buckling kitchen floor. We replaced the A/C and repaired the antiquated plumbing and electrical systems. Finally, we cleaned the ducts, which had not been cleaned since the house was built. And that was just the interior!

We also installed a new roof, new gutters, a new garage door, and a new walkway. We landscaped both the front and back, installed a sprinkler system in both yards, and built a high privacy fence around the property. In the back, where there were once mounds of dirt and mud, we created a little Garden of Eden. It would later turn out to be the beautifully landscaped backyard that enticed a family to buy the house from us when we sold it to upgrade to an even larger house.

An Extreme Makeover

After virtually rebuilding the house, I furnished it. I chose expensive, lovely pieces to grace each room. The home was a gift to my parents. Over the course of time, the Lord revealed the purchase of the house and the needed renovations were symbolic of my life! It was the reason He had me buy it!

August 7, 2003

> *My Life as a House*
>
> *I had the most wondrous conversation with Yeshua last night. He woke me up around 2 a.m. to talk. Within minutes, we were conversing about the house I was rehabbing for my parents. As I envisioned it thoroughly renovated, I bubbled, "Yeshua, that house is going to be the cutest little thing in the neighborhood when we're all done. What a hidden beauty!"*
>
> *When I made that statement, I was thinking about the house's unique window structure, cedar closets, one-of-a-kind dining room chandelier, the huge backyard and the large front porch with its stately columns.*

The house was in Memphis' High Point District. Those aspects of the house spoke of its original beauty before it fell into disrepair and became a blight in the neighborhood.

Suddenly, an image of the Fashion Fair Hidden Beauty® Crème in my bathroom flashed across my mind! Yeshua often teased me that the cream's name reflected my life. In an instant, I was hit with a realization. The house I was restoring for my parents was a metaphor for my life! The house's renovation mirrored the renovation of my life … after Christ purchased it:

My Dirty House	*My Life Before Christ*
The house was built in the early 1950's.	*I was born in 1953.*
The house was located in metaphoric capital city of Egypt.	*I am presently a resident of "Egypt."*
The inside of the house was filthy when I bought it.	*My life was filthy when Christ redeemed it.*
The house had been badly neglected, rundown.	*My life had been badly neglected, rundown.*
The house smelled moldy before I took it over.	*My sin-filled life stunk before Christ took it over.*
Seven large dogs used to have run of the house.	*Wicked spirits used to have run of my life.*
The house was infested with spiders (and other creepy critters) that we killed daily.	*My life was infested with wrong thoughts, attitudes, and behaviors that Christ killed daily.*
We hauled tons of trash out of the attic.	*Christ removed tons of trash from my head.*

My Dirty House	*My Life Before Christ*
Mounds of hidden dirt and muck had to be sucked out of the ducts within the walls, so we could breathe properly.	*Christ had to remove the dirt and muck hidden in my heart so I could live properly.*
Rotten, decayed wood, hidden within the walls, floors, and roof, had to be removed and replaced with new wood.	*Christ removed the hidden rot and decays in my life and began rebuilding me anew.*
The windows in the house were replaced because the seals were broken, and moisture buildup prevented people from seeing through them clearly.	*I could not see anything clearly before meeting Christ.*
The interior doors of the house had to be replaced to close properly.	*Christ had to close various "doors" in my life or evil would walk back in.*
The house looked adorable at first glance, but it needed a lot of work done inside and out.	*My life looked charming at first glance, but it actually needed a lot of work done inside and out.*

As I predicted, the house turned out to be simply exquisite after investing a small fortune into it. There were a lot of disappointments, hiccups, and setbacks, but it all seemed worth it after everything was done. Before the overhaul, the house looked like such a bad investment. I wondered about it daily.

God helped me see my life required as much work as that house. Surely, at times, I looked like a bad investment—so much was wrong with me.

But He did not give up. He saw the beauty I could become with some tender, loving care.

Strangers familiar with the neighborhood would often stop and ask to see the house because they remembered what it used to look like. It had been neglected for years. The change was so eye-catching and dramatic they could not believe it was the same house. It was unrecognizable. God's point exactly.

Ryan's New Home

Ryan, a budding author, started out living with me in Harbor Town, but eventually she moved to her own rental apartment in downtown Memphis. I supported her as she wrote. At the same time, Suzanne, who had cared for her terminally ill sister-in-law, Denise, left Wichita to come live with me after Denise passed away. I needed someone to run my house. I was never home. I lived on the road, crisscrossing the country, putting out fires for Denny's.

After a year of living in her own place, Ryan wanted to move to Chicago. I thought the move would help her mature in Christ. She was too close to me. She called on me to make decisions before she called on God.

In addition, she always seemed so afraid of the world. She was extremely timid. Everyone and everything intimidated her. Her voice sometimes quivered when she tried to order a meal through a drive thru. Mike and I thought the distance from me would be good for her, and a nearness to him had its advantages. The two of them could work on mending their relationship.

Ryan, Mike, and I spent three days in Chicago, looking for a place for Ryan. Ryan and I had asked God to show us just the right place for her. We had just about given up when Ryan stumbled across her dream home—a strikingly beautiful three-bedroom, two-bathroom condo in Chicago's South Loop.

Nothing but high-end features and fixtures graced the place. The ceilings in that unit were 20 feet high. Later, we would have to purchase a special pole just to change the light bulbs.

The condo was 1,800 square feet; it featured a loft off the living room that overlooked a private rooftop deck. The three-sided deck offered a spectacular, panoramic view of downtown Chicago. The space took up the top two floors of a new six-unit building. The boutique developer was also the owner. Our purchase would be his first in the building.

When I first walked into the space, I recognized it from a recent dream. I sensed God was in our previewing it that day by the way our circumstances unfolded. My only problem was the condo was $100,000 more than I wanted to spend, not including the parking space. That was an additional $15,000.

I filled out the paperwork anyway, confident the loan would not be approved. It would be my secret way out. I had just purchased a home for my parents, and I carried a mortgage on my own home. The chances of getting another loan approved were slim to none. If, for some strange reason, the loan went through, then it was simply God opening the way. I was taken aback when I got the call that afternoon! The loan had been approved!

The initial, five-year interest rate for the residence was so low that the cost of the mortgage was only $100 more than her rental apartment in Memphis! Suddenly, it seemed foolish to pay rent for something I could never own when I could purchase a spectacular piece of property for just $100 more a month.

Now I saw the property in a whole new light—as a good investment. In a few years, the place would be worth a fortune as the neighborhood developed. We could keep it in the family if Ryan remained in Chicago or we could sell it and surely make a profit.

We turned Ryan's condo into a showplace—a showplace for whom, I do not know. She probably had no more than 10 people visit her the entire time she lived there!

Ryan was in a car accident a year after she moved to Chicago. She walked away without a scratch, but her Toyota 4Runner was nearly totaled. I had it fixed, but it never drove the same. I traded it in for a luxury Lexus RX 330. That purchase spurred me to lease a Lexus SC 430 convertible for myself; it was a car I always wanted. I sold my four-door, Lexus ES 300 to Suzanne, which she still drives today.

When the dust settled, my parents lived in a lovely, thoroughly renovated home in Memphis' High Point District. Ryan lived in a stunning new condo in Chicago's South Loop. Suzanne and I lived in a beautiful home off the Mississippi River in scenic Harbor Town. Everybody drove a luxury car. I was living the American Dream—the life of a slave—and I did not know it.

April 1, 2004

A Fool for God

I could not stop crying last night. My heart was filled with awe, love, and gratitude for Yeshua. Never had the verse, "Lean not on your own understanding, but acknowledge Him in all your ways and He will make your path straight," made more sense.

Many would look at my life circumstances of the past year and the beginning of this one and conclude that I made some foolish moves. But I knew I was being moved by God's Spirit to make two of the most illogical choices of my life. Yesterday, it hit me with some force that the choices were brilliant. God was doing a larger work in our lives—beyond what the eye could see.

My Parents' Move to Memphis

I purchased a home for my parents in Memphis, Tennessee. To witness all the things that went wrong with that house, one would have concluded God could not possibly have been in the purchase. Many nights, I told Yeshua, "This looks like one of the worst real estate purchases of the century, but I know You are in it."

Just last week, the workers finished replacing the entire roof and installing gutters around the house—all that after $60,000 in other renovations and repairs. At one point, I threatened to sue the seller and the firm that inspected the house, but I had absolutely no peace about it—even though they deserved to be sued. I knew why. A lawsuit was not God's will.

A while back He showed me the house was a symbol of my life—before and after Christ. He needed me to walk through the pain, the aggravation of renovating the house. It was a perfect metaphor for the painful, frustrating renovation He was doing in my life.

Before Christ, my life was as rotten and broken as the house when I first purchased it. At first glance, I looked fine, but upon closer examination, one could see I was fraught with problems. I needed to be overhauled inside and out.

As rotten as I was, Yeshua still died for me. To the watching heavens, surely, I looked like a bad investment. I could just hear the heavenly voices, "He paid too much for her!" I looked like a mistake, a purchase that made no sense.

As soon as He fixed one area of my life, another problem popped up, then another and another. But He was patient, and in time, His tender care began to show in my life. I changed. It was hard to see what I once was. I was becoming the beauty He always knew I could be.

I stopped by the house yesterday. When I drove up, I gasped. "Oh Lord, bar none, this has to be the prettiest house on the block!" God had totally renovated the 50-year-old house inside and out. Flowers of every color were blooming in the front yard. Dark green shrubbery lined the front and side lawns. Four voluminous spider plants hung from the large, pillared front porch. Just behind them were four white rocking chairs that beckoned passersby to come sit.

I went inside to find my mother and Suzanne cleaning and my father enjoying gospel music in the family room. The house was as beautiful on the inside as it was on the outside. I stepped onto the backyard deck and looked out. The big yard resembled a little paradise compared to the mud field I purchased.

But of most importance was the joy and peacefulness of my parents. At one point, my mom started clapping her hands and dancing for my father. He could not stop laughing. I have NEVER seen them happier.

The wisdom of the house purchase hit me last night for the first time, now that all the work had been completed. My parents were only a few minutes away from anything they ever needed—the grocery store, post office, church, restaurants, bank, gas stations, hospital, and shopping malls. They were only 15 minutes away from me. The house was bigger and more elegant than their house in Detroit and everything was on one floor. The house in Detroit had four levels, which was too much for them in their old age.

I mentally went room by room through both houses to compare what they left in Detroit to what they came to in Memphis. There was no contest. The house in Memphis topped the one in Detroit, room for room.

My parents also loved the temperate weather of Memphis. Detroit was too cold. Now, my mother was only an hour and a half away from her family and the neighborhood where she grew up in Arkansas. Aunt Ernestine, who helped raise her, was dying of cancer there. My parents could now visit her often.

Last of all, my brothers and sisters in Detroit relied heavily on my parents to do things for them since my parents were retired. They kept my parents busy, which undoubtedly produced a lot of stress for them, although they never complained. Now my parents' time was their own, and I could tell they loved it. They have nice, friendly neighbors and have been adopted by their new church family. It seems God gave them just what they needed in their old age.

Ryan's Move to Chicago

With hardly any money to do such a thing, I purchased a condo for Ryan in Chicago. It was the most expensive real estate purchase of my life. I knew it was God's will that she move to Chicago. We discussed it many times. He opened numerous doors to allow me to purchase the property. While I knew He was in it, it did not make sense to me. I questioned it all for a long, long, long time.

After the move, I often asked myself, "What was I thinking?" I sent my only child, who is as shy as the day is long and beset with serious health issues, to live by herself in one of the largest cities in the world in an empty building, in a transitional neighborhood, near her volatile father, whom she fought with most of her life. What if she had a low blood sugar and was not able to make it up the three flights of stairs or even to the kitchen? Who would help her? Who could she call? On whom could she rely? The short and only answer was God.

That is exactly what happened. In the past nine months, my daughter blossomed into a confident, God-reliant, beautiful young woman. The move to Chicago forced her to grow closer to God. I was not around to buffer her against trouble. I could not hop out of bed, grab a broom, and come kill a spider in her apartment as I had done in Memphis. Alone on her own, she grew more self-disciplined and secure in who she was.

The Chicago location also put Ryan near a doctor who diagnosed her as a "double diabetic." His treatment has been amazingly effective, allowing her to shrink from a Size 22 to a 14, and even some 14s are too big.

Today, she donated three hefty boxes of clothes she could no longer fit to a friend. Ryan is also wearing her natural hair these days, after 12 years of braided extensions. She told me, "Mom, I have to love who I am, the way God made me, before I can expect anybody else to."

Her building filled up quickly—every unit has been sold or rented. All kinds of new construction have sprung up around it—condos, restaurants, shops. The neighborhood is alive and vibrant.

Best of all, Ryan's relationship with her father has never been better. Who would have guessed it? They have grown quite close. Every Saturday, he takes her to breakfast for a little "Daddy-Daughter" time. They talk multiple times a day throughout the week. Sometimes, they take in a movie together or watch one at her place. Clearly, it was God's intention to move Ryan to a higher place in Him when He moved her to Chicago. I have NEVER seen her happier.

God's ways are not our ways. His thoughts are not our thoughts. They are so much higher. Less than 18 months after my parents' house was completely renovated, my mother was struck with a debilitating illness—Clostridium difficile, commonly known as C-diff. No one knew where she contracted the toxic bacteria. It almost killed her twice. The illness turned out to be a much longer-term malady than anyone knew. It took a devastating toll on her overall health, which put my father's mental state in a tailspin. At points, we were certain he was losing his mind.

Finally, the family decided Arlene and her husband would sell their home in Detroit and move to Memphis to take care of my parents. My sister, the main breadwinner of her family, would attempt to run her mortgage brokerage firm out of her bedroom. Her husband, Charles, took the third bedroom.

It did not help matters that my sister was a pack rat. She kept stuff that should have long ago been discarded or given away. Soon stacks of contracts and paperwork covered her bed, floor, and dresser. My mother, on the other hand, was a neat freak. Everything had its place.

Suddenly, a house perfectly suited for my parents 18 months earlier, was too crowded. After a year of the two families living together, we decided they needed larger quarters—a home where each family could spread out and have its own space. We sold the Highland house, and I purchased a beautiful 5,500-square-foot estate on Garner Place in Bartlett, Tennessee.

At 3 o'clock in the morning, hours before we were to close on the new house, my father came to my bedroom, startling me out of my wits. Standing at the door in the dark, he called my name.

"Dad, is that you? What's wrong?" I sat up straight in the bed.

He came and stood at the foot of my bed. "The Lord just spoke to me. He said, 'Rachelle is Joseph.' I told your mother; we talked about it; and she told me to come tell you."

"I know, Dad. I know. Go back to sleep." What my father did not know was that the Lord had been calling me Joseph for at least four years. I just never told anyone. It was way too complicated. God was doing so much in our lives. This Joseph business was just another weird twist in the journey. There certainly was no use trying to explain it to him at that hour.

"I think we're putting you in too much debt with that house. We should call it off." He had solidly wired up the name to the purchase of our new house since Joseph was a slave in Egypt.

I explained to him we were past the point of no return. It was too late. We would lose our earnest money. We were scheduled to close in just seven hours. I had flown in for the closing. It was in God's hands.

My father turned out to be right—more accurate than either of us could have ever foreseen. The Lord quickly sold the house on Highland and allowed me to recoup every penny of the $100,000 I had invested in improvements. We used the money as a down payment on the new house. The seven-bedroom, five-bathroom estate home sat on two acres of wooded land, right off a street called Egypt-Central!

My sister and her husband had one wing of the house; my parents had the other. It was like two separate houses in one. Soon after they settled in, my sister and her husband took emergency custody of their two troubled grandsons, Marvin and Marcus. Marvin was 7 years old at the time and Marcus was six. Shortly after that, their youngest son, Charlie—Marcus' dad—came to live with them. Every room in the house was taken except for a guest room, where Ryan and I stayed when we visited.

I worked hard to maintain the three households. I lived in airports, airplanes, and hotels. Usually, I would come home just long enough to go to church on Sunday. Then, I would exchange suitcases—I always kept a spare one packed—and head back to the airport. I became a Platinum Flyer on two airlines. One must fly 100,000 miles to achieve that frequent-flyer status.

Suzanne always joked how I did not know how to work anything in the house because I was not there long enough to learn. She also observed how hard I worked for things I rarely ever got a chance to enjoy. I was a slave in Egypt. As difficult as my lifestyle was, it took a while for the Lord to get that truth through my thick skull.

God eventually used a film to crack the code for me. For years, Jeri told me I needed to see the Jim Carey film, *The Truman Show*. Not being a big fan of Jim Carey, I ignored her advice. However, one Sunday, I awoke with a deep desire to see the film. I rented it immediately after church.

January 27, 2002

Truman

Right off, I knew God had led me to rent the movie. The tipoff was the film's setting. Jim Carey's character, Truman, lived on an island in an idyllic town called Sea Haven, near a place called Harbor Isle.

Before they mentioned the name of the little town where he lived, Ryan and I marveled at the style and architecture of the houses and the outlay of the neighborhood. Everything looked so much like our own Harbor Town neighborhood. Ryan even shouted at one point, "That looks like our house!"

My mind raced. What were the chances that I would suddenly want to see a 1998 film—four years old—after moving to a place that resembled the film's setting? If I had seen the film when it first came out, the setting would have meant nothing. But now I lived on an island called Harbor Town that strongly resembled Truman's Harbor Isle.

That one oddity was enough to keep me alert as I watched the movie. I contemplated every detail. I felt God was trying to show me something about my life. It mirrored Truman's in some way.

An Unwitting Slave

Truman was a happy-go-lucky, amiable man, who was oblivious to his real-life circumstances. He had been deceived his whole life. He never knew that a corporation—a television show—had adopted him. The show chronicled, for the whole world to see, every aspect of his life—from the time he came out of his mother's womb to the present day. He was the star of the show, but he did not know it. The show was also a way to covertly showcase and promote products.

The creator of the television show placed Truman in a fake town and surrounded him with actors who formed fake relationships with him. He had a mother, father, wife, best friend, coworkers, boss and so on.

The show followed his every move and controlled every facet of his life. He followed the same routine day in and day out. Truman's life was an open book, laid bare for everyone to see. It appeared he had freewill, but the truth was the show manipulated everything around him to shape and control his decisions. The show used all kinds of plots, ploys, and deceptions to keep Truman in the dark.

Thanks to the producers of the show, Truman even developed a fear of water, designed to keep him from leaving the island and the show. Truman was an unsuspecting product of his environment. He believed whatever he was told. In so many ways, he was a slave, trapped in that idyllic little town.

One day, Truman began to suspect something was not quite right with his world. He began to explore little oddities. As he pulled back the layers of his "idyllic" life, he made one startling discovery after another.

One rogue actor—a beautiful woman who was once an extra on the set—tried to inform Truman of the truth. She was promptly kicked off the show. Although she was labeled a kook for Truman to ignore, she managed to ignite a spark of curiosity.

Finally, fed up with his mundane, humdrum, manipulated life, Truman tried to leave the island. His desire was to get to the Fiji Islands, where he thought the beautiful woman resided. (That was another lie perpetuated by the producers of the show.) When he tried to leave, he discovered he could not.

The more he sought his freedom, the uglier and more abusive the creator of the show became. He did everything to discourage Truman from leaving. If Truman found a way off the island and out of the show, the creator of the show would lose everything. He had a lot at stake. His world would come crashing down.

Truman would not give up or give in. Seeking his freedom, the determined man persisted through a horrible storm, engineered by the creator of the show. Truman was prepared to die to secure his freedom. In the end, despite his fear of water, Truman managed to get to the other side of the island, which was also the end of the set. From there, he walked off the set into freedom—and to find this true love—the one person, who against all odds, tried to tell him the truth.

The Christian Parallel

If Truman's life is not a metaphor for the Christian experience in this fallen world and our quest for the Promised Land—a place of freedom and truth—then I do not know what is! The creator of the Truman television show, which was watched every day all over the world, was a type of Satan. For his personal greatness and glory, the show's creator watched, manipulated, and controlled every aspect of Truman's life. In the same way, Satan tries to control our lives for his greatness and glory. Like Truman, we live our lives on an open stage for all rational beings of the unseen world to see, both benevolent and malevolent.

The woman who spoke truth to Truman represented a type of Christ. It was her boldness in telling Truman the truth, to her own peril, that ultimately resulted in Truman's freedom. And do not miss the significance of his name. Truman represented man in search of truth. For most of his life, Truman did not know just how restricted and manipulated his world had been. Unseen forces controlled him.

For years, Truman was in bondage, a captive or slave to his world, and he did not know it. He had been lulled to sleep by an idyllic life in the little sleepy town where he was born and grew up. He never knew anything else. He was never truly happy or fulfilled in Sea Haven because he was not truly free. However, he found his emancipation in the end.

God had gotten my attention. In many ways, I was just like Truman. I had a measure of what appeared to be freedom, but was I really free? Finally, I was ready to listen.

February 2, 2002

A Slave in Egypt

When Ryan walked into my room this morning, she found the floor covered with spent tissues on both sides of the bed. I cried most of the night. I had a trying day the day before. Unsolved issues mounted as new challenges rolled in. At one point, I became so frustrated with my circumstances I was ugly to a woman over the telephone. Right after that bout of rudeness, God cut off my phones. They all went dead!

I was in the middle of several projects I needed to wrap up. Now what was I going to do? Rather than grow angry or anxious, I shut down my office and went to my room to pray.

I wept to the Lord, confessing my sin. My sin was ever before me. I have so many issues; it looks like I will never overcome them. I have recounted them to the Lord on many occasions. As I lay across my bed, lamenting my sin, but trying not to go to a place of self-pity, the telephone suddenly rang.

I sprang straight up in the bed, "Well, look at that!" I marveled. I picked up the receiver to hear a recording from the telephone company informing me our phones were fixed. I knew God had repaired our phones in response to my confession.

Last night, I tried to cut to the root of my issues. "Lord, help me crystallize why I am so unhappy!" I must have cried out to Him for an hour imploring, "Why, why, why … am I so miserable?"

I could not put my finger on it.

"I live in a palace compared to most of the world. I have an excellent job that pays well. I can't remember ever being hungry. I am as healthy

as an ox. I have clothes on my back—fine clothes. I have clothes in my closet with the price tags still on them. I stay at first-rate hotels, eat in five-star restaurants, and I am driven around in sedans and limousines everywhere I go. I have a lot of wonderful friends, the best parents in the world, a brilliant daughter who loves and seeks after You. She is not into drugs or sexually active. Why is my heart so downcast?"

Then I thought about the horrible things that had happened to people I knew or read about, many of them Christians.

"Lord, no one has thrown acid in my face. I haven't accidentally run over my baby with my car or left her inside to suffocate or freeze to death. I haven't lost the use of my arms and legs in a car accident. My family hasn't been hacked to death with a machete. I haven't seen the inside of a concentration camp or a slave ship. I haven't been raped or sexually abused. My plane has never been hijacked and used as a missile to topple skyscrapers. I haven't been blown to pieces by a bomb."

By this time, there was no controlling my tears. "I have two eyes, two ears, and a nose that work. I can walk, run—even dance." Now I was screaming in anguish. "Why am I so unhappy? Please tell me. WHAT IS MY ISSUE? WHAT IS WRONG WITH ME?"

"When did you become unhappy?" I heard the Holy Spirit ask. I thought for a moment. It had been during the last five years.

"You weren't always unhappy," He noted. That was true. As a matter of fact, I had been a positive, joyful person most of my life. The unhappiness was a recent phenomenon.

He then led me on a mental journey back to the height of my joy when I had no real problems to speak of. I had an influential job. I felt I made a difference in the world. I had a good reputation. I had lots of friends and I was active in both the church and the community.

Then a new thought came to me. Although I was a pillar in my church, deeply involved in many ministries, I was no threat to Satan's kingdom. I thought I knew a great deal about spiritual warfare, but I truly knew very little then.

During the past five years, I had come to learn, by painful experience, just how pervasive wickedness was in the world. It is deeply ingrained in the very fabric of virtually every institution in the world, and it deceives and enslaves people at every age, in every epoch, ultimately leading to eternal death.

This realization took hold of my heart. My present unhappiness was a direct result of God revealing truth to me about the world I lived in. I was unhappy with my earthly estate and the estate of my brethren! For the first time in my life, I felt like a literal slave—trapped by the presence of sin and its miserable effects everywhere I turned. So, it did not matter how well I lived in the present darkness, I was still a slave.

I was acutely aware the enemy watched my every move, and that he had relentlessly tried to thwart God's good purposes in my life. He tried to beat me down and to discourage me at every turn. Every day, it was a battle simply to survive. That was when my crying turned to uncontrollable sobbing.

"Oh, Lord, I am ... we are ... all SLAVES! SLAVES! We're surrounded by structural evil everywhere, in every place. WE ARE ALL SLAVES!" The Lord simply let the truth sink into my soul. "I am like Joseph in Egypt!" For the first time, it occurred to me that although Joseph rose to become second only to the Pharaoh, exchanging his pit for a palace, he was still a slave because he was in the world. He wasn't free! Finally, spent from crying, I told the Lord, "You are our only hope."

Now that I understand the true state of my condition, the Lord fully opened my eyes to the Egyptian bondage that surrounded me everywhere I went. The whole world was Egypt!

February 23, 2002

The Big Eye

I had to attend a glitzy gala on the West Coast this weekend. The event was star-studded. My daughter and I stayed at the Century Plaza Hotel and Spa in Century City. We were placed on a high floor. The room was spacious and sunny.

Right outside our hotel room window, front and center, was a water fountain shaped like a gigantic human eye; it was the logo for one of the big networks. The human eye is also an Egyptian symbol. The spiritual significance of the eye did not escape me. God never lets me forget where I am. I am in Egypt!

March 1, 2002

More Egyptian Symbolism

I had to attend a business conference in Detroit this weekend. I took Ryan with me so she could see her grandparents. She slept in her old room. I took my room. Everything in my room was the same—except for one small addition.

My mother had taken an oversized Egyptian vase that I had given her a few years back and placed it in my room, right at the door. That placement made it one of the first things I saw when I entered the room and the last thing I saw when I left it. The Lord does not want me to forget where I am. I am in Egypt.

In Memphis, Egypt's heartland, I attended a church called Temple of Deliverance. That is exactly what I found there—blessed deliverance! God set me free *spiritually!* Although I was in Egypt and had walked with the Lord more than 18 years, I discovered a freedom in Christ that I never tasted before.

My pastor, the late G.E. Patterson, presided over Temple of Deliverance and the entire Church of God and Christ (COGIC) denomination. For the first time, I saw people sing, shout, and dance in the Lord because THEY WERE SAVED! THEY WERE FREE! They were redeemed by Christ and "got it" in a way I had not seen other Christians "get it."

They were thankful for trials. They rejoiced in them. That just meant "more Jesus," because every time trouble came knocking, the Lord answered the door. He showed up and showed off for them in ways I had not seen Him do in the lives of other Christians I had been around.

I learned to praise my way out of storms. I discovered much of my deliverance was in my praise. It is a powerful weapon in spiritual warfare. Praise opens prison doors. Praise moves mountains. My grasp of this truth at this time was not happenstance. God had a mountain range waiting for me just over the hill. What I learned at Temple of Deliverance would help me traverse those mountains.

Chapter 26
Called Out of Egypt!

The time eventually came for me to leave "Egypt" and all that was familiar to me. In the season of my internment, I had come to know my Savior in a whole new way. I had learned to appreciate and esteem Him in ways I had not before.

Only then did I understand the perplexing dream the Lord had given me seven months after I first arrived in Memphis. He wanted to give me hope. Egypt was just a temporary pit stop. It was not my home. One day, I would leave and never return.

August 30, 2002

A Dream: Flying to a Strange Place, a New Home?

I had a strange dream early this morning. I feel compelled to record it here. I'm not sure that I understand any parts of the dream but recording it may help me make some sense of it.

The dream opened with me entering a large office complex, looking for a FedEx store. I felt I was in Florida. My young nephew Chris was with me. He entered the building before me, trying to locate the office before I could. I told him to slow down as I entered behind him.

Once inside, I surveyed the entire lobby. It did not look like a lobby I had ever seen before. Instantly, I knew where the FedEx office or FedEx kiosk was—downstairs. I headed for the steps.

I stepped down on the first stair of a steep, carpeted staircase and then decided not to proceed. The stairway looked much too dangerous. The stairs were steep, and there were no handrails! A person could fall off the edge.

The second I stepped back up, I started to fly. All I could see was gray, but I could feel myself flying! I flew a long time with no scenery in many directions. Then, I stopped. I opened my eyes to find myself in my bed or, so I thought.

I reached over to look at the clock on my nightstand. I could not make out the time because the tabs that showed the numbers were stuck. I could see the tabs fluttering around 7:15 a.m. or 7:34 a.m. I started to shake the antique green, oval-shaped clock. I could not un-stick the tabs.

Then the window caught my eye and I rose out of bed to look out of it. I was horrified to see I was not in my bedroom in Memphis anymore! I had flown to an unknown place, a place I did not recognize. Where was I?

The scene outside had a country setting. All I could see was green grass and trees. Suddenly, I desperately longed to be home again. I missed it! I became terribly upset, nearly hysterical.

I jumped back in bed crying. Urgently, I started to pray. With my hands to my face, pressed against my pillow and cried. "Lord, please help me! I know how to reach You and talk to You where I used to be, but I don't know how to reach You in this new place! Please, help me!" I heard footsteps. Someone was coming!

Terrified, I jumped out of bed and slid underneath it! I held my breath and tried to pull the sheets and bedcovers down the side of the bed to hide myself. Someone began speaking.

A tall, slender man had entered the room. He was talking to me. I kept quiet in my hiding place. He was on one side of the room, and I was hiding underneath the far side of the bed. He could not see me, yet he knew I was there.

Still talking, the man reclined across the bed. The weight of his frame pressed the mattress and box spring closer to my head. He talked in a kind, relaxed tone. He lay in the bed talking with his hands resting behind his head and his ankles crossed. Somehow, I could see him from underneath the bed.

Finally, he coaxed me out. We became friends instantly. He said he wanted to show me around. He had a warm sense of humor. As I walked down a hallway, I was stunned to see a lot of my belongings. They were stacked on two black bookcases! With every object I spied, my mouth dropped open a little wider. How did my things get here? The house had a cluttered feel to it. It was small, casual, and eclectic.

As I followed him down the hallway, the tall, slender man, who resembled the actor Will Smith, said, "Let me show you your room." He said something about the room being "a big 50 square feet" in size. For some reason, I expected to see a large room, but the room was not large at all. It was small and cozy.

The bed was covered with a heavy satin, purple bedspread. I surveyed the rest of the room. It looked rather cluttered, although everything seemed to have its place. I saw a dresser to the right. Then, off to my left, I spotted a small Black baby girl lying on the bed. I didn't see her before. "Oh, there's a baby!" I said.

"Yes!" he answered.

When my eyes popped open, I was relieved to see I was in my own bedroom. It had been a remarkable dream! But what did it mean? I grabbed my notebook and pen from my nightstand and began to record the dream and its possible interpretations.

It appeared I would be carried away from my present home to a new one. I speculated the move may be tied to a new ministry of some sort. My new home (and new life) would be small, modest—quite different from our Memphis dream house. Other insights I gleaned from the dream were these:

1. There are no shortcuts. The FedEx office or kiosk in the dream represented a shortcut—a fast, express way to get something done. Shortcuts are dangerous. This was represented by the steep, downward path to the FedEx office. (The devil offered Jesus a shortcut to glory in the desert.) Sometime in the future, I will be tempted to take a shortcut. God says, "Don't rush in like a child! Take it slow!"
2. I will be way outside my comfort zone and homesick for the familiar. It will be a terrifying time for me.

3. It will seem as though time is standing still for me in this new place. Things will appear as if they are not moving. I will feel stuck in time.
4. The baby girl in the dream represents someone or something I must care for, nurture. She is my responsibility. I believe it is a budding ministry of some sort.
5. The Lord will raise up someone tall and slender who looks like Will Smith. This man will make me feel right at home in my new place or in a new endeavor. The person will be warm, winsome, and charming. He will show me the way around.
6. My new home will be small, casual, eclectic, and cluttered with my things. It may be in Florida.
7. Although I will experience considerable discomfort in this new place and long for what used to be, I will be surrounded by green pastures with lots of trees.

I knew God would show me more in time. Nearly three years after the dream, on a day like any other day, the Lord spoke to me about leaving Memphis. "I want you to put your house up for sale," I heard Him say to me as I worked out on the treadmill at the downtown YMCA.

"Put the house up for sale? Where am I going?" I asked.

"Orlando." He knew that would be music to my ears. I had come to abhor everything Memphis represented in the spirit realm.

"Why Orlando?" I kept walking.

"You need to be close to the work."

What work? This made absolutely no sense to me. My work was in South Carolina. I was busy as ever at Denny's, and I flew to Greenville-Spartanburg *every* week.

Nevertheless, I put the house up for sale. Within two days, a couple from Sarasota, Florida saw an Internet posting. They drove all night to see the house. They put a contract on the property the same day they saw it.

They left the offer on the kitchen counter, agreeing to my full asking price.

Just as they were leaving, another couple walked in to preview the house. The woman gasped as she entered the living room and looked toward the kitchen. "Let me run back and get my tape measure out of my car," their agent said.

The Sarasota couple and their agent stood just outside the courtyard staring at one another. Ten minutes later they returned and amended their contract to offer an additional $5,000. I agreed to their offer on the spot.

The couple asked to move the closing date up by one week. The husband was a doctor, and he needed to start his residency at St. Jude Children's Hospital, which is located close to Harbor Town. I moved up the closing date by a week to accommodate their request. I did not realize at the time that doing so meant we would have lived in Memphis ("Egypt") for *exactly* 3½ years, to the day!

There was no way I could have known in the dream the Lord had given me three years earlier that I was looking at my home in Florida. It wasn't the house I would live in for three years when I first arrived in Orlando. Nor was it the temporary one after that, where Suzanne and I would live for five months after becoming homeless. It wasn't even the one after that, where Suzanne, Ryan, and I would live for 2½ years as the Lord rebuilt our lives.

He had given me a glimpse into where I would be living when I was fully immersed in "the work" and the life He had called me to in Orlando, Florida. The work He used to break me free from the world's bondage. There would be no shortcuts getting to this place!

Shrinking me down to nothing to be fitted for fulltime ministry would prove to be a terrifying experience. The dream was an accurate depiction of what the transition would be like for me. Downsizing my life was necessary for me to identify with those to whom He called me to serve.

He called me to minister to the "least of these." I needed to know what it felt like to be counted among the poorest and the least. It was a long way down in the eyes of those observing my descent, but it was up in God's eyes. And, as He relayed to me on more than one occasion, it was a marvelous sight to behold.

On July 4, 2005—Independence Day—Suzanne and I left Memphis and everything symbolic of Egypt and headed for Orlando. When we departed, I did not yet realize that God was leading me out of bondage and into a "wilderness experience," where there would be further testing.

I would be tested just like the children of Israel were tested after God led them out of Egypt. The desert is where God gets Egypt out of His children once He has gotten His children out of Egypt. It is a barren place where God tests and proves His people; and through the tests, He teaches them to rely on Him for everything, to make a full break from the Egyptian system.

All children of God must go through the desert before they can enter His promises for their lives. We cannot enter His promises with our minds in shackles. Everything that prevents us from seizing His promises for our lives, must be removed. In the desert, we learn to worship God fully in Spirit and in Truth.

Chapter 27
Fleeing to the Wilderness

Through a series of bizarre occurrences, God placed us on the eastside of Orlando in a lovely, gated community called The Preserve. Originally, I had flown to Orlando with a checklist. I picked out what I thought was the perfect rental home. It had all the features I was looking for—two large bedrooms, two big bathrooms, and a spacious kitchen. It had lots of windows to let in the sunlight. It was also close to a supermarket, bank, post office, dry cleaners, and park.

A week before we were to move, God gave me a dream in which I narrowly escaped a train wreck. Barreling down the road at 80 miles an hour, my car miraculously made a 180-degree turn just seconds before hitting a speeding train. I had no idea what the dream meant until a friend of mine, Marshall Rice, whom I had not seen or heard from in years, called to see how I was doing in Memphis. I told him I had just rented a place for Suzanne and myself in Orlando, where he lived.

He admonished me for not calling him first. Although he was a long-time staffer at Campus Crusade for Christ, he had just become a real estate agent. He informed me there were many Campus Crusade families, serving as missionaries in foreign countries who needed someone to lease their homes. Renting one of their homes would help them with their mortgage expense while they served.

I assured him I would be happy to forfeit my deposits and cancel the contract I had just signed with the rental company, if doing so would help a missionary family. But he had fewer than seven days to find us a place. All the arrangements had been made for us to move into our new apartment in one week.

He called me two days later with three possibilities. One house was ready for immediate move-in. The owners, a missionary couple, had purchased another home closer to Campus Crusade's offices. Due to a back injury, the husband could no longer endure the long commute from his old home. The house was 1,000 square feet larger than the rental unit and cost only $200 more per month.

I called the owners that day. They faxed me a rental contract to sign and fax back. With that settled, I set about undoing all my original, meticulous plans. I cancelled my contract with the rental company, called the movers with the change of address and redirected the postal service. I rescheduled the cable, electrical, and telephone companies. Because of the tight timeframe, we would have to move into our new place, sight unseen. Every time I was tempted to worry about taking such a risk, I remembered the dream.

We pulled up to our new home less than 30 minutes ahead of the movers. I ran inside to figure out where to put all the furniture before the truck arrived. I was instantly enamored with the quiet beauty of my surroundings. Although smaller and less luxurious than our showplace in Memphis, the house was much larger and nicer than the rental apartment.

But it was not the house that captivated me; it was the panoramic view of a quiet lake and green golf course that gave me a deep feeling of tranquility. I later learned the community had nine such lakes and innumerable breathtaking views of the golf course.

Eventually, I would spend many quiet mornings and evenings sitting on soft blankets of grass by still waters, allowing God to refresh my soul. It would be the fulfillment of a dream the Lord gave Jeri shortly before our arrival.

In her dream, the Lord decided I had been fed too much fast food because of my hectic lifestyle. As a result, I was spiritually anemic. The fast food was symbolic of "short, quick hits of time" spent with Him. I was surprised to learn that He equated the amount of time I spent with Him to "fast food!"

In the dream, He told Jeri that He had now prepared a "feast" for me in the "Green Banquet Room." No more fast food. My Green Banquet

Room turned out to be the golf course by those still waters where I spent long mornings and evenings with the Lord. There, He nourished my famished spirit.

Although the house was spacious, it was not as large as our Harbor Town house had been. So, we gave away a lot of our things the day of the move, including three television sets. (Eventually, the Lord would remove all televisions from our home.) Months after we moved in, my parents and sister, who still lived in the large Bartlett estate, came to visit. They returned home with a trailer filled with more items that we gave away. God was beginning the process of delicately extricating us from our possessions and freeing our lives from the influences of popular culture.

The entrance to The Preserve was manned by a uniformed guard—24 hours a day, seven days a week. We lived on Royal St. George Drive. Only after we moved in, did God inform me that our new address was significant. He counseled me one morning, "Let it be a sign to you." For years, I did not understand what He meant by this. But after a trip to the Coptic churches in Ethiopia, I began to gather some pieces of the puzzle.

"That's Jesus. That's Mary. But, who's that guy?" I asked the Coptic priest.

"That's St. George, the patron saint of Ethiopia." I later discovered St. George was a patron saint of several countries. Until that exchange, it never occurred to me that St. George referred to an actual person. I never read about anybody named George in the Bible. However, in the mural paintings of these Coptic churches, St. George, a warrior of royal lineage, was always depicted slaying a green dragon; and in some paintings, he was saving a maiden in distress.

On the plane ride back to the States, the Lord dropped a curious detail into my spirit that I pondered the entire return trip and for years to come. My landlord and his wife moved to GREEN DRAGON STREET after vacating the property Suzanne and I rented on ROYAL ST. GEORGE DRIVE! Of the thousands and thousands of streets in Orlando, what were the chances they would move to Green Dragon Street?

The two addresses meant nothing to them. They meant nothing to me until that very moment on the plane. Both addresses were signs to me, but what message was the Lord trying to convey?

Chapter 28
Founding The Ephraim Project

Five months after arriving in Orlando, the Lord gave me a dream that would change my life *forever*. In the dream, there were two little girls, sisters—one taller than the other. I knew the two sisters represented two modern-day descendants of ancient Israel because of what He had been teaching me about the 10 lost tribes of Israel during my quiet times.

The taller one symbolized the Northern kingdom—the 10 tribes that, in time, became known as Ephraim. The shorter one symbolized the Southern kingdom, comprised of tribes of Judah and Benjamin. The two sisters were starving in Ethiopia.

The taller one, resting on a pallet on the ground, was dying in need of medicine and hope. She spoke to me in the dream. She was just about to give up. She broke my heart. I vowed in the dream that I would bring help. Then, I woke up. That dream would be the catalyst for the founding of The Ephraim Project.

January 20, 2006

A Dream: My Little Sister in Need

I had the most haunting dream last night! The dream opened with two little Black girls struggling to walk out of a room. The girls appeared wobbly from starvation. They both were nearly bald, and they were dressed in the same aqua-print, sleeveless, shapeless shirts. It was clear they were sisters. One was slightly taller than the other one. The shorter girl disappeared from the scene, leaving the taller one alone.

In the new scene, the taller of the two sisters was lying face down on a pallet. She had given up on life. As I observed her, someone said to me, "Her calorie intake is down. She is dwindling away." I had such pity for her. She had no mother, no one to comfort her. She was dying partly from starvation and partly from hopelessness. I bent down to tap her gently on her back. That is when I noticed I was a giant.

"Can I have a word with you?" I asked. The little girl lifted a bit from her mat to wipe away her tears. Then, she looked up at me and said

the strangest thing: "I'm having a heart attack. Do you have any heart attack pills?"

I told her I did not. Her skinny arms and legs dangled in the air as I picked her up with my gigantic hands. I held her in my arms. I noticed how thin she was—just skin and bones. I rubbed the bottom of her tiny feet. I looked around for help. I vowed I would do everything in my power to get that little girl what she needed to thrive. Suddenly, the dream ended.

After eluding me for a full day, the meaning of the dream hit me hard the following night. The key to interpreting the dream was the two little girls. God showed me two sisters for a reason. And one was taller than the other for a reason.

In Scripture, the Prophet Ezekiel referred to the Northern and Southern kingdoms of Israel as two sisters. After I realized who the two sisters represented, the rest of the dream fell into place. The two sisters characterized a line of desolate descendants of Judah and Ephraim, residing in Ethiopia, Africa. The older (taller) sister symbolized the Northern kingdom that fell in 722 B.C. It was scattered to the nations roughly 100 years before the Southern kingdom. The older (taller) sister represented today's Ephraim.

Interestingly, a week before the dream, I met with Rabbi Kokeb Gedamu, a Messianic Ethiopian Jew and good friend. He and I were introduced years earlier when I first discovered my Ethiopian-Jewish roots. Rabbi Kokeb and his wife, Menalu, shepherded a congregation of Ethiopian Jewish believers in Philadelphia, Pennsylvania. (How this couple managed to get to the U.S., via the Sudan, Egypt, Israel, and Canada, is one of the most harrowing testimonies I ever heard.) Together, they founded the House of Israel International Ministries (HIIM), a nonprofit organization that helps Ethiopian Jews. They help those who have been airlifted to Israel and those who remain in abject poverty in Ethiopia.

Rabbi Kobeb had a first-hand, working knowledge of the conditions under which his people lived in both countries. Through him, I learned there were at least 40,000 Ethiopians starving in the country's remote mountains and in the capital city, Addis Abba. They were the descendants of the ancient Hebrews, tracing their roots to Judah or one of the other tribes.

Many had become believers in Yeshua—Messianic Hebrews. These, particularly, were locked out of Israel because of their belief in Jesus Christ. They were also rejected by their fellow countrymen because of their desire to return to Israel, their motherland.

In desperate need of food, clothing, and medicine, they were dying where they stood. There was no one to help them, to comfort them. Many had given up on life. It was the devil's desire that they become extinct.

When I finally realized who they were, I cried for their preservation. I wept hard and long. I begged God to intervene. I asked Him to move heaven and earth for them, to stir the hearts of kings to move on their behalf. They were my people. They were His people, and if He did not rescue them, they would perish. I sobbed until my eyes were swollen.

At the end of my prayer, the Lord told me I had what I asked for. He instructed me to move in faith and, when I did, I would discover I had what I needed.

January 20, 2006

Birthing a Ministry

I am so clear now what The Ephraim Project is to do! Yesterday, I began taking steps to solidify my IRS charitable status and open a checking account for The Ephraim Project, Inc. I am expecting a bonus in about three weeks. I will start The Ephraim Project with those funds. It should be close to $100,000.

I also wrote down a list of people to contact. Perhaps, they can help me send a container of clothes, shoes, and medicine to these desperate people. I asked Rabbi Kokeb to arrange from someone on the other end to receive the container of goods. I will also provide him with cash to dispense among the villages' elders when he goes to Ethiopia this spring. They will aid the people. I know as I move in faith, I will have the Lord's full backing.

For weeks, I could not speak to anyone about the dream without crying. A few days after I had the dream, I made preparations to purchase a shipping container the size of a large semi-tractor trailer, to fill it with all manner of goods, and to ship it to Gondar, Ethiopia. God had shown me that Gondar was where many of ancient Israel's descendants presently resided. Not all were put on slave ships. Some never left Africa.

I worked for three weeks, in my own power, to make the shipment happen. I got nowhere. I called several CEOs I knew from the restaurant industry. Not one returned my call. Then one day, Marvin Bozard called me, out of the blue. He was from LIFE International, a ministry of Campus Crusade for Christ. He offered me 12 bales of used clothing, each weighing 1,000 pounds. It was mine for the taking. He also offered to help me with the shipment. He had shipped scores of containers all over the world, and he could help me with mine. I accepted.

I did not know at the time that this relationship would open doors for me at the highest levels of the Ethiopian government. It would also expedite the establishment of The Ephraim Project, a private foundation, dedicated to serving the poorest of the poor.

The 12 tons of used clothes were valued at $60,000. Was it possible that I could use this donation to accelerate the processing of my application for tax-exempt status with the U.S. Department of the Treasury? It was a long shot, but worth a try. I attached the LIFE International donation letter to our thick application to be classified as a 501(c)(3) private foundation. I requested our application be expedited to take advantage of the generous clothing donation. At the time, the process of becoming a nonprofit organization took nine to 12 months, and nearly 80 percent of all applications were rejected.

We applied on March 15, 2006 and were approved seven weeks later, on May 6, 2006. I could hardly believe my eyes when I opened the letter and read the first six words: *We are pleased to inform you ....* It was clear God was with us. He swiftly opened a door we could not open for ourselves.

I devoted my entire annual bonus to the project. Using that money and the generous in-kind donations from other humanitarian relief organizations and individuals, we filled the shipping container with used clothing and shoes; sleeping mats and blankets; two sets of computers, printers, fax machines, copiers, cameras, heavy duty surge protectors; mass quantities of toiletries (e.g., deodorant, facial soap, toothpaste, toothbrushes, lotion, shampoo, conditioner); face cloths and towels; school supplies and toys for children of all ages, from blowing bubbles to basketballs to dolls.

The plan was to ship the container from Orangeburg, South Carolina to the Port of Djibouti in Northeastern Africa, where it would be taken to Ethiopia and trucked through the mountains to Gondar. But the day it was scheduled to leave, we got a call from our customs broker on the ground in Djibouti: "As of today, the Ethiopian government will not allow used clothes to be shipped into the country. It hurts the local manufacturers."

That looked like a setback, but I saw it as a divine setup to do something more, something better. Also, based on dreams and other revelations the Lord had given me, I knew the project would not be easy. Unexpected things would happen. But God promised I would succeed where others had failed. I would blaze a trail. I had to trust Him on that.

Two days after learning the new restrictions, I purchased another shipping container of the same size. We set up another date to transfer all the used clothing and shoes from the original container to the second container. Marvin filled the second container with other merchandise from his warehouse, including mass quantities of new and used schoolbooks that covered a myriad of subjects. I paid for that container to be shipped to Liberia, Africa. There, the textbooks could be put to good use since English was the official language.

In the meantime, Marvin called in all kinds of favors to refill the Ethiopian container. Two of our major donors were Samaritan's Purse World Medical Mission and Global Aid Network (GAiN). I cannot express the elation I experienced when I saw pallet after pallet of medical supplies, brand new clothes from leading retail distributors, stacks of refurbished computers and printers, and lots and lots of other merchandise being loaded into the container—added to what we had already collected.

I would not know until we completed Ephraim's 990-PF Tax Return the following year that we had amassed $583,000 in donations, and that the container was worth millions when converted to Ethiopian currency!

It should have taken four months to get the shipping container from Orangeburg, South Carolina to the mountains of Gondar. It took almost a year because several ministers in Ethiopia's central government had their eye on the container. It seemed everyone wanted it.

Because Ephraim did not have the proper credentials to take possession of the container in Ethiopia, we had to transfer title to another ministry upon its arrival in Africa. This meant losing control of the container. Its contents could end up anywhere. Whom could we trust? We had a few false starts, but we ended up choosing Chuck Colson's Prison Fellowship. Many nights I cried out to the Lord, on my knees, asking for the container to reach the intended recipients. I did not know God had put plans in place to personally shepherd the container to His chosen destination.

After being held up in customs for months, the container finally reached the residents of Gondar, the surrounding villages, and the doctors and staff at Gondar Medical Hospital. God moved the highest levels of government to get it done. His first move was to arrange a conference in the States. At this setting, I met, then President of Ethiopia, Girma Wolde-Giorgis, the third highest ranking official in Ethiopia.

I was invited to the conference and then asked to speak—no doubt a divine appointment set up by the Orchestrator of the Universe. While there, I also met a neurosurgeon. He was an older Caucasian gentleman, who was quite talkative. He was no ordinary neurosurgeon. He was a neurosurgeon who trained Ethiopian neurosurgeons.

Mr. Neurosurgeon smoothly managed to work His way into my circle during the entire symposium. Everywhere I went, he was there. At times, this made me a bit uncomfortable. I did not quite know how to read His almost too-friendly, solicitous manner.

At one point, he handed me a large stack of historical papers on the tribes of Ephraim and some other topics. He said he copied them at the library for me. I had misspoken about Ephraim at an earlier informal session, where he corrected me. "The papers will show you your error," he said. I kept wondering when he had found time to go to the library—in the middle of a summit meeting. I graciously accepted the papers and then discarded them in the wastepaper basket in my room before I left the conference.

At the final dinner, Mr. Neurosurgeon came to my table, crouched down near my chair and asked if I had ever been to Las Vegas. I was thrown by the question.

"Why?" I asked.

He explained that I could see Gladys Knight there. He said I reminded him of her because she and I both were, and I quote: "Easy on the eyes." (Note: The expression, "Easy on the eyes" is one of my favorite lines from the animated cartoon *AntZ.*) After that, he asked to take a picture with me. Someone took a quick snapshot. I never saw him again.

Slowly, it dawned on me that the Lord had done what He said He would do one day. He came to me disguised! And as a *neurosurgeon* no less! (He forgets nothing!) I did not realize I had been divinely visited until the summit was well over and the Lord began to tease me about it. I would not learn the significance of the Gladys Knight comment until a few days after the conference. Days later, whenever I thought of the Lord, I would begin to hear Gladys Knight's song, *You're the Best Thing that Ever*

Happened to Me, play softly in my spirit. The music started out of nowhere. Whenever I meditated on the lyrics, they made me weep.

That surprise visitation was to be the beginning of several *physical* visitations from the Lord. He came as someone different each time. And in each one, He (or someone else) would ask to take a picture. I would never be given a copy of the picture. From the outset, the Lord warned me about His visits: "If you're too busy or too religious, you will miss Me!" I missed Him *every* time!

As the Lord would have it, the president of Ethiopia and I hit it off well, so I seized the opportunity at the conference to ask for his assistance with my container. I gained the confidence to do this from a dream the Lord had given me. In it, He showed me being warmly received by ministers of the Ethiopian government. President Wolde-Giorgis instructed me to visit him when I returned to Ethiopia, and he would investigate the matter. He kept his promise. When Suzanne and I arrived in Addis Ababa later that year, the president had people waiting at the airport to escort us to the royal palace. She and I sipped tea and nibbled on cookies in his palatial office as he made phone calls.

On that same trip, I also had a private meeting with Ethiopia's Minister of Justice, who desperately wanted the container to help prisoners throughout the nation's penal system. Unlike the United States, families of prisoners in Ethiopia bear the burden of supporting their incarcerated loved ones. If the family is poor—and the vast majority are—or the prisoner has no family, the man or woman lives in extraordinary want.

After that, the Lord arranged still another meeting. This time, Suzanne and I also had the pleasure of dining with the Deputy Prime Minister of Ethiopia, the nation's second in command. We had dinner with him and at least eight other ministers of the central government at our hotel in Gondar.

Late one afternoon, we returned to our hotel to see military personnel with large guns slung over their shoulders, surrounding the building and on the roof. Guards were everywhere. We did not know the deputy prime minister and his entourage had traveled from Addis Ababa to Gondar to have dinner with us. We scrambled to prepare.

After dinner—to the sheer terror of the Campus Crusade nationals—I personally circled the table to pass out Bibles to all the ministers. Later, I learned that was a bold and unprecedented move in that culture. The locals were speechless as each minister, some Muslim, graciously accepted my gift. When the time came, these men worked together to get the container out of Addis Ababa, where it had been stuck for months, to Gondar.

In the end, one-quarter of the goods and merchandise in the container was distributed to prisoners throughout Ethiopia. This delighted me to no end because the Lord told me upon first arriving in Ethiopia: "Ray, don't forget the prisoners." I never quite understood what that meant. Now I did.

Rekebnaba Geremew, a director of one of Gondar's largest schools, made sure that the remaining 75 percent of the container's contents was distributed fairly and equitably throughout the villages. The medical supplies went to Gondar Medical Hospital. Once emptied, the shipping container was converted into a schoolroom in Gondar. It was the fulfillment of a dream the Lord gave me in late August 2006.

August 22, 2006

A Dream: Dead Snakes in My Path

My second dream of the night was also strange. It opened with me running along the grass, while other people meandered down a concrete path. As I ran, I looked down to see a brightly colored iguana. It wasn't moving. I jumped over it and kept running. A short distance later, I saw a brightly colored snake coiled in the grass. While it was rather large, it did not move either. As with the iguana, I jumped over it and kept running.

Just as I turned to look back at it, I tripped over another coiled snake. It was gargantuan—something someone might see as a zoo attraction. I

> *fell over it, but hopped back up quickly, expecting it to attack me. But it never moved. In fact, it felt dead when my foot touched it. I ran toward the people along the path, pointing toward the snake. "Did you see that thing?" The dream ended.*

I knew the dream was a positive one even while I was dreaming it! A dead snake is *always* a good sign in a dream. The immovable or dead creatures in my path indicated God would restrain the devil's attacks against me as I ran the uncharted course He had set before me. My route would be something new and unprecedented, something never done before.

Shipping the container was a mammoth undertaking for me. Watching my dream finally become a reality also represented a monumental victory. But imagine my surprise when I learned the container was only a tiny piece of a larger puzzle. God was working toward something much bigger. In fact, shipping the container felt almost like a ruse to get me to Ethiopia, and in front of the president of the Amahra region, where Gondar is located.

We visited Gondar, while checking on the status of the container. When the plane wheels hit the tarmac, I blurted, "Ah, I'm home!" I sensed it in my spirit! I felt it in my bones! I knew my ancestors had walked this land.

We were met at the airport by two regional government officials. They were holding a sign with my name on it. Who were they? We were not expecting anyone to meet us.

They greeted us warmly and informed us that we had a meeting at 4 p.m. with the president of the Amahra region and his administrators. A car would come to the hotel and escort us to the meeting. To this day, I do not know who God used to arrange the meeting.

I pulled from my suitcase the one skirt I brought on the trip. By then, it was completely wrinkled. There was no such thing as an in-room iron or ironing board in these parts. I had no idea what the meeting was about, but I sensed the Lord had planned something wild and wonderful.

When I entered the room with Marvin and two others in our party, lights flashed, and cameras clicked. Reporters were present. Our guests invited me to sit at the head of the table next to the president. I broke the ice when I told the president he looked exactly like my brother Earl, which he did.

Looking straight ahead, I sat down at the longest conference table I had ever seen in my life. I was the only woman at the table. The officials present introduced themselves. They all spoke of their roles in the regional government. I still did not know why we were there.

After the introductions, the president began to speak. "We understand you are trying to get a container to Gondar." *Okay, this is about the container*. "We want you to know we appreciate everything you're trying to do for us. But if you really want to help us, we need water." I didn't hear what came after that. A million little puzzle pieces came together in my head.

Years ago, the Lord told me, "One day your people will be looking for water, and you will bring them water." This always confused me. I am from Michigan. Michigan is surrounded by five lakes. Why would my people be looking for water? So, I concluded someday members of my family would be looking for *spiritual* water—Jesus Christ. And I will speak the truth to them about Jesus, the Living Water. That is not at all what the Lord meant.

I looked around the conference table at these people, who so closely resembled my kin. As they talked about water, my mind raced a million miles a minute. *Oh ... my ... gosh! These are my people! These are MY PEOPLE! That is why he looks like my brother! Yes, I'm Ethiopian! This is what the Lord told me! These people are "my people looking for water!" Is God amazing or what?!* I tuned in just in time to catch the president's next words.

"So, is Allah God or is Jesus God? I tell you, the one who brings us water—his God is God. He is the one who can have our souls." To this day, I believe the Lord put those words in his mouth. They were meant to challenge me.

No, he didn't. No, he did not just say that! The dare worked. The gauntlet had been laid. The battle was on now!

"Jesus is God! And He will bring you water!" I said with complete and utter confidence. Later, alone, in my hotel room, I moaned and whined to the Lord, "Oh, Ishi. Another fine mess! Where am I going to get water?"

I would soon learn, as with everything else, the Lord had gone before me. His plan was for The Ephraim Project to join forces with the House of Israel International Ministries. Together, we would bring freshwater wells to remote Jewish villages in the isolated mountains of Gondar. Some had tried and failed because of the rough terrain. It was much easier to drill wells in the flatlands of Kenya than the highlands of Ethiopia.

Moreover, Satan employed all kinds of tactics to discourage missionaries from reaching these desperate people. Sometimes local officials prevented passage. Other times, tribal leaders forbade village entry. During certain times of the year, heavy rains rendered the treacherous trails impassable. Recurring vehicular and equipment failures hindered and discouraged others. Blocked at every turn, many gave up after a while. However, God opened the way for us just as He indicated He would in that late-August dream of 2006.

Rabbi Kokeb had already installed his first freshwater well when he invited me to join him. The need was astounding. In one village, the women, girls, and sometimes, small boys, walked three hours to the nearest water source with 40-pound clay jugs strapped to their backs. This was a daily one-way trek. The walk back was even more arduous because the jugs were made heavier by the water they held.

Many elderly women were permanently bent at a 45-degree angle because of carrying water all their lives. Unfortunately, much of the water was infected with all kinds of contaminants, including feces from cattle that drank from the same source. Using that water frequently caused many of the children and elderly to fall ill. Some died.

Rabbi Kokeb and I worked together on the next project to install freshwater wells to one of the region's largest villages. It was a three-hour drive from Gondar. Because it comprised roughly 1,500 men, women, and children, we provided this village with two wells.

We used nationals to help us install the wells just *outside* the village walls, so the Coptic Christians and Muslims could share in the water. Why not solve the water problem for all of them, and maybe bring peace and reconciliation between the groups? And while we were at it, why not introduce them to the One, who made the water possible?

It is not hard to imagine the impact the installation of nearby freshwater wells had on the villagers. It fundamentally changed their lives. No longer did the women have to devote six hours a day to retrieving dirty water for cooking and household chores. Their time could be devoted to other things, such as making tools or pottery to sell in the marketplace. No doubt the lives of the Coptic Christians and Muslims were also positively affected by the wells.

Soon everyone wanted to know, "Who brought the water?" We had the Perfect Answer. We partnered with The JESUS Film Project team in Addis Ababa, to bring the story of Jesus Christ to the region. We set up a large screen in a wide-open field and, at nightfall when everyone had gathered, we showed the film.

Most of the villagers had never watched television before, much less a film. They sat on the ground, looking up at the screen, mesmerized by the story of Jesus. The story is taken from the Gospel of Luke and told in the viewers' heart language. Many thought the actor playing Jesus *was* Jesus!

They sobbed and moaned profusely when Jesus was crucified, and rejoiced—jumping up and down, hugging each other—when He was resurrected. In the United States, I had only seen that kind of excitement at Super Bowl games. "He brought you the water! He brought you the water!" our team yelled to the villagers in Amharic.

Wherever this film is shown, there is a point where it is paused, and the viewers are asked if they would like to invite Jesus into their lives. These villagers (and their neighbors) were given the opportunity to invite Christ into their lives too. Hundreds raised their hands! When I saw this, I knew I had found my life's calling. I would bring water and then the Living Water to my people!

Back in the States, both Rabbi Kokeb and I raised money to install more wells. The money just seemed to come to us. The cost could range from $5,000 to $16,000 per well, depending on the terrain and well placement. Within 18 months, 17 freshwater wells were installed.

Meanwhile, HIIM was testing a new prototype. The new well had the capacity to pump and redirect water to the villagers' small farms, allowing them to grow crops to feed their families. They could then take the rest of their harvest to market to sell, and eventually break the cycle of grinding poverty.

The Ethiopian government awarded the project 10,000 hectares of free land—the equivalent of 24,710 acres—for 10 years to turn into farms for those families. Eventually, our water program caught the attention of some officials in Israel. They pressured the local officials to make us remove all mentions of Jesus Christ in connection to the wells.

Rabbi Kokeb simply renamed the program, "Wells of Living Water," and kept going. Seemingly, the officials did not realize that Living Water was just another name for Jesus Christ. In time, the two nationals overseeing our operations in Ethiopia fled to the United States, in search of political asylum. Both won their cases. Despite the dangers, I felt I had found my true calling in life. Soon I would resign from Denny's and dissolve my company. The time had come to transfer another kind of wealth.

Chapter 29
Leaving Corporate America

My exit from Denny's was divinely guided. God gave me no less than 10 dreams on the subject! One of the dreams God used to guide me into His waiting purposes for my life involved me preparing to fly. He gave me this dream on March 12, 2003, four years before I left Denny's.

In that dream, I finally reached a mountain summit. The heights were dizzying, and I was terrified. A friend's daughter, Tasha, was sitting at the top of the mountain swinging her legs when I finally reached it. In real life, Tasha is the most fearless young woman I know bar none. Tasha, a second-generation Haitian American, has achieved some remarkable successes during her lifetime because of her fearlessness. After graduating first in her class and interning at Johns Hopkins University, she is now a medical doctor, specializing in gastroenterology.

In my dream, Tasha was about 10 years old and holding a baby. And, of course, she was not the least bit terrified. I, on the other hand, was trembling, shaking like a leaf as I tried to turn around on the tiny ledge to sit next to her. She was facing outward. I barely managed to do the same.

Then, suddenly, I heard God's voice echoing through the mountains. He called me by name and commanded me to fly! I took the baby girl, who was symbolic of our embryonic ministry, from Tasha and I prepared to leap off the mountain.

God gave me another dream a year later, in 2004, in which Denny's senior management team entered a restaurant to celebrate some hard-won victories. But I was denied entry. I was left outside alone with a young woman who held a little baby girl.

I took the little girl, symbolic of Ephraim's young ministry, and climbed a steep set of stairs. (I would go up after leaving Denny's—way up!) The three of us entered an Italian restaurant with a harvest decor.

A year and a half later, that dream came true when the new vice president of human resources suddenly decided I could no longer participate in the Company's equity bonuses because I was not a Denny's employee. After 11 years of faithful service, that was a first. I became increasingly unhappy working in Denny's new chilly environment. But God warned me in a dream it was still too early to leap. Everything was not yet in order.

April 28, 2006

A Dream: Don't Jump Ship!

I had a dream on Wednesday, April 26. In the dream, God provided important insight into my work-ministry circumstances. I was on a ship. On the deck of another ship people beckoned me to leave my ship to join them.

There was some distance between the two ships. I would have to dive into the ocean and then swim to the other ship to join them. I decided I could do it. So, I climbed on top of the deck railing, stretched out my arms in a diving position, and prepared to jump.

Suddenly, the people on the other ship said, "No, stop! Take off your glasses."

I did not realize I had on eyeglasses. I removed my glasses. Surely, they would have been lost if I dove into the water wearing them. I prepared to dive again.

They stopped me a second time and instructed me to do something else that was also wise. I did it. After that, they instructed me to do one more thing before coming to their ship. In the next scene, I saw myself meticulously scrubbing clean each step I took as I backed out and exited the ship. The dream ended.

I knew the dream pertained to my departure from Denny's. Just before I drifted off to sleep, I queried the Lord about simply "taking a leap of faith" out of Denny's and into fulltime ministry. I thought about offering my resignation and simply trusting Him to help me make the transition.

Through the dream, the Lord was telling me, "Don't leap! There are things you must do before you leave, things you haven't thought about." These things would be in my own best interest, and they would also benefit Denny's.

God wanted me to leave Denny's in good shape, with all my projects wrapped up and tied with a neat, tidy bow. That was why He showed me cleaning each step as I backed out. An orderly, thoughtful exit would result in a clean break. A leap would create havoc and confusion and hurt my witness. I was certain I was not to make any drastic, immediate moves to leave Denny's.

A year later, the time came to leave. God used the timeless story of Ruth and Naomi to inspire and direct me.

March 25, 2007

Let Go of the Old Season!
(Based on the Book of Ruth)

Today, in his discussion about womanhood and what makes a good woman in God's eyes, Pastor Tims continued in the Book of Ruth. We studied from Chapter 3, having finished Chapters 1 and 2 during the previous weeks. The theme this Sunday was "Change Your Clothes!" That meant for us to realign ourselves to God's New Season. Prepare for a new kingdom assignment.

In Chapter 1, Ruth experienced an unexpected setback—a challenge, a problem. Her husband died. Her sister-in-law (Orpah) and mother-in-law (Naomi) also lost their husbands. Ruth, unlike her sister-in-law, chose to leave her native country, Moab, and everything familiar to her, to cleave to her mother-in-law in pursuit of something better in Israel (Bethlehem).

In Chapter 2, Ruth strove hard to "work it out." She did not quit in the midst of adversity, but she chose to play the hand dealt her. In Bethlehem, God led Ruth to glean in the fields of her kinsman-redeemer, Boaz.

In Chapter 3, Ruth received a little counseling from her "coach and mentor," Naomi, who knew the customs and traditions of her homeland. And here's where God began to speak to me ... like a coach and mentor. He wanted me to see I was now in Ruth's position:

1. *It's the end of the Barley Season. Ruth's window of opportunity is just about to close. The season is about to shift, and she must adjust. A door is about to shut.*
2. *The end of any season means the beginning of another, but Ruth must act quickly. She needs to seek, look, and study her situation.*
3. *Coach Naomi tells her four things to do to get ready for the new season. Boaz needed to see Ruth in a different light. She needed to take off everything that represented her past:*
   - *Wash yourself—symbolic for getting the "old season" off you.*
   - *Anoint yourself—symbolic of being filled and anointed by God's Holy Spirit.*
   - *Change your clothes—symbolic for changing your mindset, attitude, disposition, and speech to fit the new season. Leave the past in the past and head boldly into the future. You can't be dressed "in the past" to enter the future.*
   - *Don't announce yourself. He will notice you. This is symbolic of God's favor being poured on you because you embraced the new season by washing and anointing yourself and changing your clothes. He knows you need help. He saw you gleaning.*

Pastor Tims offered some other insights that resonated with my spirit. Again, as he spoke, I felt God's Spirit speaking directly to me:

1. *The children of Israel had to spend time in the "wilderness-holding place" to erase/eradicate their Egyptian mindsets—their "slave mentality"—before they could enter the Promised Land. "You need to get rid of your old mindsets before you can take hold of God's promises for you," Tims counseled.*
2. *Before Joseph was taken before Pharaoh after being pulled out of the pit, he shaved and put on new clothes to fit his new season. His new clothes matched his confidence in God. "Tell me your dream and I will interpret it," he told Pharaoh. "Prior to going*

before a president of a country, as Joseph did, change your clothes before you get there!" he advised.

3. *God wants to change your season of welfare and gleaning to one of prosperity. He has planned something better for you. Trust Him. He wants to take you to a better system.*
4. *When you take hold of the new season, conduct yourself like you are worthy of the best. Change the energy you give off to others. Carry yourself with confidence. Know you are a royal priesthood ... the seed of Abraham. God qualified you for the assignment. Go dressed like you own the company, Mrs. Boaz! Live the part.*
5. *Think BIG. Dream BIG in the new season. Pastor Tims told the story of two fishermen—a pro and an amateur. When the pro caught a big fish, he removed the hook from the fish's mouth and tossed it into a chest. The amateur kept throwing his big fish back into the sea. When questioned about this by the pro, the amateur said all he had at home was a small frying pan. ("Change your frying pan!")*
6. *People want to align themselves to someone who is confident. Convince yourself you ARE a special child of God. When He made you, He broke the mold. You are the apple of His eye, the head and not the tail.*

You are "New Wine" for a New Season.

At the end of the message, I felt the sensation of the Lord pressing heavy on my head. It is a feeling of weightiness that I get when the Lord is very near to me. The weight of His Presence bears down on my skull. It feels as if I am carrying something on my head.

Walking out of that sanctuary I knew I had to leave Denny's almost immediately. I recognized it had to be sooner than July 31—a date I had toyed with based on a case I was handling for the Company. I was confident I had to decide that day.

Two hours after I returned home and prayed, I emailed Nelson and told him I was leaving Denny's in 12 business days, on April 10, 2007. The Lord wanted to do a new thing with me. He wanted to take me into a new season, where I would become what He always told me I would be to Him—New Wine.

On April 10, 2007, I officially resigned the Denny's account after 12 years of service. After I submitted my official written resignation, Nelson only talked to me with a lawyer present. That was until I questioned him about it. We had been friends. What happened? I soon learned I would not be receiving the year's severance I expected, on the technicality that I was not an employee.

I had poured my life into rewriting The Denny's Story. The Company would no longer be known for racial discrimination, but for racial *and* gender inclusion. It was now a model for other Fortune 500 companies to follow.

For 12 years, I had been treated like a Denny's senior executive in virtually every way. I ran multiple departments, gave and received annual performance evaluations. I participated in its quarterly and annual bonus programs ... until the last year. Most people outside the Company thought I was an officer. They did not know I was a consultant, and Denny's and I wanted it that way. I sat on the Management Committee—a small core of senior executives who ran the Company—from Day One.

Notwithstanding all that, I felt like "the Joseph whom Pharaoh forgot." Offering the severance package would have been a gracious act. Instead, Nelson was quite bitter about my resignation. I learned about his anger from others inside the Company, and I saw it in dreams.

Following is a short excerpt from a long dream the Lord gave me four months before my official resignation. In the dream, He called me out of Denny's—out of Corporate America. He warned me that my departure would not be received well.

December 26, 2006

Answering the Lord's Call

I had the longest, weirdest—perhaps most telling—dream of my life early this morning. The dream pointed to some things I could expect to happen to me in the future. I sensed God preparing me for an unpleasant experience. Being dead-to-self will be the only way through it.

A Dream: "Joseph!"

In one of the last dream segments, I was walking with a small group of stragglers. It began to thunder. That meant a storm was coming. A Figure stood on the other side of a small, black chasm. I was on the side with the stragglers.

Suddenly, the Figure called me to get my attention: "Joseph!" I looked. It was the Lord! He motioned for me to come with Him. I glanced at a woman who was among the stragglers. Then, I looked at Him. I looked back at her. I knew I had to decide. Do I stay with them or do I jump? Finally, I leapt across the chasm to the Lord's side.

The woman and other stragglers began to berate me. With ugly scowls on their faces, they said nasty things about me as the Lord and I walked away arm-in-arm. Neither one of us looked back. I heard myself say, "I don't care. You can't hurt me. I'm already dead." That meant I had resolved to die to my selfish goals, dreams, and ambitions. I had replaced them with the Lord's.

In the next scene, the Lord walked me to a flying contraption and strapped me in. Then, He fastened Himself in. The flying machine resembled a theme park ride. I knew we were about to fly. We took off.

We flew high in the sky, so high my head started to spin. I became so frightened, I shut my eyes. The Lord finally said, "Open your eyes." When I did, I could see for miles and miles in all four directions. He said, "All of this is yours."

In that dream, the Lord clearly confirmed the Joseph-like call on my life. For years, He had been telling me I was a Joseph, but that was the first time He called me Joseph in a dream. I knew the call had something to do with helping pull many people through a time of great spiritual and physical want. At this point, it required me to take a small leap from Denny's into whatever the Lord had planned. He warned me that my departure would greatly upset the "powers that be." They would feel forsaken. He also revealed that some were certain I would not make it. They were confident I would ask to return.

The Joseph Call would require me to die-to-self in a way I had never done before. This would be the only way to get through it. In heaven's eyes, I would fly high in the Lord when I left my corporate life behind. In the very end, I would inherit it all. ("The meek shall inherit the earth.")

Near the conclusion of my stint at Denny's, on a flight back to Orlando, the Lord gave me a powerful revelation. I was sitting at the gate, waiting for my plane, when I distinctly heard in my spirit: "You're more like the Samaritan woman than you know." The Lord told me, like the Samaritan woman at the well, I had poured my life into six pseudo husbands. That is, I had freely emptied my gifts and talents into six CEOs or other powerful executives to whom I reported during my career in Corporate America.

"Count them," He said. I pulled a pen from my purse and began to write down names on my coffee napkin, starting with Don Dempsey and ending with Nelson Marchioli. I counted and recounted. The number was the same each time—six! "It's time to stop pouring your life into dead things," He whispered.

I had spent 30 years in Corporate America, and I had given these men, who were not my Husband, the best years of my life. I was both discouraged and encouraged by the revelation. Suddenly, I felt I had squandered most of my life on Whoppers and Grand Slams. (God would have to show me later this was not entirely the case.) I was encouraged because after the Samaritan woman met the Seventh Man—the Perfect Man—she never turned back. He flipped her world. Her *real* Husband redeemed her squandered time.

I left Denny's and dissolved IBS, thinking Suzanne and I were going to live in Ethiopia. On our last trip, we even tried to find a place to live. At the end of that trip, officials from the central government quietly pulled me aside. They informed me that everything I had done up to that point had been illegal because The Ephraim Project was not a registered non-government operational agency (NGO) in Ethiopia.

They sent me to a lawyer in Addis Ababa, who told me everything I had to do to become a legal entity in Ethiopia. As I listened, I could hardly wait to have a private moment with the Lord. "Ishi, what is this? You got me out here doing all this stuff ILLEGALLY?" I confess I was more amused than anything else, and He knew it. He often used my childlike faith (or stupidity) to clear paths that appeared blocked, to start something new.

As soon as I returned home, since I had already resigned from Denny's, I began working on my relocation with the Ambassador of Ethiopia. He resided in Los Angeles. We agreed his office would handle my papers to clear the way for The Ephraim Project to become an NGO and for Suzanne and me to become residents of Ethiopia. It turned out the only part of that plan that was God's was my resigning from Denny's.

I never heard back from the Ambassador of Ethiopia. After sending my completed application packet, my many phone calls went unanswered. God had effectively blocked my path. I should have known something was amiss when He gave me a dream that ended with the destruction of my passport. In the dream, my passport fell from my hand into a tight space, from which I could not retrieve it. It landed next to a bottle containing a thick, milky substance. The bottle overturned, spilling its contents on my passport, and ruined it. The Lord was, in effect, telling me, "You will not be traveling out of the country anytime soon."

I quickly learned that as a sign of the "bride to come," I had to do more than just bring water to the thirsty. Next, God would also show me how to bring food to the hungry multitudes. That same year, The Ephraim Project began feeding Orlando's homeless. We started by feeding six people. Today, six years later, we oversee an operation that feeds more than 1,500 homeless men, women, and children weekly. Over the course of those six years, the Lord had to perform a LOT of *interior* work in me.

Unbeknownst to me, when I left Corporate America, I was still a long way from experiencing and knowing God in the way He wanted me to. I couldn't the way I was. Now that the Lord had gotten me out of "Egypt," it was time to get "Egypt" out of me. He needed to change my ways of thinking and doing things, so I could walk lockstep with Him into His glorious purposes for my life.

Chapter 30
Purging My Life

Those first few months out of Denny's, the Lord gently, tenderly comforted me as He held a mirror up to my life. It was not a pretty image. I was so ashamed! Filled with shock and remorse, prostrate on the floor, I cried daily tears of repentance. I did this not because He kept rehashing my faults and failures, but because daily I discovered new "un-Christlike" things about myself that tore my heart to pieces. In "Egypt," I often behaved like the Egyptians. Until He pulled me out, I was too busy "making bricks"—working like a slave—to notice.

Some days, I cried until my eyes were swollen shut. How could I have been so off? I had no idea how ineffectual I was as a believer in Christ. I thought I had accomplished so much! I had been so busy "doing," I had not stood still long enough for God to show me the spiritual issues that kept me from being all He created me to be.

Eventually, He dried my tears. He helped me understand that I was being called to a higher level of consecration in Him. He, then, used a vacuum cleaner, of all things, to explain I was in the midst of an extreme *spiritual* makeover.

July 19, 2007

The Vacuum Cleaner

In the middle of preparing a speech I have to give next week in San Diego, Suzanne decided to tidy the house. I thought she went to her room to nap, but the next thing I knew she was trying to vacuum the floors. Something was wrong with the vacuum cleaner. She brought it to me. While I wanted to work on my speech, the Holy Spirit kept nudging me to help. Finally, I relented.

We did everything we could to that vacuum cleaner. We could not identify the problem. I found a small, dirty filter and cleaned it right away with soapy water. Suzanne cleaned off the second, larger filter. It, too, was quite dirty. Cleaning the filters helped, but they were not the source of the problem. The vacuum had lost all its suction.

Suzanne explained that it worked the last time she used it, but not very well. In fact, it had been losing power over time. She also reminded me that I paid a lot of money for it. We debated in the store rather we should buy a cheap one or this one. We finally chose to make the more substantial investment, thinking it would be worth it in the long run.

We took the machine completely apart! At one point, Suzanne wondered if we would be able to put it back together. But even dismantled we could not see the problem. Of course, we prayed throughout the ordeal. "Lord, please fix it! Please show us what's wrong! Please, give us wisdom."

We wrestled with that thing for nearly two hours. I was not ready to throw in the towel on it because we could see it had ample suction on the inside. It just was not working on the outside.

Suzanne examined the long hose. While it did have dust and residue along its wall, it was clear all the way to the bottom. Or so we thought.

She beckoned me over. "Look at this." I pulled the plastic hose straight and peered deep inside. "Something's in there! There's stuff stuck down there! That's what's blocking everything!" I announced. She agreed. "We have to cut the hose!" I concluded. She disagreed.

"Suzanne, there's no way we're going to get that stuff out of there unless we cut the hose and pull it out." She still disagreed. "What do you suggest?" I pressured her. She had no answers. She just did not want to do something so radical.

"Suzanne, listen to me. We can cut the hose, pull the stuff out, and duct tape it back. Or, we can let it sit here and look pretty and be useless!"

Finally, she gave in. I ran to get a razor blade. We discussed the best place to cut. I made a quick slit at the farthest end of the hose, near the base. Dirt and big dust balls spilled out of the cut.

Suzanne retrieved a plastic bag to hold the trash we pulled out. There was a lot of it—three piles. We even found an ink pen from a resort hotel in Orlando. We pulled out everything we could see.

I retrieved a wire clothes hanger from my closet and made it into a long, wiry stick. I stuck it in the other end of the vacuum to push any remaining debris to the opening, where we made the slit. Unable to do more, we taped the hose and put the machine back together. I told Suzanne, "If this doesn't work, we have done all we can do, and we just have to buy another one."

She plugged in the machine; I flipped on the switch. Oh, my goodness! That vacuum had so much power! It even sounded different! We had made a mess on the family room floor. It sucked the mess right up. I marveled at how clean the rug was after Suzanne was finished vacuuming. It looked new! The vacuum cleaner performed like a brand-new piece of equipment.

We praised God, gave each other a high-five and then gave God an imaginary high-five. Suzanne went to work on the rest of the floors. When she was done, they were beautiful.

A Power Purge

In the pre-dawn hours this morning, I could not stop telling God how pleased I was that He had pulled me out of Denny's. I had not realized what a drain it had been on me. Life was so different now. "I was blind, but now I see," I joked.

The uncertainty of my financial circumstances had pulled me closer to Him. I spent more time with Him than ever before. For weeks, He had been putting His finger on things that were wrong in my life—things I could not see before. Tenderly, He had been showing me issues I needed to address. Surely, I was in the midst of an extreme makeover. He was making me over from the inside out.

This is what the Lord meant years ago when He said, "Get your house in order! I will be bringing you home soon." He was referring to my life—not my Last Will and Testament and the state of my financial affairs!

I have never felt closer to Him. I am no longer running around trying to fix the world. I leave that to Him. These days, I just like to sit in His Presence and talk ... about anything.

Finally, we landed on the subject of the vacuum cleaner. "Your life is like that vacuum cleaner," the Holy Spirit counseled. The more I thought about it, the more sense it made. My many hidden issues kept me from walking in the fullness of His power. I needed to be purged!

I got excited every time I thought about how that vacuum worked after "surgery." How powerful it was! Suddenly, I could not wait until He put me back together and sent me out to do what He created me to do.

I pulled seven truths from my experience with the vacuum cleaner:

1. I may look okay from the outside, but if dirt, dust, and debris pile up on the inside, I cannot work as I should. I lose power.
2. I may not lose my power all at once, but over time—until I have none.
3. Cleaning up little things in my life here and there is good, like cleaning the filters; but I must get to the root cause of my issues.
4. The root cause is often hidden from the human eye. It is difficult to get at and sift out, but God sees it.
5. God has made a substantial investment in me. He gave His life. He sees my potential and will conduct "surgery" on me if He has to. He will remove the debris in my life to get me working as I should, as He always intended.
6. Surgery hurts, and it may leave scars; but if it is not performed, I will be useless and good for nothing.
7. When God is done, I will even SOUND better!

A Fresh Anointing

By November 2007, seven months after my resignation from Denny's, something had happened to me that I was not aware of. A fresh, new anointing had come over my life. Lying prostrate on the floor before the Lord all those many months had changed me. God would have to show me just how much.

I was asked to speak at Holy Ground, a church in Greenville, South Carolina. I flew into town and stayed at Jeri's house in Simpsonville. She agreed to attend the event with me. It started at 7 p.m. We thought we would be home before 10 o'clock. We planned to make popcorn and watch a movie.

The event coordinators had not given me a topic. When they first asked me to speak, I was told, "Just come and share your heart. Tell us what God is doing in your life." I took their advice, literally.

I typed up what God was doing in my life—the plain, naked truth. And I decided to do something I had never done. I would read this out loud word for word—no bells, no whistles, just the facts—from a sheet of paper.

When it came time to speak, I walked to the front, took the podium and began reading my testimony. Essentially, I told them the nasty, filthy mess I had been and shared how God began to gently, tenderly clean me up, once I agreed with Him about my condition.

While the content may have been poignant, my quiet, flat delivery had to be one of the most boring ever. When I was done, I stepped down and took my seat. I just sat there with my head down. Then something happened.

Women dressed in fine suits and high heels began to make their way to the front. One by one, they began to lay prostrate on the floor! Some quietly cried, others rocked and sobbed! I had no idea it was happening because I never lifted my eyes.

Finally, one of the event coordinators tiptoed over to me and whispered in my ear, "We think … uh … maybe, maybe you should pray for the people." I stood up and looked around. Women were laying prostrate on the floor, just broken. Only the Holy Spirit could have used my words to move them like this!

I got down on my knees and reached for the woman nearest to me. I touched her and began to pray. "Dear Heavenly Father…." Before I could say another word, she slumped to the floor, slain in the Spirit. I looked at her. She was out cold. I hardly knew what to say. I fumbled through a short prayer and moved on to the next woman.

I looked at Jeri standing in the rear of the room. She stared at me, wide-eyed. She knew what I was thinking, and I knew what she was thinking. We were both thinking the same thing. This all was a wondrous move of the Holy Spirit, and we just needed to enter in and wait to see what He would do next.

At one point, I looked up to see a long line of men, women, and children in front of me. They had formed a prayer line. They wanted me to pray over them, one-by-one. Again, I looked at Jeri standing at the back of the room. She looked at me and shrugged her shoulders as if to say, "It's God! Go with it!"

Someone put a chair underneath me and I started. It seemed to go on forever. Some were slain in the Spirit, some were not. But after I prayed for the first 10 to 15 people, jubilation broke out all over the hall. People started singing. Someone began playing a piano. People began dancing with one another. They had been set free! From what, I could not tell. Only God knew for sure.

Someone grabbed me and together we began to do an entirely, unrehearsed Hebrew dance. Two women began yelling, "That's the dance we saw in our dream!" Apparently, God had given the women the same dream of His people dancing in jubilation! I must have danced for 30 minutes straight. I was exhausted when I finally stopped, but God was just getting started.

Before the evening was over, Gina Hockaday, a powerful woman of God I met at the event, joined me upfront in prayer to set free a young lady suffering from several demonic spirits. As we warred over her in the Spirit—calling the demons by name and commanding them to come out—she wretched and vomited. All over the hall, the people stood with outstretched hands and prayed while we warred over her.

When it was all over, the young lady collapsed in our arms with a smile, tears streaming down her cheeks. She was free! And she knew it!

God had given me a fresh, new anointing of His Spirit! Now I was seeing the manifestation of it. That anointing had the power to heal and set captives free. There is no amount of money in the world worth it.

Jeri and I arrived back at her house at about 1:30 in the morning. I was as limp as a dish rag. I could speak only in a whisper during the next few days. My voice and body were spent.

The Sin of Presumption

Critical to my spiritual transformation during my stint in the wilderness was the eradication of another debilitating sin in my life—the sin of presumption. It was as large and looming as the sin of covetousness had been. The Lord made it clear to me that my call would be thwarted if He left the sin unchecked. When He chose to reveal mysteries to me about the end of the age, He did not need me running off, half-cocked and independent of Him, muddying up His cosmic plans. That was a misuse of His glory. That was the sin of presumption.

Nobody knows the eternal plans of God. Not even the angels can figure out all that God is doing. He cannot be second-guessed or anticipated. He is inscrutable!

As I grew more in Him, He needed His glory to be manifested in my life for people to see. At the same time, I needed to learn how to "carry" the weight of His glory properly. I should not attempt to drive or control Him or the process. It was okay to hope, dream, and ponder about the wondrous things He was doing in my life, but it was not okay to plan my life around these wonders. His plans were much too big, too mysterious for my tiny, finite mind to understand. I was to be led by His Word and Spirit. I was to wait on Him. He was the Architect ... The Castle Builder!

The Lord first sought to teach me about the sin of presumption through the life of King David. Just as King David was guilty of the sin of presumption in the handling of the Ark of the Covenant, God showed me I was guilty of the same sin when I tried to anticipate His plans and run ahead of Him. God will not be led or driven anywhere, by anyone, at any time. He leads, we follow.

The Ark of the Covenant was a visible sign that the invisible God of the Universe was dwelling in the midst of Israel. It was a symbol of His Presence and Glory. God made a pledge that He would be ever-present among His people (Ex. 6:6, 7). The Ark was a shadow of Christ, Immanuel-to-come:

1. The Ark contained the two tablets upon which the 10 commandments (Law) were written by the hand of God. (Christ came to fulfill the Law.)
2. The Ark contained a pot of manna that was the miraculous food (bread) provided by God in the wilderness to keep His people alive. (Christ is called the Bread of Life and we need Him daily to keep us alive.)
3. The Ark contained Aaron's rod that had blossomed and budded. The budded rod signified to Israel that Aaron and his tribe (Levi) were chosen by God to serve as His high priests, His ministers. (Christ was chosen by God to serve as His High Priest. He would be God's representative to the people and the people's representative to God.)
4. The lid of the Ark was called the Mercy Seat or the Place of Mercy. (Christ is the personification of God's mercy upon fallen people who cannot save themselves. He demonstrated His mercy when He clothed Himself in flesh and came to earth to atone for the sins of the people. Under the Old Covenant, once a year, the Mercy Seat was sprinkled with the blood of bulls and goats to make atonement for the people of Israel.)
5. The Ark was placed in the Holy of Holies and separated from the rest of the Tabernacle (and later the Temple) by a heavy veil. (After Christ died on the cross, the veil in the Temple was split in two, signifying that Christ had, once and for all, atoned for the

sins of mankind. Fallen man no longer had to be separated from God.)

Thus, the purpose and significance of the Ark of the Covenant was fulfilled in Christ.

During the time of the Judges, when Israel was at a historic low point spiritually, God allowed the Philistines to capture the Ark. Israel had presumptuously carried it into battle, thinking it would help them win, despite their waywardness from God. God would not let them use His glory that way. They suffered a veritable slaughter at the hands of the Philistines.

The Philistines kept the Ark for only seven months since God sent a plague among them that ultimately forced them to give back the Ark to Israel. But even the Levites who first took the Ark back suffered a serious loss because, once again, they did not handle the Ark correctly. God would not allow His glory to be handled in a presumptuous manner. The Ark finally found a resting place among a righteous family in Israel, and there it stayed for years.

Samuel—raised up by God to be a prophet, reformer, and Israel's last judge—did not seek to bring the Ark back to the Temple during his lifetime. The nation was too wayward under King Saul, a willful, rebellious leader. In time, God anointed and raised up a righteous servant-leader, King David. He would bring the Ark to Israel, to the city of Jerusalem.

But even David, God's chosen servant, had trouble bringing the Ark home. Uzzah died because he accidentally touched the Ark when it nearly tumbled off the oxen cart. David should not have been transporting the Ark to Jerusalem by cart. He did not follow God's prescribed method of having the Ark carried on the shoulders of God's priests.

Finally, after three months—adhering to God's prescribed method—David took the Ark from where he left it at Obed-Edom's house, to the

Tabernacle in the City of David. Once accomplished, David danced before the Lord with all his might. Israel and David's house were blessed because of the Ark. God's Presence and Glory dwelled among them.

King David could not fulfill God's call on his life without God's manifested Presence and Glory. As Israel's anointed king, it was imperative he bring the Ark to the City of David. In the same way, God told me I could not fulfill His call on my life without His Manifested Presence and Glory. And, like David, I would have to learn how to handle it, how to carry it properly.

Despite all this understanding, I made repeated stumbles. I did one amazingly stupid thing after another, based on a vision or dream the Lord had given me. The presumption always caused me, and particularly Ryan, a lot of pain.

It would start simply enough. The Lord would give me a dream, a vision, a word of knowledge, a revelation or a string of revelations, and I would run headlong with it into a rabbit hole. No amount of head knowledge about this sin could rescue me from it.

God allowed me to experience the painful effects of presumption, time and again, but like the sin of covetousness, I just could not seem to shake it. Fortunately, God had a plan. As Suzanne says, "God knows how to tame His children."

The Lord dealt with the sin of presumption in my life the same way He dealt with covetousness. He set me up for a big fall. The fall would serve as the catalyst for breaking me free, once and for all, from this sin.

In late February 2008, I found myself writing approximately 50 family members, friends, and acquaintances about a catastrophic earthquake that would hit mid-America. It would affect many states from the north to the south and split the nation along the Ohio, Missouri, and Mississippi Rivers. There would be massive flooding and a devastating loss of life.

I had the audacity to specify the date of the earthquake and the time—April 19, 2008 at sundown, around 6 p.m. I told them to pray to God and ask Him specifically what they should do and whom they should tell.

Over and over thoughts tumbled in my head: *I have this knowledge! I believe this is what God is showing me. How can I not tell them? What if they knew and did not tell me? I would be furious. What if I kept quiet and some of them died and then others found out I knew about it and did not say anything?* On and on I went.

It did not help matters that on the day I decided to write and post the letters, I found a book of stamps stuck underneath the tire of my car while parked at the post office. The book contained the exact number of stamps I needed to complete the mailing. A sign from God!

When I told Ryan what I had done, she was both incredulous and mortified. "Oh, Mom, please! No, you didn't! Please tell me you did *not* do that. Pleeeeeeeeeese!" I was so confident I had done the right thing.

"I'm going to have to leave the country after this!" she moaned. She immediately called her father in Chicago. She wanted to warn him that he would be receiving a letter from me and what it contained.

"If there's an earthquake anywhere in the U.S. within two weeks of that date, I'll become a believer!" he vowed. He could not stop laughing.

Of course, as the Lord would have it, no earthquake struck on April 19, 2008. I was in an airplane when the quake was supposed to hit. When we landed, everything seemed normal. I asked the Lord about the quake.

"My mercy endures forever," He answered crisply. We'll talk about the quake later."

He was not pleased with what I had done. I was humiliated beyond measure before my family and closest and dearest friends. But I would learn in the coming days and weeks that His mercy extended to me too. I waited with considerable trepidation and fear for a fallout that never came. I surmised I had caused a lot of people a lot of grief and pain. I would be labeled an alarmist and certifiably crazy. No one would ever believe another word I said. Why should they? I felt I should be stoned to death as a false prophet.

But the Lord had a plan.

Although a catastrophic earthquake did not strike on April 19, 2008, a 5.4 magnitude quake shook several Midwestern states along a 450-mile stretch on April 18, 2008 at 4:40 p.m. It touched parts of Illinois, Indiana, Michigan, Missouri, Kansas City, Nebraska, West Virginia, and Kentucky. It was felt as far south as Atlanta, Georgia, rattling homes, schools, businesses, and the nerves of several million Americans.

Apparently, that was close enough for Mike. He felt the quake in Chicago and solemnly declared me a psychic and himself a believer. Among the recipients of the letter, several told me later the warning shook them awake spiritually. They felt they had drifted in their walks with the Lord, and the letter helped them reorder their priorities. The prayer warriors among the group were convinced their fasting and prayers stayed God's hand. Others never mentioned it and, by the grace of God, continued to be my friends and seek my advice and counsel in spiritual matters, which simply floored me. Virtually, all were glad the country was not hit.

I heard of one man—a friend of a friend I told—who was angry with me that the earthquake did not occur because he made a lot of preparations. Later, I wondered, while he was taking measures to protect himself and his family, if he had taken the time to prepare his heart.

As for me, the Lord waited patiently until I came out from underneath the covers. His only comment to me was: "Don't *ever* do that again!" That was it. We never spoke of it again. I was tamed.

Chapter 31
Two Signs of the Coming Rapture

During my first year after leaving Denny's, God performed two miraculous wonders to confirm there was a point to all that was happening to me. I was not just on some crazy random journey. He was doing a profound work. I was a sign of His bride who would be raptured out of the world one day soon and into His presence in heaven. He desired to give me a glimpse of how the blessed event would occur.

On May 29, 2007, fewer than 60 days out of Denny's, God quietly performed the first marvel. He made the handle break off my curling iron—while I was using it. Then it disappeared!

One minute the piece to my curling iron handle was there, and the next minute it was gone. I was in the room with it when it disappeared. I was standing right next to the piece. I saw it. Just as I reached down to pick it up, it was no longer there! It had vanished! I could not find it anywhere. This is how it will be for those left behind after the rapture of the church.

Roughly four months later, on September 28, 2007, the Lord performed a similar, but different feat. He transported my prayer shawl from the backseat of my moving vehicle to the living room table at my house. He did it in such a way that I knew I had not mistaken what happened. Suzanne was a witness.

In this second wonder, God demonstrated how He could take an object in one place and move it to another without anyone seeing. One minute, on the way to New Destiny's early-morning prayer service, the prayer shawl was in the backseat of my car. When exactly it disappeared from the backseat, I still do not know.

When I arrived at church and opened the back door of the car to retrieve it, the shawl was gone! I placed it on the backseat with my purse when we left the house. Initially, I forgot it. I specifically went back into the house to get it. Suzanne waited for me in the car while I went back.

She and I must have spent 10 minutes searching the car after we arrived at church. When we returned home after the prayer service, we found the shawl sitting on the edge of the living room table! Normally, if I was not using the shawl for prayer, it remained folded in a matching knitted case and placed in a special chest in my bedroom, where I kept all my sacred items. That week, I kept it in a tall basket in the dining room because I used it daily at New Destiny's prayer services.

Later, I learned the second reason the Lord took the shawl that particular morning. He used the opportunity to anoint my uncovered head with His Spirit in special preparation for what would come next in my life.

June 1, 2007

The Mystery of the Disappearing Hot Curling Iron Handle

I had THE ABSOLUTE most wonderful experience last night! It was both perplexing and spine-tingling. I knew God was demonstrating something very special. I had washed and blow-dried my hair. I was about halfway finished curling my hair when, suddenly, the black plastic shell that covered the handle of the hot curling iron broke off and fell to the floor.

In my peripheral vision, I saw it lying on the white tile. The floor was bare except for the black handle piece and a white throw rug.

With the plastic covering gone, all that remained was the metal handle. I decided I would complete the curl I was on and then try to reattach the shell to the handle since the metal was almost too hot to touch. I finished the curl and reached down to pick up the piece. It was gone!

Since the cabinets extend all the way to the floor, there was no way the handle could have fallen underneath. Stupidly, I looked INSIDE the closed cabinets. I looked three or four times. I searched underneath the flat rug lying on the floor—another stupid move.

Although I saw where the handle landed, I felt compelled to search the ENTIRE BATHROOM! It was gone. I knew God was responsible for the missing handle, but what was He trying to teach me? Remarkably, He allowed me to finish my hair without the plastic covering to protect my hands!

A Hidden Rapture Message

Later, it occurred to me why the Lord took the handle piece. Joshua and I will disappear just like that curling iron handle. We will be a sign to Christ's bride—the true church—that she will be taken in the same manner in the rapture. One second, she will be present and, the next second, she will be no more.

It will happen in the twinkling of an eye. It will happen in the presence of people, yet no one will see it. People will search and search for her, but they will not find her. Those remaining will know something strange, odd, and supernatural occurred, but they will be at a loss to explain it.

September 28, 2007

The Mystery of the Translated Prayer Shawl

As Suzanne and I prepared to leave for New Destiny's early-morning prayer service, everything seemed normal. Little did I know I was about to experience the supernatural.

"Oh, I forgot my prayer shawl," I told Suzanne as I brushed past her to go back into the house to retrieve it. She went to the car, parked in the garage, and waited. I headed through the laundry room and into the dining room, where I kept my shawl in a tall blond basket during our special prayer weeks. After a special week of prayer was over, it would be returned to a chest in my bedroom. The shawl is from Israel, a gift to me from my Cousin Debbie. I use it as a covering when I go to the altar to pray.

I grabbed the shawl, raced out of the backdoor and locked it. I opened the back-passenger door of my car on the driver's side, threw in my purse and the shawl, and slammed the door shut.

"Are you sure you don't want your Bible?" I asked Suzanne. I saw her Bible sitting on the washer in the laundry room as I headed back to the

car with the shawl. When I first passed her to retrieve the shawl, I saw it in her arms.

She explained she had been reading it and inadvertently brought it with her when it was time to go. Since we would be praying and not reading, she took it back inside. It would be safe in the laundry room until we returned. We drove to church.

When we arrived at church, Suzanne grabbed her things. I turned off the headlights and jumped out of the car. I opened the back door to grab my things. My prayer shawl was gone! How could that be?

"Oh, you must have forgotten it," Suzanne said.

"No, no, no! That can't be! I threw it in the backseat! I saw it lying next to my purse when I shut the door! I saw it, I'm telling you!" I was wild with excitement.

She and I searched the car over and over. We turned on the interior lights.

"It's not here!" I concluded. I had the ridiculous thought that maybe it somehow fell out of the car before I slammed the door. But I distinctly remember seeing it in the backseat. We both agreed God was behind the missing shawl. He would make His purpose known in time.

Once inside, I decided to find a lone pew to express my praises and petitions to God out loud. Then, I abruptly changed my mind. "Nope, I want to pray at the altar," I whispered.

As I knelt at the altar, I was very aware that my head was uncovered. Usually, during these times of prayer I cover my head with the shawl. It makes a private tent (tabernacle) for the Lord and me to commune. Today, I used my two hands to cover my eyes and block out all distractions. I prayed and sang to the Lord for 10 minutes. Chills ran up and down my body as I prayed. I could feel God's anointing on me.

Everyone was instructed to come to altar. We would have a time of corporate prayer. We usually form a big prayer circle before the altar. But by this time, the anointing was so great on my head, I struggled to stand! Once up, I fell back down on my behind! I tried to stand up again but thought better about it. I crawled up an altar step and remained on my knees.

After about 15 minutes, I could no longer remain on my knees. I was too weak. I simply draped myself over the altar steps. The corporate prayers continued a few feet away. They were powerful and strong. Many of the prayers picked up on themes I had discussed earlier with the Lord during our time together.

Near the end of the prayers, I could not even speak. All I could do was agree in the Spirit with what was being prayed. Finally, the prayers ended.

The anointing was so heavy I could not get up on my own. Suzanne had to steady me on my feet. She held me as we walked slowly to the car. I slid into the driver's seat and waited. Gradually, the anointing lifted enough so I could cruise home. By the time I pulled into the garage, I felt normal again. When I walked into the house, I immediately spotted the prayer shawl sitting on the edge of the dining room table!

"You left it here?" Suzanne asked as she walked in behind me.

"NO WAY!" I yelled. "Remember, you waited for me to go back and get it!" I walked her through how ludicrous it would be for me to run in the house for the express purpose of retrieving something and then putting it down and running out of the house without it. She agreed.

Besides, I distinctly remembered opening the backdoor to the car and throwing in the shawl next to my purse. I saw them both together before slamming the door. But I did not need to go through a whole, long explanation. I knew what had happened and why. God revealed it to me in an instant.

The missing shawl was a demonstration of how God can transport and translate objects or people from one place to another without anyone being the wiser. It was the first time in my life I experienced Him removing an object from one place and putting it somewhere else. He will translate His bride from earth to heaven without anyone seeing the event. I suspect the translation will mirror those experienced by Enoch, Elijah, Philip, and Paul in the Bible.

There was another reason why God took my prayer shawl that day. He literally anointed my head with His own oil! He poured Himself—His power, authority, Spirit—directly on my head that morning in preparation for what was coming next. I would not understand this until my visit a month later at Holy Ground Church, where I gave the most boring, driest speech of my entire life—one that shook hell and loosed many captives.

Chapter 32
Slaying Giants

As God began to make me over, He showed me giants in my midst. They would surely keep me from seizing His promises for my life if I did not contend with them in His strength. Before He could slay them, I needed to acknowledge their existence and trust Him wholly to deal with them. He desired my utter confidence in Him when I encountered these Goliaths in my life. He recruited my friend Denise Wiggins, a prison inmate in Memphis, Tennessee, to help me face the challenge.

September 7, 2007

Facing the Giants

In her last letter to me Denise wrote: "I want you to watch the movie, Facing Your Giants. *(Actually, the film is called* Facing the Giants.*) I saw it earlier this summer. In a handwritten note, I informed her I had already seen the movie and enjoyed it.*

As I wrote, the Lord quickened my spirit. Suddenly, I remembered two weeks earlier, New Destiny Christian Center showed Facing the Giants *at Thursday night Bible study. Suzanne and I returned home without staying since we had already seen the movie. Now I suspected God had wanted us to stay to see the film that night since my friend, whom I deeply respect, was asking me to view it.*

*I sensed it was really God urging me to view the film again. And, I felt Denise's use of "your" (*Facing Your Giants*) was also from Him. He wanted to speak to me through the film, to glean something specific about and for my life that I missed the first time.*

For the children of Israel to seize the land God promised them, they had to face the giants in the land. Ten of the 12 spies came back with negative reports. "We are like grasshoppers in their sight!" The giants instilled fear in the people.

Only Caleb and Joshua believed God. But the people retreated in fear, believing the report of the 10. This angered God. Thus, God allowed them to wander in the desert for 40 years. A generation later, their children took the land.

I knew at some point in the future, I would cross over into God's promises for my life. To take hold of what He had prepared for me, I would have to face my giants. Even then, I was facing some colossal issues. I asked God to help me not retreat in fear. "Let me be like my ancestor David," I prayed. Next, I rented the movie.

September 10, 2007

The Film: Facing the Giants

True to my word, I rented the movie, Facing the Giants. *Suzanne and I watched it together and it was a true blessing. In the film, Mr. Bridges stated to Mr. Grant, the head coach of Shiloh's football team, "God has opened a door for us that no one can shut." I felt the same about my life. God was opening doors for me that no man could shut. But if fear kept me from walking through those doors, I would never seize God's promises for my life.*

Following are the truths I gleaned from the film on how to defeat the giants in my life:

1. *God puts us in "impossible" David-and-Goliath situations to show off His power to an unbelieving world. This is how He receives glory from our lives. We must know if He brought us to it, He would see us through it ... if we trust Him.*
2. *God answers prayers that lead to His glory.*
3. *We must have a vision for our lives that is outside ourselves. Visions attached to self are too small and not worth fighting for. When things get tough, we quit.*
4. *We can "give the game away" when we are focused on wrong things, apathetic, or operating in fear.*
5. *God's saints should not be moved by sight (the size of our giants). We should be moved by God's Word (His promises).*
6. *We must stay humble before God and others, but confident in the Lord's power to bring us through.*

7. *The devil will send arrows our way to discourage us, especially at our lowest points (e.g., betrayals, accusations, frequent and multiple problems.)*
8. *We must lay our lives at God's feet and let Him have His way with us.*
9. *We should never think or speak defeat. Just keep believing God.*
10. *God will keep us safe in the shadow of His wings as He works out His Providence in our lives.*
11. *We should prepare our "fields" by faith to receive God's rain (blessing) in our lives. God will send the rain when He is ready.*
12. *We must use our spiritual weapons (God's Word, prayers of thanksgiving, praise, intercession, etc.) to defeat our giants.*
13. *We must apply God's Word to our practical, everyday living. We have to "do" it, not just hear it or read about it.*
14. *Sometimes God will blind us to our circumstances so that we do not know how far we have come or how far we have to go. He simply wants us to trust Him and keep pressing forward.*
15. *After the trial, we will discover we can do more than we ever dreamed possible with God's help.*
16. *In everything we do, God wants us to take time to love one another—be supportive, encouraging, and instructive.*
17. *God will allow our "Goliaths" to outnumber us and to be much bigger, greater, faster, stronger, and more powerful, so there will be no mistake when the dust clears that He slew the giant. He will outsmart our giants every time.*
18. *God will take saints who trust Him to places they technically are not supposed go under natural or normal circumstances.*
19. *We should always strive to give our very best to God even when we think we have nothing left. Keep pouring. Do not quit on Him, no matter how badly it hurts. We are an offering ("living sacrifices") to the Lord. He allows circumstances to envelope us, only to burn off the bonds and dross. Do not lose heart. Let Him finish the job of refining and perfecting.*
20. *A big movement always begins with the diligent, persistent prayer of a righteous remnant.*
21. *The most spiritually attuned saints, whom God uses most mightily, are usually obscure, unknown, ignored people (e.g., praying blind man).*
22. *The righteous can pray for years and then, without warning, God's Spirit can rain down blessings of deliverance on many.*

23. *Corporate prayers are the most powerful, bringing widespread blessings to many.*
24. *Although fulfilling our destiny can take years, we can have fun getting there, if we choose to be living sacrifices to the Lord.*
25. *God desires that we dream big dreams. If we do not give up on them and persevere in Him, He can make them come true for His glory. (Coach Grant began to dream big after seeing God answer prayer. He started to dream of the Eagles going all the way to the state championship.)*
26. *God desires that we praise Him for our victories and defeats. It does not matter if we win or lose. We should bless and praise His name always.*
27. *God will allow circumstances to unfold to test our allegiance and trust in Him. Will we still praise Him in the face of a bad report? Some of the reports may later prove to be false or inaccurate!*
28. *God will do miracles in our midst—things we cannot do for ourselves—when we trust and honor Him. In due season, He will give us the desires of our hearts.*
29. *God is so generous; He will give us "double for our trouble" (like Job) once we come through the fiery trial.*
30. *We should never give up because with God all things are possible—even if it is the fourth quarter of our lives and all looks lost! He can shift the wind in our favor!*

Slaying the Giant of Fear

Fear of lack and fear of the future were the first giants I had to face. The Lord wanted to show up and show out for me in ways I had not let Him before. He wanted me out of safe harbor, out of the boat, and out in the deep with Him. That is a scary place to be.

The first order of business was to take away my purse. I could not rely on money any longer in any way. The Lord gave me a dream in which I was going into battle, and, at the very last minute, I looked at my large handbag and tossed it aside.

He started by directing me to empty my bank accounts. In short order, I gave away $50,000 to a ministry engaged in a large expansion project and $40,000 to another trying to stay afloat. I whittled away the rest on living expenses and making offerings every Sunday morning and Thursday night at New Destiny. I decided never to leave church without first offering the Lord something, even though I had no income.

In time, with not even a dime left to my name, I would learn to rely on Him to supply my every need. To my utter shame and surprise, learning how to rely solely on the Lord, turned out to be one of the most terrifying experiences of my entire life.

During those first few weeks after my resignation, all I could do was lay prostrate on my bedroom floor before the Lord. Like a leaf in the wind, my whole body shook from fear. I had *never* experienced that before.

In my mind, not only was I going down, but I was taking my whole family with me. Financially, I supported my mom and dad, my sister and her husband, their two grandchildren and son, Ryan, and Suzanne. I was responsible for all the mortgages.

I was amazed (and ashamed) at my lack of faith! I had always considered myself a woman of strong faith, but there I was, on the floor trembling in terror. Why hadn't Denny's given me a severance? Had it, life would have been so much easier, or so I thought at the time.

Every single time I found myself on the floor shaking, the Lord met me there. He was so gentle, sweet, and patient.

"What are you afraid of?" He asked one day.

"I don't know, Ishi. I don't know." He and I had been through so much together. What was I afraid of?

"I'm here. I am not going to leave you. You have nothing to fear," He promised. I felt myself relax a little.

The Lord continued: "He who dwells in the secret place of the Most High...say it, go ahead, say it ...." I started repeating Psalm 91 after Him, verse by verse. And with each verse, I felt tension leave my body. I had never memorized that Psalm before, and yet I was recounting it word for word! I could hear God's voice softly speaking each verse before me! By the end of the Psalm, I was completely tranquil. We went on to talk about other things.

The next day, it was as though I had forgotten everything we discussed the day before, as if the Psalm 91 recitation never happened. I found myself back on the floor shaking. And so, it went.

Each time, the Lord would join me on the floor. He would quiet my racing heart. After I was calm, we would talk about other things and I would get up and go live more life. I would be okay until my American Express bill or Fidelity statement came in the mail. I could not open them. My stomach would drop at the sight of the envelopes, and I would be right back on the floor.

In time, I came to love that space on the floor by my bed. I loved it more than sitting quietly by the still lakes that dotted our housing complex. It became my favorite place in the whole world. Lying prostrate there, the Lord would soothe me with His truth and love.

I confess I had a tough time, at first, being still and allowing God to do what He desired to do in my life and in Ephraim's ministry. I experienced several false starts with the ministry because I felt I should be doing *something*. In addition to the water wells, we also had a dream of repairing Gondar's Angerab Dam. It provided the 260,000 residents of Gondar and the surrounding villages with 83 percent of their water.

It was an extensive project. Due to leakage and high erosion from surrounding hills, the dam had a projected life of only another four to seven years. Perhaps, I could raise funds for that since we did not seem to have a problem with well funding.

I spent an entire day writing an introductory proposal to the foundation of a major Fortune 500 company, seeking a grant. The foundation had a superb history of helping developing nations with large water projects. My proposal was fact-filled from all my research on Gondar's dam issue. I had managed to secure two separate engineers' reports on my last visit to Ethiopia. The data bolstered my argument. I thought I made an eloquent case for support.

At the very end of the day, God moved my hand across the keyboard, and, just like that, the proposal was gone—completely erased! How could I have not saved a single version? I was furious with myself until I heard the Lord whisper, "Be still."

In another instance, I wrote a newsletter promoting our water-well ministry to family, friends, neighbors, and business acquaintances. I sent the promotional piece to practically everyone for whom I had a mailing address. I wanted to let them know what I was doing and to drum up support for the wells. It was such a worthy cause. I raised $3,500.

It was my first and last ministry newsletter for the next six years. The Lord let me send it, and then He asked me not to do it again. He would provide everything I needed. I did not have to chase mammon. I was not in Egypt anymore! "Chase Me, and I will give you what you need!"

The Holy Spirit taught me some powerful lessons about "letting go and letting God" during that time. The Lord wanted me to rest in Him, to be still, and let Him work out all my problems, big and small. He wanted me to allow Him to create His own opportunities for the ministry. Only He knew where He was taking us. He invited me to come alongside Him and participate. It was not to be the other way around, which is what I was used to doing all my life.

It took me a while to realize He was calling me to have a sweet adventure with Him. He was the driver. I could come along for the ride. As we went, He would give me specific things to do. In all matters, I was to rest in Him. He was not calling me to wring my hands with worry, but instead to be constantly awed by His manifold wisdom as I watched Him be God.

July 6, 2008

"Be Still!"

God spoke so clearly to me this morning during my time alone with Him. He used several unrelated passages of Scripture to tell me what He has been telling me for more than a year now: "BE STILL AND KNOW THAT I AM GOD! Stand still and watch Me deliver you from every threat to your life. I will deliver you into a broad place."

Today, He asked me to consider two persons He had placed before me—my older sister Nanette and psalmist Dewayne Woods. Both suffered from terminal illnesses.

Nanette had been diagnosed with chronic lymphatic leukemia and Dewayne had been diagnosed with AIDS. Both struggled beyond all imaginings. Both thought they were not going to make it. Both stared death in the face. No doctor on earth could help them. Then, after years of suffering, God did what no one else could do. He healed them. Every aspect of their testimonies brought Him great glory.

Shortly after I left Denny's, Nanette called me.

"Are you near any water?"

"Yes, I have a lake right outside my door. I looked out the sliding glass doors of my family room. "It can't be more than 10 feet away." She was silent for a moment.

"You know how much I love being near water. I think I need to come visit you. I need to make peace with God." That was her way of saying she was losing her fight with cancer, that God would be taking her home soon.

"Come, come!" I encouraged her. "It's very peaceful here. How soon can you get here?" We set a date.

At this point, my personal accounts were dwindling fast, but I made a mental note to purchase a chaise lounge for her. She could put her feet up, stare at the water, and talk to God all day long. "Suzanne and I will take care of you," I promised. We rang off.

She called me a week later, sobbing. She could barely speak. My brother-in-law had gambled away the money she was going to use to purchase her plane ticket. He lost every dime at the racetrack. The trip was off. She could not come.

Suddenly, I remembered on my very last trip home from Denny's, I received a free plane ticket from Delta Airlines. They had overbooked the flight. I overheard a desperate bride-to-be screaming at the agent.

"No, no ... you don't understand. My wedding rehearsal dinner is in a few hours! I must get on *that* plane!" For the first time in my life, I was not in a hurry. I gave the woman my seat and Delta gave me the voucher.

"Wait a minute, Nanette!" I interrupted her crying. "Let's get Delta on the line." I made a three-way call. A Delta representative came on the line right away. I asked if my voucher was transferable. She confirmed it was. She asked me what I would like to do. We made Nanette's flight arrangements to Orlando. It did not take 10 minutes. When we all hung up, I knew God had arranged everything. He wanted her in Orlando as badly as she wanted to come.

The evening before she came, I still had not purchased a chaise lounge. I had weeks to do it and now I was down to the last day. For some reason, I kept forgetting. I would remember long after I passed Lowe's, where I had planned to buy it. Now, I was too tired. Maybe I could get one on the way to the airport. I grabbed a quick bite to eat and then decided to go for my evening stroll with the Lord.

Not more than five houses from our house, I spotted a cream-colored chaise lounge sitting by the curb of my neighbor's house. It had been put out for garbage pick-up! It looked barely used!

Instantly, I knew it was for Nanette. But just to make sure, I walked around to the side of my neighbor's home to catch a view of the backyard from the golf course. Two brand new loungers, replete with a table and four matching chairs, were placed around the screened pool. I scurried back around to the front, grabbed the lounger, ran back home and placed it in our backyard beside the lake. I marveled at God's provision ... and tenderness.

When Suzanne and I met Nanette at the airport the next morning, I could hardly believe my eyes. She was a wisp of a person. She had lost so much weight. Her soft hair, cropped very closely to her head, was completely gray. She walked slowly with a cane. However, she was in good spirits.

"You've got to come to church with us tomorrow. You will love it. Every Sunday, it's like going to Disney World to me." Although she told us not to plan anything around her, she agreed to come. Not only did she join us Sunday morning, she went back with us that evening to hear a man named Dewayne Woods in concert.

Dewayne opened the concert with an incredible testimony of how God cured Him of AIDS. Years ago, he tested positive for the virus. He took all kinds of medications. Then, one day, he challenged the Lord.

"You know I travel the country singing about how You are a healer. Why don't you heal me?" With that, he stopped taking all his medications. His health plummeted. He did not care. He decided to worship God all the more. On his deathbed, he made up new praise songs. Then something happened. He started to get better.

On his next routine visit to the AIDS clinic, they took a blood sample. For some reason, it took an unusually long time for the nurse to come back to him. He waited. The doctor was called into a room. Then, others joined him behind closed doors. Finally, Dewayne was called in.

The doctor apologized. Somehow his blood sample had become mixed up with someone else's. They could not figure out how it happened. They needed to take another sample because the sample they had for him did not have the AIDS virus. They pulled another sample and got the same result.

Eventually, Dewayne's case was taken before a national board that certified he had AIDS for many years and now he was free of the disease!

Dewayne's testimony energized my sister's faith. That night, without telling a soul, she prayed a simple 11-word prayer: "I know You can heal me. Why don't You heal me?" She went to sleep in pain. She woke up pain-free—a first since being diagnosed with the disease eight years earlier! She told no one.

The next night, she went to bed without pain and woke up again without pain. That was it! I could overhear her on the telephone from my bedroom, which was adjacent to hers. That morning, she called her doctor's office in Detroit to make an appointment. Next, she told Suzanne and me about her two pain-free nights and day. Interestingly, her doctor told her the day before she left for Orlando that her white blood cell count had reached a new high. She would have to undergo more chemotherapy when she returned.

On May 31, 2007, Suzanne and I were headed out the door to go to Thursday night Bible study when the house phone rang. I grabbed it. I saw Nanette's number.

"Hey! Let me call you back. Suzanne and I are late for Bible—"

"No, no ... I just wanted you to know I got my results back today. There is no trace of cancer! Everything is normal!"

I could not stop screaming! My sister came to Orlando looking for water. She found Christ, the Living Water, ready to answer her prayer!

God told me that in the same way Dewayne and Nanette could do nothing to save themselves I could do nothing to save myself, to change my situation.

"You can't fix it," He warned me. "But at the right moment, I will. And it will bring Me great glory." In the meantime, I was to simply trust Him. There was nothing to fear.

Whenever I was tempted to fear, I deliberately recalled Nanette and Dewayne's "impossible" situations. An inexplicable peace always came to my spirit. Then, I could rest—heart and mind, trouble-free. My watch-phrase became, "In Him, I must rest."

Slaying the Giant of Debt

During my last year at Denny's, God put me through a 12-week Crown Financial Course. It screwed my head on straight, once and for all, regarding the management of His finances. Even today, I still refer to my Crown course book. Everything Crown teaches is based on sound Biblical principles.

After taking that course, becoming debt-free and staying debt-free became my all-consuming desire. God allowed me to pay down some of my debt while I was still at Denny's, but not all of it. I was roughly $750,000 in debt—the sum of two mortgages—when I left.

When I resigned the Denny's account and dissolved IBS, my personal expenses were $15,000 a month—$5,000 for each of the three households. I paid the two mortgages and our rent until I could not anymore. It took 17 months to completely exhaust all my accounts. That included the $90,000 the Lord instructed me to give away to two ministries at the onset.

Three months before I became completely penniless, God gave me a heartening dream in which I had to face three enormous giants. But rather than being hostile, the giants were helpful to my family and me. Whenever I grew anxious about the future, I pondered the dream. It worked to ease my mind and to help me remember God was in control. Somehow, some way, He would make these giants serve His purposes for my life. My job was to trust Him.

July 7, 2008

A Dream: Helped by Three Huge Giants

In my second dream of the night, I found myself perched with Arlene and my mother in a tight, high place. I cannot recall all the activity that took place up there, but I remember my sister clipping a long, dangling earring to my cheek rather than to my ear. She did this because we did not have enough room to maneuver. We all laughed when she clipped the earring to my cheek.

Suddenly, three huge giants appeared. They were dressed like ancient warriors. One reached out his hand to help me. I held his big hand as he walked me down a steep incline to safety.

The three giants stood by, observing me as I began to scoop up and discard handfuls of ashes off the lining of a mink coat! The lining of the coat was light aqua. At one point, I separated the lining from the coat. I found a damp towel and began wiping it clean until I had removed all the ashes. The dream ended.

Escorted to a Safe and Prosperous Place

In the dream, God acknowledged my family and I are in a very tight spot. We do not have a lot of room. That is, we do not have a lot of money to do much with these days. But we remain in good spirits. At a time set and appointed by Him, my help will appear out of nowhere. God will use those things that appear to be huge threats to my life—things so much bigger than I—to help me.

Like Cinderella, God will raise me up from the cinders of my old life. Once I get rid of the ashes and residue of my past, the Lord will lead me to a place of prosperity, symbolized by the mink coat.

The aqua lining of the mink coat represents Yeshua. Aqua means water, and He is the Living Water. As the lining of a coat is hidden from plain view, God's astounding plan and provision for me will be concealed from people. He is the one guiding me to a safe, prosperous place.

The estate I had purchased for my parents in Bartlett, Tennessee went into foreclosure first. Wells Fargo held the mortgage to that home.

Despite having two other mortgages with Wells Fargo in the recent past—both successfully paid off—the bank dealt with me like a deadbeat criminal. I was astounded by the contrast in treatment.

Bank representatives called every few days to harass me about payment. I did not understand this because I explained my situation to them in writing and recounted it many times over the phone. Finally, I realized it was a tactic of the enemy to discourage me, to provoke worry and perhaps cause me to act rashly. When I realized what was happening, I made a deliberate choice not to fret, and I stopped taking their phone calls.

As God would have it, my parents, who lived in the house, moved back to Detroit to live with Earl, long before the bank took it back. They never knew the trouble I was in. They simply had grown homesick for Detroit, packed up everything one day and left. They missed their friends and their church back home.

Arlene and her family, who also lived in the house, eventually left too. They remained in Bartlett where they rented a beautiful house, fewer than two miles from the original house. My brother-in-law landed a job with a transportation company that helped cover the rent. This allowed their grandsons to stay in the same school district.

No longer looking to me as their source, my mother, father and sister's relationship with Christ blossomed. Their faith in Him strengthened into something I had never seen before. It was a thrill to see them walk daily in God's miracles as I was doing!

Since I had $100,000 worth of equity in the house, the bank sold it at a great price. Wells Fargo lost nothing in the transaction, and the family that bought it shortly after it went into foreclosure got a great deal. I suffered no tax consequences. Everyone was happy, including me. When the bank took the house back, a weight was lifted off me and replaced with inexplicable joy. Most people would weep at such a loss. I felt liberated!

The foreclosure on Ryan's condo in Chicago did not commence until the one on the Bartlett house was almost complete. This made life very manageable. Sovereign Bank held the mortgage to the condo. My experience with Sovereign Bank was vastly different from my experience with Wells Fargo.

The people at Sovereign were nice. There was no harassment. They gave me time to try to sell the property since I had nearly $250,000 of equity in it.

Many buyers came, fell in love with the place and never returned. One woman backed out of our contract a week before the closing, forfeiting all her earnest money. It finally became clear to me God was not going to let us sell the condo. That would have put too much cash in my hands. I was not supposed to have a purse during this season. Money in the bank would defeat His purposes for my life.

Because of several failed attempts to sell the condo, it took almost 18 months for the bank to take the property. This, too, turned out to be a strategic part of God's plan.

Our real estate agent was in the middle of a nasty divorce. He had to vacate his home quickly. With nowhere else to live, he asked to stay in the condo while he tried to sell it or until the bank took it over. Ryan had gone to stay with my sister in Bartlett, taking only a few items. The agent offered to pay rent, cover the utilities, and keep the fully furnished space clean and presentable for prospective buyers. After a little nudging from God, I accepted his offer.

As it turned out, he stayed a full year, and he kept his word! He gave me $1,000 a month, which I sowed into Ephraim's nascent ministry. Also, Sovereign Bank gave me $1,000 when I turned over the keys to its agent. I used this money to keep the ministry afloat.

Truly, it was an instance of God using a giant to bless me as I journeyed to a new place of freedom in Him. In the end, we used the earnest money from the failed contract to move Ryan and her things to Orlando. Her household items furnished our empty townhouse—the one Suzanne and I moved into after five months of homelessness. Ryan joined us in Ephraim's budding ministry. By this time, we were serving meals to Orlando's homeless every Friday and offering other humanitarian aid.

When I could no longer pay the mortgages on my homes, many family members and friends advised, "File for bankruptcy to protect yourself!" But God said, "Be still! I am your Protector!" I could wallpaper a house with the solicitations I received from law firms offering their assistance. I discarded every mailing and ignored every phone call. I would not budge.

Mike was quite angry with me because Ryan lost her condo. "Your mother could get a job tomorrow making $250,000 *anywhere*!" he screamed. I refused all calls from headhunters because God kept saying, "Don't chase money! Chase Me! I'll provide!"

I also knew it was not God's will that I continue to finance Ryan's extravagant lifestyle. It handicapped her in ways I could not see, and it undermined her reliance on Him. Just as He was my Provider and Protector, He was hers. He wanted a chance to prove it.

Changing Our Cars

Just as the Lord pulled us out of our luxury homes, He changed out our luxury cars. In dreams, a car often represents a person's Kingdom assignment—his or her God-ordained call or purpose during a specific segment of life. Clearly, God was not calling us to a life of luxury. He was extricating us from it.

I was happy when the lease on my Lexus SC 430 convertible came to an end, which was four months after I left Denny's. I found myself trying to hide it from potential ministry donors. I often parked it out of sight when I drove to meetings.

I will never forget one vendor's reaction to my car. He was doing a lot of print work for Ephraim. He was impressed with our water work in

Ethiopia and talked about giving us a discount. We finished, and he walked me outside.

He stopped mid-sentence. "Is that your car?" I nodded. A look of disdain came over his face. I understood why. That car made me look like a high-flying con woman on a mission to fleece unsuspecting donors. He never spoke of the discount again, and I was too embarrassed to ask him about it.

The car was a burden in other ways as well. Two years into the lease, I had to purchase four brand new tires—run-flats, the type of tires required on my Lexus wore out quickly. I barely drove the car because I flew so much. Yet, within 24 months of leasing the car, I had to shell out $2,000 to replace the tires. There were other subtler costs as well. As one Memphis parking attendant reminded me one day, "Ma'am, you cannot drive a car like that and not leave a big tip."

When I returned my Lexus convertible, the leasing company wanted an additional $1,800 for the car to cover repairs for minor scrapes on the side panel and a small pock mark on the windshield. I really did not have it to give. After hanging up the phone, I ran to my bedroom, fell on my knees, and asked God for help. He told me to call my insurance company. He would take care of the rest.

State Farm asked to see the car. I directed the agent to the dealership. He made an appointment that week to inspect the vehicle. By the time he arrived, the car had been sold!

I called the leasing company to protest. The woman apologized profusely for the mishap. She promised to call me back after speaking to a supervisor. When she did, I learned I no longer owed anything. I was completely free of the car. The four-figure monthly car payment was a thing of the past.

Just before leaving Denny's, I purchased a new Mazda 3 with my last paycheck. I paid cash. I bought the car in Chicago and allowed Ryan's friend, Joseph, to drive it for three months. Four weeks before the lease expired on my Lexus convertible, I flew to Chicago to retrieve it. I drove the Mazda for only seven months before God asked me to gift it to a missionary friend, Melody Copenny. I could hardly believe His request.

Melody had been praying for a car for more than a year. She felt strongly God did not want her to go into debt to purchase it. So, she prayed, believing, somehow, He would work it out.

After a year of praying, she had saved less than $1,600 toward a car. Her ministry coworkers teased her, "How long are you going to wait? You need to go on down to the bank like the rest of us and get a car loan." She ignored their taunts and advice. I knew God could do it. For weeks, I joined her in that prayer.

Then, one day, during one of our weekly prayer sessions, I prophesied the Lord would give her a car. I was confident of it. I just did not know He planned to give her mine! Even that modest Mazda 3 was too much luxury for what God had in mind for me.

At first, I kept trying to avoid the subject. But the Lord persisted. Finally, I told Him, "Okay, okay ... listen. This is how we can do it. After You give me a car, I will give her mine." I said it twice and spoke slowly so there would be no misunderstanding.

Shortly after that conversation, the Lord woke me up in the middle of the night with a specific command: "Go get the title from the box in your office and put it in your nightstand drawer." I did as He instructed. I climbed back in bed. "You will give the title to Melody. She needs the car. You don't."

Really? I had owned a car since I was a freshman in college. I could not imagine suddenly not needing a set of wheels. The Lord put me back to sleep. In the predawn hours, He gave me a dream to show me exactly how the car would transfer from me to Melody. He was going to throw a party, and I would present the title to Melody there. He even gave me the date of His party!

The next day, I received a call. I was asked to speak at an in-home, weekend retreat. The event was sponsored by the Impact Movement, a Campus Crusade for Christ ministry that serves minority college students. The ministry could not afford to underwrite an off-site event for its participants, so the leaders decided to sponsor a sleepover at the home of a staff member.

More than 15 young missionary women were expected to attend. The food would be provided by the staff and attendees. All kinds of games and activities had been planned. It would be a time of sharing and bonding in Christ. The date of the sleepover was the exact date the Lord had given me in the dream!

Less than two weeks later, it all happened just as He said it would. At the retreat, God shut everybody's mouth—including those who had teased Melody—when I handed her the title and the keys to my car. She drove me home the next morning, and we met the following Monday to notarize the title. Then, she drove me home one last time. I watched as she disappeared down the street with my Mazda.

While kneeling by my bed in prayer later that afternoon, I felt someone whisk past me, put something on my nightstand, and leave. After my prayer, I found a set of car keys. They were Suzanne's spare set.

"No longer say, 'That's Suzanne's car,'" she later instructed. "My car is your car. It belongs to both of us now." She was true to her word. I drove Suzanne's car more than she did for nearly a year. It was our sole vehicle for ministry and personal use until God gave us another.

God eventually gave the ministry a 1998 Ford Windstar passenger van with nearly 100,000 miles on it. It was so beat up and dirty, I could hardly stand to sit in it. Large parts of the dashboard were falling off and ceiling liner was falling down. The van also had a stale odor inside that I could not get out. I still remember how we got it.

One night before going to bed, Ryan put an ad on Craigslist, requesting a free van for our ministry. The posting was against their guidelines, but we did not know it at the time. The next morning before she got up, we received a call from the owner of Izzy Automotive in Kissimmee, Florida. He told us to come get the title and the van. Izzy informed us that he had never looked at Craigslist before; he just happened to be curious that morning. Right after his call, we received notice that our ad had been removed because it violated Craigslist's policy guidelines.

In time, I came to adore that van! It had several quirks that made it ideal for our ministry. All the seats were missing except the two in front. That made it more like a cargo van than a passenger van, which was exactly what we needed. On the passenger side, there was an 18-inch wide space that ran from the side door to the back. It allowed us to comfortably carry our long serving tables. The van was so worn and dogged that we did not mind all the spills that came with hauling hundreds of pounds of food and drinks from the food bank every week. Wear and tear were always a concern with the Lexus.

That beat-up, raggedy van was a hard-working "hoopty." We hauled food, furniture, people, and all manner of things in it nearly every day. My Lexus convertible, which Suzanne always referred to as "the selfish car," did not have a backseat. No one ever rode in it except me.

The van was free. The Lexus, at the end of my four-year lease period, costs $63,000. The van served hundreds weekly. The Lexus served one. Do the math. Which one do you think pleased God more?

We drove that Windstar van for more than a year before the transmission blew. I had it towed to Kissimmee, and I transferred the title back to Izzy. No one knew it, but I cried when it was time to let it go. I could hardly believe how emotionally attached I had become to it and how many lessons God had taught me through it! I patted the Windstar's hood just before leaving it in the parking lot, "Like my grandma used to say ... 'You done good, Girl! You done *real* good!'" It had served the Kingdom well.

God graduated us to a much better looking 1998 Ford Windstar with far less mileage. It had been an old mail delivery van. Jeri purchased it for the ministry from the insurance payout she received after her daughter, Jeanette, totaled her car. Miraculously, Jeanette crawled out of the wreckage without a single scratch.

Rather than use the entire check to purchase a replacement car for herself, Jeri decided to split the payout with me. Of course, I would not hear of it. So, she went through Ryan.

She used half of the money to purchase the van for the ministry and the other half to replace her car. As only God could do, after purchasing the ministry van, she found the exact same car that had been totaled—same model, same year, same color, same mileage—for exactly half of the insurance payout. It was as if God split one egg and brought forth two.

That van also served us well, but, after a year, its transmission went too. I will always believe it happened because I asked God to give us a van with air conditioning. That van only had a heater. It was murder driving in the hot Florida sun without cool air. The open windows and the miniature fan I had clipped to my sun visor were my only relief. In the summer, when I stopped at traffic lights, sweat poured from my face. Right after my prayer, the transmission failed. I junked our second van in as many years, for $400.

Five months later, in August 2011, a generous donor in Davie, Florida gave the ministry a lightly used 2008 Dodge Grand Caravan. When I slipped into the driver's seat, I could not stop shaking my head in wonder at God's provision. The dashboard and ceiling looked brand new. The previous owner used the van for work; it was her company car. Every three years, her company gave her a new vehicle as well as the option to purchase her old one.

She told me God woke her up one night and told her to purchase the van for our ministry.

"But Lord, that's a lot of money!" she protested.

"You just spent $10,000 on your daughter's wedding," He reminded her.

The next day, she called to tell me she had just ordered a new car and as soon as it came in, I could come get her old one. It took five months, during which I was never without transportation. God moved the hearts of volunteers to let me drive their cars. Some were expensive, luxury vehicles with features I had never before seen in a car.

Within six months of arriving in Orlando, Ryan sold her luxury SUV to help with family and ministry expenses. We joked that the sale of her SUV had to be the easiest automobile sale ever.

A man named Mr. Fox drove to Orlando from Jupiter, Florida with his girlfriend. The car was for her. He purchased Ryan's SUV for top dollar, sight unseen, even after discovering a large dent in the front fender. Ryan had not bothered to tell him about the dent over the telephone. He did not care. He still thought it was a great deal. Ryan was carless for two years, but God got her everywhere she needed to go.

No More Shackles!

Many family members, friends, and colleagues were convinced I had suffered a nervous breakdown when I left Corporate America. I heard their whispers: "How could she have walked away from all that money? What is she going to do now? She should have never left that job before she had another one! She'll go back!"

No one realized I was answering that bell! The Creator of the Universe was calling me to join Him in a great cosmic adventure. What was money compared to that? What was *anything* compared to that? In the process, He removed my shackles. I was liberated and loving it! I was completely and totally debt-free—a lifelong dream realized, albeit attained in a way I had not imagined.

The Lord was taking me someplace I had never been. The ride was enlivening and exhilarating! At the same time, I was becoming someone new, someone better. He was detaching me from the world. It required my total trust in Him. He assured me I would not be disappointed.

To most people, I looked as if I was going out of the world backwards. But I knew differently. God was accomplishing something much bigger than the human eye could see. Daily, He performed miracles on my behalf, showing Himself mighty and an Ever-Present Help. I could hardly wait to get up each day just to see what wild and crazy thing He would do next!

I had put all my eggs in His basket. He was not about to let that basket fall. He had wooed me into the wilderness, and spoke tenderly to me, and He used my "Valley of Achor" ("Trouble") to open a new way of living. He gave me a vineyard of my own to tend for His glory.

Slaying the Giant of Homelessness

In early 2008, I informed my landlord of our dwindling financial resources. I explained that by September, I would no longer be able to pay the rent. With this knowledge, he put the house on the market. He had put up the property for sale before, but, when no one bought it, he pulled it off the market. When he put it back on the market a second time, I was convinced it still would not sell. I fully expected God to keep all buyers at bay since we had founded Ephraim's headquarters there, and we were using the house to accomplish such good work for the Kingdom. I was wrong.

One day, a young Muslim couple with a little boy came to see the house. The woman fell in love with the view of the lake and golf course. The family put a contract on the house and gave us six weeks to vacate.

I was confident the contract would fall through. How could God sell the house from underneath us? Besides, Suzanne and I were in the midst of sending a humanitarian container to Haiti. We needed the house to help the people of Haiti with their food crisis. Somehow, we knew God would work it out for all parties involved.

We concentrated on the container and left our precarious living situation to the Lord. We seized the opportunity to send not only food, but other items as well, including some of our own furniture. The entire house, including the garage, was filled with stacked boxes of donated, non-perishable canned goods and other staples. Many of the nonfood items were things salvaged from the streets in our complex.

We lived in a relatively wealthy neighborhood and were constantly amazed at the nice things people discarded. We made a habit of getting up very early to peruse the neighborhood on the days the garbage trucks came. Our neighbors' "trash" would become someone's "treasure" in Haiti. Up until that point, I had never gone through anyone's trash, so I was not aware of how wasteful Americans were. Many people discarded perfectly useful items, only to replace them with something new or different. Some people tossed brand new things.

We had no idea how we would ever afford to ship the container to Haiti. We were too broke. But we both felt God's Spirit leading us to collect items for such a venture. Sure enough, when we had collected enough food and items to fill a 20-foot container, an anonymous donor stepped forward and gave us $4,000 to ship it to Haiti! Later, another donor paid for both of our airfares to travel to Haiti to check on the container! The day we left, we learned we would have one week upon our return to vacate our home. Still, I was hopeful.

In Haiti, our days were so filled with ministry that we did not have time to think about our own problems. In one meeting at a Christian school, I got so caught up in the Lord's compassion for His people, I promised to send money back to purchase 12 bicycles for the 12 schoolteachers. They faced great difficulty getting to and from school every day. They walked miles each way in the hot sun.

The director assured me he could purchase the 12 bikes in Haiti for as little as $100 each. I promised they would all have their bikes within a year. I planned to purchase a bike a month until the year was done. We pulled numbers to determine the order. They rejoiced and praised God as though it had already been done. I walked out of the meeting thinking *What just happened? Where am I going to get $1,200?*

While we were in Haiti, Suzanne led several souls to Christ, including her brother, who died a week after we returned from the trip. She wept with gratitude to the Lord for sending her home to Haiti to minister, especially to her brother. The day we left Florida for Haiti, he left Port-au-Prince to travel to Cap Haitian, where we would be staying.

It took him two days to get there by bus and on foot. He had no idea she was coming. He simply had not been feeling well and felt he should get out of the city and to the countryside for rest. The two were so glad to see each other. It had been years since their paths last crossed. They spent the afternoon together. It was during this time, Suzanne led him to Christ. Later, I prayed for his healing. He seemed to improve.

I did not agonize over personal circumstances while in Haiti until the very last day. As I thought about what we were facing upon our return, I felt a slow panic start to set in. In seven days, we would be homeless. We had a house still filled with furniture—nice things, expensive things—and nowhere to put them. I managed to pay our last month's rent just before we left. The security deposit we paid three years earlier covered that last expense. But now what? God was ready with not one, but two dreams, to quell my mounting fears.

September 11, 2008

Hopeful Dreams in Haiti

In Haiti, I had a BIG change of heart regarding our home on Royal Saint George Drive. I felt we needed to leave. If I were in my landlord's shoes, I would not have done anything differently than what he had done. If my tenants could not pay the rent, I would put the house up for sale; and if I got a buyer, especially in this difficult market, I would take it. The sale of the house would pull his family completely out of debt. How could I not want that for them?

We needed to move, but we had no place to go, and we had no money. A slow dread started to come over me. God knew. He gave me two dreams—one, two days before we left Haiti, and the other on our last day there. Both were constructive and reassuring.

First Dream: Walking Up High and Gliding in Air

In the first dream, I found myself walking high above the pedestrians on the street. That was a good thing because it meant I was walking in a high place in the Lord—above the crowd. In the dream, I wore a brown skirt, white blouse, and backpack. The backpack was a clear sign of homelessness. Most homeless men and women carry everything they own in backpacks on their backs.

As I walked, I came to a narrow wooden plank. While the plank was not terribly long, it had no sides. It would be dangerous to cross. I knew I was in trouble the moment I stepped on the plank. I lost my balance and started to fall. I reached out to try to break my fall, but that was not necessary.

The backpack suddenly became a jetpack! It allowed me to glide far above the pedestrians below! What a thrill! I glided smoothly past the narrow plank and on to my destination.

Clearly, God was showing me I had nothing to fear. Yes, I was about to enter a tricky place in my journey—and it would look scary to me—but things were not as they seemed. The Lord would uphold me as I journeyed. He was letting me know as Suzanne and I prepared to transition from our home to a place only He knew of, we would be okay. He would keep us safe. I would get through that tricky spot easily and continue to my destined end.

Second Dream: Guided to a Safe Spot

In the second dream, I was driving along in a little jalopy. Someone was sitting in the passenger seat next to me. I do not know who it was. I felt it was Ryan or Suzanne. Looking out at the water to my left, I took a curb too fast and lost control of the car. The car swerved into a large opening of a building. It was dark inside, like a tunnel. I could not see a thing.

I took my hands off the steering wheel, covered my face with crisscrossed arms and began to scream. As we prepared to crash, I apologized to my passenger: "I'm so sorry! I'm so sorry!" I just knew we were going to crash and die. I also felt somehow, we would end up drowning in a body of water.

I screamed and waited ... and waited ... and waited. Finally, the car came out of the other end of the building and coasted perfectly into a parking spot, overlooking the water. The dream ended.

The moment I woke up from this dream, I had to smile. God was telling me not to worry. While it looked like my life was about to crash—and I was taking Ryan and/or Suzanne with me—that was not the case. He was in control of the car. Yes, I would go through a brief dark tunnel of sorts, and I would not know where I was going, but we were protected. He would take us to a safe spot and park us there.

I mulled over both dreams on the plane ride home. They encouraged me greatly. Suzanne and I soon landed in Ft. Lauderdale. It would take us 3½ hours to drive to Orlando. I suggested we pray the entire way. We took turns praying aloud.

I prayed first, laying out our case before the Lord. Then, Suzanne prayed. That is all it took. The Lord's answer unfolded in my mind. We had already determined, like Ruth and Naomi, we would not split up. Besides, we had only one car.

Suzanne and I knew we needed to live someplace where we could continue to serve the homeless. We were confident God did not want us to give up our ministry. Over time, it had become our whole "reason for being." It delightfully consumed our days. God had performed so many miracles to keep it going, and it seemed to be growing weekly.

After Suzanne completed her turn at prayer, the thought came: *Call George and Susan Mamboleo.* Susan and George, a Kenyan missionary couple who worked for Orlando-based Campus Crusade for Christ, were the perfect answer. *Why hadn't I thought of them before?*

It never occurred to either of us, before that prayer time, to ask the Mamboleos if we could stay with them. They were the perfect answer. Both husband and wife were extraordinary servants of the Lord, and they lived in a large four-bedroom, three-bathroom house. Their adult children had moved out.

Laura Acosta, the wife of my landlord and an intercessory prayer warrior, joined Susan Mamboleo and me at the Mamboleos' home for weekly prayer. The three of us had prayed together every Tuesday for more than a year. We had grown close during that time. Also, before I left Denny's, when I had an income, I was a big supporter of the couple's missionary work in Kenya and other parts of the world. Driving, I pulled out my cell phone and dialed the Mamboleo's home.

"Sure, you can stay with us," Susan said without a moment's hesitation. She did not even ask George. "I have a room for you, and I have one for Suzanne. You can sleep upstairs and use the guest bathroom up there. Suzanne can sleep downstairs and use the downstairs guest bathroom."

The Mamboleos had space for only one additional car. Had I kept my Mazda, there would not have been room for it. Susan and George welcomed us with open arms. In Kenya, they were accustomed to many people living under one roof as a big extended family. They had missed that when they came to America.

The next day, Susan came to our house to help us collect some of our clothes to take to her house. She told me about a storage company near her home that was running a fall special—the first month's storage was free. The second month, I would only pay half price. Also, the company had a large moving truck I could use at no cost, if I rented a storage space. I just had to pay for the gasoline.

On moving day, three women showed up at our door, including Laura, to help us move. I marveled at how God used our brains to get a near impossible task done. There was not much brawn between the five of us. The Lord worked through every snag we encountered. When we reached an impasse, we stopped and prayed. Then, BOOM! The answer came to one of us. "Oh, I know! I know what we can do!" one of us would shout excitedly to the others. God gave us all turns at being smart. Surely, He was in our midst.

The move was one of the hardest things I had ever done in my life. I hauled furniture twice my weight for hours. Except for our two bedroom sets and a few pots and pans that we put in storage, we gave everything away to four families.

One family lived right next door. They owned a big, beautiful house. Except for a gracious hutch in their foyer—a match to my sofa table and end tables—their living and dining rooms were completely empty. The first time I walked into their home, three years earlier, and saw the hutch, I suspected they would get my living room set one day. Perhaps, it would happen when we went off to Ethiopia.

We made countless trips back and forth between the two houses, hauling the contents of the living and dining rooms across the lawns. Nothing was boxed but our books.

The Mamboleos received my oak office furniture that wrapped around three walls. They took pictures, mirrors, wall hangings, bookcases, and a lot of other valuables. Two other friends took everything else—virtually everything in the kitchen, including the kitchen table and chairs, and everything in our guest bedroom. God had already shown me in a dream, the latter two pillaging through our house. So, at the end of the day, I used the truck to deliver the heavy furniture to them on the other side of town.

God was in *every* detail. When it was all over, I looked like I had been in a fight and lost. I was so sore, battered, and banged up. I had bruises and cuts everywhere. But God proved to be an amazing help! He turned a very, *very* difficult situation into a true wonder.

At the end of it all, I marveled at how He managed to pull it off with just five women. I felt like I was now knee-deep in some grand adventure with the Maker of the Universe. I could hardly wait to see what other problems would surface just to experience what He would do next.

Perhaps the most astounding part of the move was God more than paid for it all. I started the move without a cent in my pocket, but by the end of the move, I had been given more than $1,400. The moving truck and movers were free.

As if that was not enough, one of the movers, Melody Gardner, filled up the truck's gas tank before we returned it. She went into the gas station to buy a drink. When she returned, she matter-of-factly announced, "God just told me to give you everything in my purse." She dumped her purse's contents in her lap, counted $176, and handed it to me. By the end of the move, I had enough money to purchase all 12 bikes for the Haitian schoolteachers! No one had to wait. And, I had cash to spare.

The Mamboleos took us into their home and asked for nothing. We could not tell them how long we would stay, and they did not set a deadline. Only God knew the answer. We were a good match. While they could provide shelter, they had very little food. While we had lots of food because of our ministry, we did not have a home. So, we shared.

Intriguingly, it turned out my small room in the Mamboleo's house had just been painted deep red—all four walls and the ceiling. I instantly perceived it to be symbolic of Christ's blood covering over my life during my stay there. I filled the empty room with a wicker dresser, a twin bed and a lamp, all of which I had collected from our trash pickups.

Susan and George allowed us to use their home freely to serve the homeless just as we had been doing in our own home. Susan often helped us prepare the desserts. We never missed a Friday. None of our homeless guests ever knew we were homeless too.

We lived five miracle-filled months with the Mamboleos. God's provision came from some of the most unexpected sources and it was nonstop. Our first day in their home I asked God to bless them like the Ark of the Covenant blessed Obed-Edom's house during the time of King David. He heard my prayer. He poured blessings on them, and us, and on our respective ministries.

On the same day I read how Elijah's prayer provided the Zarephath widow with an endless supply of flour and oil, we were given seven 40-pound bags of regular flour, three 40-pound bags of whole wheat flour, and nine cases of cooking oil. Surely, God was making a point. We would always have more than enough, abundantly more than we could ever ask for or imagine.

Our cups and cupboards ran over. All our hearts burst with gratitude to God for the new living arrangement. All of us, except the devil. Surely, he had expected Suzanne and me to have given up by this time. But by God's grace, we persevered.

One day, driving home to the Mamboleos, I became aware of a large signboard that marked the name of their complex. I had missed it countless times before. It was called Bridge Waters. The moment I spotted the sign, I heard the Holy Spirit: "They're a bridge over troubled waters." I knew He was referring to the Mamboleos. I knew then Suzanne and I would not live long with them. A bridge helps one get to the other side. One does not live on a bridge. It is strictly for crossing over.

In late 2008, I found a letter in Ephraim's post office box from General Mills, the former parent-company of Burger King Corporation. It stated I had qualified for a pension on my 55th birthday that was about six weeks away. It was a complete and total surprise.

I stood in the middle of the post office and wailed, holding the envelope to my chest. I did not care who saw me. Payment would commence on January 1, 2009. The monthly pension of $1,274 ended our homelessness and marked the beginning of an extraordinary, new way of living.

Slaying the Giant of Self-Sufficiency

Suzanne and I had been staying with the Mamboleos only a few weeks when the enemy pulled out another gun and aimed it straight at my head. Surely, he had found the bullet that would finally stop me. I received a notice from the Internal Revenue Service, questioning my 2006 personal

Tax Return. The IRS asked for proof that I donated $190,000 to charity that year.

When we lost our home, I lost most of my personal papers. At the time, it did not appear to be a big deal. It seemed my old life did not matter anymore. It also did not help that I deliberately destroyed a lot of my documents after I dissolved my consulting firm in August 2007. I burned them in a ceremonial bonfire in the townhouse parking lot where we lived. I felt led by the Holy Spirit to do it.

The papers represented my old life. God had revealed to me in several dreams that out of the ashes of my old life, I would emerge a new, sleeker, better version of my former self. When He was done, I would be unrecognizable to those who knew me before. "Who is this coming up from the wilderness, leaning upon her Beloved?" (Song of Solomon 8:5).

In 2006, I employed the services of four separate accounting firms—two in Atlanta, one in Memphis, and one in Orlando. One firm worked for my consulting firm; one worked for my private foundation; one worked for my oil and gas company; and one oversaw my personal taxes. The firms worked together to produce their respective returns. Need I say my 2006 personal tax return was complicated? I am not sure I ever understood it.

The day I received the notice, I was scheduled to work for a local food bank at the Orlando Convention Center. I decided to bow out and work on my tax problem. I had to locate my 2006 tax return, but I had no idea where to start. I called Zack Fulmer at Ron Blue & Company. He was the one who had invited me to participate with the food bank. I told him my issue and that I was unable to volunteer.

"I have your tax return right here on my computer," he said. I was stunned. He pulled it up. Anything I wanted to know about it, he could tell me. It had completely slipped my mind that I worked with Ron Blue & Company during my last year at Denny's. We had been working on a plan for me to become debt-free when God took over. Zack had several years of my tax returns in his possession. I felt God in our midst. Zack emailed me the return.

Now, I needed the backup data. I was not sure if I had it. So much had been lost in the move (and bonfire). I did, however, keep my old checkbook registers. I could pinpoint checks written to charities from it.

Thus, began the long, arduous, frustrating process of calling charities to reproduce old receipts and ordering cancelled checks from the bank. Each check cost $10—a lot of money to someone who did not have any.

The devil did not make it easy. I had to order the same checks from the bank two and three times because my electronic orders kept mysteriously disappearing. Copies of checks to the bank's fax machine were never received. The fax machine almost always stopped working whenever I entered the bank. This was not my imagination. It happened so often that even the bank employees made note of the phenomenon. Eventually, we resorted to snail mail. Some of those requests made it, some did not. I repeated steps two, three, sometimes four times to get what I needed. Flummoxed, the bank started waiving all charges.

Before I could send the information to the IRS within the prescribed deadline, a decision was made by the Utah office that I owed the money! I was never given a chance to respond to the notice! I did not even realize what had happened until I asked to meet with someone locally, face to face. I had a suitcase full of data. It was too much to send out-of-state, too much to explain by letter.

The local arbitrator explained to me during our initial meeting that the buck stopped with him. This was my final opportunity to make my case. I had somehow lost the first one without even knowing it.

By that time, the IRS had delved way beyond my charitable donations. It wanted to examine my entire personal tax return and those of my other enterprises to determine to what extent they impacted my personal return. My problem had exploded into a full-blown audit.

By the grace of God, the arbitrator was a gracious, understanding man. He made many phone calls to Denny's and others on my behalf. He knew I was in way over my head, and he tried his best to help me.

In the end, after several visits, he made complete sense out of my returns. Everything was in order. However, I could only produce $160,000 in receipts or cancelled checks. I signed a document agreeing I owed the IRS $30,000 plus interest. The agent readily discerned there was no malfeasance on my part, so he cancelled all penalties.

Where would I get $30,000? My next option was to present the IRS with an Offer-in-Compromise (OIC) to prove I could not pay. An OIC can be a complicated document. One must prove he or she is unable to pay the whole debt but is willing to pay part of it over time. I could not make an offer for nearly a year because I had nothing to offer.

At one point, I did receive $12,500, half of a $25,000 returned deposit from our 2005 oil drilling project. But I had already promised to use $5,000 of it to buy Amharic-language Bibles for one of Rabbi Kokeb's Ethiopian mission trips. With God, a promise is a promise. It is a vow. I made the commitment long before the arbitrator concluded I owed the money. In fact, for the longest time, I was utterly convinced I owed the IRS nothing and could prove it.

Moreover, I knew God oversaw the timing. Everything had unfolded in the precise order He wanted it to. I was being tested. All of heaven was watching. Will she break her promise to buy Bibles in order to make a deal with the IRS and save herself?

When the time came to review my OIC, my decision to fund Bibles did not sit well with the U.S. Treasury Department. I was told it would weigh heavily in its decision to accept or reject my offer. I used the remaining $7,500 to pay that year's taxes. The amount included a steep penalty for cashing out what remained of my retirement fund—$40,000—and giving it to a local ministry the year before. I acted out of obedience to the Lord. If I had kept that money, I could have paid off the entire IRS debt! In fact,

Suzanne and I would have never been homeless had I kept the entire $90,000! Surely, God's ways are not our ways.

Finally, a friend stepped forward and gave me $5,000 to offer the IRS. I offered $5,000, to be paid within one year. I had to release at least 20% or $1,000 with my OIC proposal. I asked to be allowed to pay the remaining portion of $4,000 within one year. But my plan was to surrender it all within 90 days. One day, I would repay my friend.

I was hopeful that my OIC would be accepted. I used another friend's recent OIC settlement as a benchmark. She had just settled her case with the IRS months before. She owed a whopping $100,000, and the IRS settled with her for a repayment sum of $2,000, to be paid over two years! She hired an attorney for $5,000 to present her case. But God told me He was my Attorney. I was not to seek the help of another.

My proposal bounced between several IRS offices for nine months. Periodically, I would be notified that my offer was missing certain requested documentation—documents I knew I provided because I kept a copy of everything I sent. I resent it anyway. In the meantime, my debt grew to more than $34,000.

Finally, my OIC was assigned to an agent. He sent me a letter, asking *a lot* of questions. I answered them to the best of my ability. He sent an even larger packet, asking dozens of additional questions. I cried when I opened the packet. I was given a small window to respond because his office was in the middle of renovations and would be closed at points.

I produced a document the size of a mini-telephone book. I express mailed it within the timeframe given. I tracked the package several times until it arrived. Although it was delivered and signed for by an IRS representative, and I received a return-receipt verifying delivery, I was told the agency never received it. They claim I missed the deadline. All my protestations fell on deaf ears.

Since I missed the deadline, the agent filed a federal lien against me. The day after he filed the lien, the package mysteriously showed up on his desk. Although the agent had already pulled the trigger, he felt he owed me the courtesy of at least looking at the packet. By the end of the day, he felt his rejection of my offer was in order. The federal lien would remain. By that time, the debt had ballooned to more than $38,000!

When the dust settled, the IRS determined I owed $38,437.42. I would have to pay $400 a month from my $1,274 pension until the debt was paid in full. Interest would accrue as I paid down the debt. I estimated it would take me eight to ten years to pay off. After two years and four months of fighting, it had come to this? I could not stop crying. Then I came to my senses. I had been using the wrong weapons!

I cancelled the rest of my day. I drove home and grabbed my Bible, a notepad, and pen. I sat down and recorded 12 Scriptures from God's Word, in which He promised blessings and deliverance to those who helped the poor. My favorite was Psalm 41:1: *"Blessed is he who considers the poor; the Lord will deliver him in time of trouble."* Surely, I was in a time of trouble. As I meditated on these verses, I could feel worry fall off me. Peace permeated my entire being. Joy started to bubble up.

I wrote down the 12 verses and took them to God's throne room. He and I had a frank discussion over the promises. I recounted each one to Him: *"And, Lord, here You said …."* By the time I was done, my spirits were in the sky. My eyes were as big as saucers, looking to see what He would do next. I had no doubt something was going to happen!

I did not have to wait long. Within 48 hours of my prayer, a woman called me. She heard about my debt and the IRS ruling. She instructed me to meet her at Bank of America that Saturday morning at 9 o'clock. Her only request was that I never reveal her identity. I agreed. That morning, she transferred $38,437.42 to my account. I sent a certified check to the IRS the same day.

The following Monday, I called the agent to tell him to be on the lookout for the check. He was astonished. He had not been expecting that phone call. "You must have really been praying," he responded in complete wonderment.

"Yes!" I replied. "I can hardly believe it myself. No one is more amazed than I." Later, I learned the money the woman gave me was more than half of her life savings!

The IRS debacle turned out to be one of the biggest blessings of my life. Through it, I learned I could trust the Lord to the bitter, utter end of every circumstance—no matter how insurmountable it seemed. I did not have to jump through hoops, fret or worry, or rely on my limited knowledge and restricted resources, nor did I need to ask people to save me from my circumstances. God stands ready to hear and answer my cry. He will marshal *whomever* and *whatever* to do His bidding on my behalf. I can rest in Him. The battle is His. And He *always* wins His battles.

Chapter 33
Grasping the Big Picture!

According to Revelation 12:6, 14, the number of days the woman in Revelation 12 would dwell in the wilderness would be 1,260 or 3½ years. One day, the Lord instructed me to calculate the number of days between two significant dates in my life—July 5, 2005 and December 16, 2008. Since Susan and I fled "Egypt" on July 4, 2005, July 5 represented our first full day in the "wilderness."

December 16, 2008 represented my 55th birthday. On that day, I became eligible for a pension from General Mills. That pension opened the way for us to secure a place of our own and to build whole, new lives in Christ. Thus, December 16, 2008 marked the end of our wilderness experience.

Words cannot express the shock I experienced when I discovered there were *exactly* 1,260 days between the two dates! It was more evidence that I was who the Lord said—a symbol of a fulfilled Israel in the latter days as well as a sign of His "bride to come."

God used those 1,260 days to get "Egypt" out of me. When Susan and I walked out of the wilderness and into God's promises for our lives, the trials and testing did not cease. They continued. However, we weathered adversities quite differently. We developed a complete and utter dependency on God that we did not have prior to our wilderness stretch. There would be no "going back to Egypt" to look for *any* kind of help *ever*. We looked solely to Him for *everything*.

I discovered the last 3½-year segment of my life was significant in yet another way. God revealed those tumultuous 1,260 days or 42 months foreshadowed Israel's 1,260 days or 42 months in the wilderness during the 3½-year Great Tribulation! After that time of travailing, as it was with me, she would never again "go down to Egypt" to look for help. That is, she would never again look to the nations of the world to come to her aid. She would look to Jesus Christ, her Messiah.

January 30, 2008

Foreshadowing Israel's Coming Tribulation

In the Old Testament, Israel's genealogy is broken into three sets of 14 generations, starting with Abraham. From Abraham to David, there were 14 generations; from David to Judah's Babylonian captivity, there were 14 generations; and from Judah's Babylonian captivity to the coming of Christ, there were 14 generations—42 generations in all.

Forty-two, according to Ed Vallowe's Biblical Mathematics—Keys to Scripture Numerics, *is the number for Israel's testing, suffering, and oppression. Israel's oppression under the Tribulation beast will take 42 months—1,260 days or 3½ years.*

I knew my first two 42-month terms in Detroit and Memphis, respectively, were not coincidences. They had a purpose. Both were periods of severe, brutal testing, designed to challenge and change me, to transform me into someone I had never been before. I wrestled with the Potter almost daily as He sought to mold me into a usable vessel.

Today I realized for the first time, the significance of the season I am presently in. I am now living the 42-month stretch Israel will live during the Great Tribulation! I am a pattern for her. Next year at this time, my stint as a pattern for her will be complete.

God revealed that He divided my life into three distinct sets of 42 months (three sets of 3½ years.) These periods were times of painful testing. But the "wilderness" phase—the one I'm in now and will complete next year—tried my faith the most. The three sets of 42 months or 3½ years break out as follows:

1st 42 months or 3½ years	*Detroit*	*Beginning of Sorrows/Birth Pangs*
2nd 42 months or 3½ years	*Memphis*	*My Tribulation in Egypt*
3rd 42 months or 3½ years	*Orlando*	*My Great Tribulation/Wilderness*

During the first 42 months in Detroit (i.e., Beginning of Sorrows/Birth Pangs), I could not understand what was happening to my life. It just flipped upside down. That period of my life was marked by great turmoil and perplexity. That is also when I began to experience literal birth pangs! They would come out of nowhere. It was a spiritual pregnancy. I was extremely unhappy during that period in my life. I had never been more sorrowful.

During the second 42 months (i.e., My Tribulation in Egypt), God moved me to Memphis, Tennessee, which is named for the ancient city of Memphis, Egypt. I lived in Harbor Town, right near Pyramid Arena—an imposing mirrored pyramid with a large statute of Rameses the Great prominently displayed in front. The Mississippi River ran through Memphis, Tennessee, just like the Nile River ran through Memphis, Egypt. That was also a miserable time in life for me. I was surrounded by trouble on all sides, tossed and afflicted daily. God used that period to refine me, to burn off the dross and bonds in Egypt's fiery furnace.

After bringing me out of Egypt, God led me to the wilderness. He used the last set of 42 months (i.e., My Great Tribulation/Wilderness) to try, test, and prove my faith in Him. It was a wondrous time of deep spiritual nourishment. I came to know God intimately. In the wilderness, I was forced to walk by faith as never before. After 2½ years of it, I saw dramatic differences in myself. The transformation God wrought was remarkable, a miracle! At that time, I predicted my desert experience would be completed in January 2009! Then, I would be fully ready to take hold of God's promises for my life!

I am confident Revelation 12:6 and 12:14 foretell what will happen to Israel, or a remnant of her, during the 3½-year Great Tribulation. She will repeat my wilderness experience. After Satan incarnates the Antichrist, Israel will be greatly persecuted, but God will protect a remnant. She will be given two wings of a great eagle (supernatural reference to God) that she might fly to her place in the wilderness. There she will be nourished for 42 months, 1260 days or 3½ years from the presence of the serpent (Revelation 12:14, 6).

God will open the spiritual eyes of the Jewish remnant in the wilderness, as He did mine. He will feed and nourish her both physically and spiritually. She will come to understand who God is and what has been happening to her as a people since the crucifixion, resurrection, and ascension of Christ. It will happen during intense visible and invisible warfare. When God removes her spiritual blinders, she will finally understand, accept, and embrace the truth that Jesus Christ is, indeed, her Messiah and the Savior of the world.

Her experience will be very much like mine. She will gain extraordinary, supernatural spiritual insight and discernment during this time. During my 42 months in the wilderness, I came to comprehend more truth than all the previous years of my life combined!

She will repent and cry out to her Messiah. He will answer her cry and rescue her. She will, in effect, "deliver" the Messiah to the world. God will unite the whole house of Israel—Judah and Ephraim—at that time!

Interestingly, God showed me another connection between Israel's genealogies and my foreshadowing of Israel's destined path. It took three sets of 14 generations or 42 generations for Israel to produce the One destined to rule earth's throne forever, Christ, the Messiah. It is through three sets of 42 months—three sets of 3½ years—the Lord brought forth His wife, Israel. It took that long for Him to free, transform, and prepare her for Himself.

Gene Edwards, author of *The Divine Romance*, described the nation-to-wife metamorphosis this way:

> *"... in late afternoon, it began to appear, first as a tiny speck on the horizon, gradually growing until it became a moving sea of humanity. It was His people, lately set free from slavery ... The fleeing refugees were coming into clear focus now. He could make out Moses in the lead .... He stared at this moving mass of humanity until the image before Him blurred and began to change in form, and finally, became one person. His eyes now saw not a multitude of people, but only a*

lovely young girl, coming up from Egypt, crossing the hot sands and moving toward Him.

Soon she will enter the land I have promised to her. There she will reach full womanhood.' In the eyes of earthen man, she was a nation, but through the eyes of God she was a woman. A nation, yes, but in His sight a composite woman who foreshadowed His bride" (Chapter 15, pp. 55-56; Chapter 18, p. 65).

Edwards proffered, as Eve was bone of Adam's bone, the woman was destined to be spirit of God's Spirit, essence of His Essence. Eve was hidden inside of Adam and brought forth from Adam and joined to him, and the two became one flesh. Likewise, the woman, hidden in God from the earth's foundations, one day would share His Spirit. The Spirit of the Lord would indwell her, making her one with Him.

Although of His Spirit, she would still have to be freed from Egypt's bonds and conformed to His image. That would take time. Just as it took the nation of Israel three sets of 14 generations or 42 generations to bring forth her Messiah, it would require three sets of 42 months to transform the woman to His likeness, to give her His mind and heart.

Chapter 34
Seizing His Promises

On January 1, 2009, I began receiving the small monthly stipend of $1,274. After five months of being virtually penniless, the amount seemed like a fortune to me, and not a small one. The pension ended our homelessness. God, over time, used it to show me how to live within my means and His miracles. I had no debt to speak of and no need to create it. The Lord moved Suzanne and me into a spacious 2,000-square foot townhouse, close to everyone and everything we needed for ministry.

The landlord hired a firm to determine if I alone qualified as a responsible tenant since my name would be the only one on the lease. I held my breath and waited for the results. God had already revealed in a dream that the townhouse was where He would put us, so I simply waited for Him to perform a miracle. He did.

My rental application was approved, despite the loss of two homes to foreclosure. The landlords—an older Christian couple, who owned the property outright—loved the idea of us running our ministry to the homeless from their home. They even reduced the rent and agreed to pay the condo association fees. It also helped that Melody Gardner lived right next door. She was like a daughter to the couple. She also vouched for our integrity.

Suzanne and I and, later, Ryan, lived in the three-bedroom, three-bathroom townhouse for nearly 2½ years, living miraculously off my small pension and whatever else God put in our hands. We ran the ministry within its four walls and needed most of the space there to do it. The only personal space we had were our individual bedrooms upstairs.

We never had a personal or ministry need that God did not meet. The Lord melded our personal and ministry lives into one. We became Ephraim and Ephraim became us. There is not enough paper or time to recount all the wonders the Lord performed for the ministry and all the ways He stretched and supplemented our small income, part of which we often used for ministry expenses.

We never felt a need for long. A prayer would go up, and the answer would come down—quickly! We would pray for something in the morning and by that afternoon, it would be in our hands. Sometimes we did not even pray. We would just discuss the need. Then, there would be a knock at the door, or the telephone would ring, and we would be offered what we needed. Sometimes, we would wake up to find things sitting right outside our front door on the porch—anonymously left. I would just shake my head in wonder and dance! My heart-song became, "Ishi, what have we needed that You have not provided?" We both knew the answer: NOTHING! Surely, we were not in Egypt *or* the wilderness anymore.

Suzanne and I had been attending New Destiny for almost 18 months when God suddenly opened my eyes regarding Pastor Tims. One Sunday, I was sitting in a pew enjoying his message when he began to joke.

"I know what they say about me out there! Yeah, I know what they call me. That's that 'Will Smith' pastor!" My mouth flew open. I had to force myself to remain calm *and* seated. God had just given me a critical puzzle piece! I sat there flabbergasted.

He's the man in my dream! He's the tall man in my dream who looks like Will Smith! He's the one who shows me my new place ... my new ministry! Then, I saw the words, "New Destiny Christian Center" at the front of the church in a whole new light. I had stared at those four words for more than a year and never made the connection. *He's the one that God is using to craft my new destiny!*

He started the first day I arrived. I often told people going to New Destiny was like going to Disney World. I could not wait to get there. And when I left, I left flying! God poured truth into my spirit through this man and his ministry, and I was like a BIG sponge. I could not get enough.

I would take notes on all his sermons and then go home and type up what God said to me through them. I could hear God instructing me through him, telling me what is coming next. And the praise at New Destiny was out of this world. We praised God on our feet for an hour *before* the service even began. You could feel God's pleasure.

Psalmist Darwin Hobbs often visited New Destiny as a praise and worship leader. His songs dripped with God's anointing. I could listen to one of his songs, and the spirit of oppression would just fall off me.

God gave me a dream once in which I was incarcerated. Darwin Hobbs appeared in my prison cell, grabbed me by the arm, and together we walked out of the cell, right pass the prison guards into freedom. The Lord was confirming a truth with this dream, one I learned at Temple of Deliverance in Memphis. My deliverance was in my praise. Nothing could set me free faster than praising God.

In the "Will Smith" dream, Pastor Tims and I hit it off immediately. He made me feel comfortable, unafraid. In real life, I never had a close-up encounter with him except once and that was quite brief. But I liked him. His personality was so much like my own, it was scary.

He once told the congregation when he was a little boy, after watching a television show, he wanted to be Superman. He wanted to fly! So, he grabbed a towel, tied it around his neck, and jumped out the second story window. His point was for us to imagine what God could do with a fearless, wild personality like that, harnessed for His glory.

His story reminded me of a vision the Lord gave me once when I was well into my forties. I saw a quick flash of myself as a grown woman, running right off a cliff. A large Figure was standing at the edge, waiting. I could see everything, but the Figure's head. I knew it was the Lord. He reached out with both arms and grabbed me by the waist in midair. He held me there, my little legs still running like a cartoon character. He was showing me I often leapt without forethought. At the same time, He made it clear to me that He took great pleasure in my bravery and boldness. They showed faith in Him.

One day, shortly after I had resigned from Denny's, the Lord gave me a simple instruction: "I want you to start washing dishes at New Destiny." So, while I patiently waited for my NGO papers from Ethiopia (that would never arrive), I washed dishes for "Hope for Destiny"—New Destiny's ministry to the homeless.

Every Sunday, New Destiny would send buses to downtown Orlando's homeless shelters and invite the homeless to the 11:00 a.m. worship service. After the service, these men, women, and children enjoyed a multicourse meal in the gym at large, linen-covered banquet tables.

They also received clothing, shoes, toiletries, haircuts, blood pressure checks, reading materials, counseling, and prayer. Around 3:00 p.m., coordinators loaded the buses to return our guests to their shelters. We served between 60 and 70 homeless guests each week.

At first, Suzanne and I simply washed dishes. Then, God decided to promote us. When some servers did not show up, we would put on hairnets, plastic gloves, and aprons and serve the food to our guests *and* wash the dishes.

There were many Sundays when we swept and mopped the gym floor, took out the garbage after serving the food, *and* washed the dishes. It was nothing for us to be there for seven hours on Sunday. We would leave the house at 10 a.m. and return home around 5:30 p.m.

We did that every Sunday for more than two years. In the process, we learned how to operate a commercial kitchen. We worked hard for God. But He worked even harder for us.

One Sunday, while working in New Destiny's kitchen, I noticed a top cabinet separating from the wall. The screws were loose. I was careful not to touch it. Someone would have to fix it on Monday. Unfortunately, I did not warn Suzanne.

At some point she touched it, and the entire cabinet separated from the wall. The corner of cabinet hit Suzanne square in the middle of her forehead as it fell to the floor. I looked up just in time to see her standing completely dazed in the middle of the kitchen floor. Later, she told me she saw stars.

She collapsed on the floor. Several of us in the kitchen grabbed her and pulled her to a hallway bench. Someone yelled, "Call 911!" Suzanne begged them not to. While there was no spewing blood from her forehead, I could see a large gash right in the middle of it.

A doctor, who was a member at New Destiny, was summoned out of the service. She held up fingers in front of Suzanne's eyes.

"How many fingers do you see?" she asked.

"Two ... three ... one," Suzanne responded correctly. "Just let me go home," she begged. I took off my apron to take her home.

"Let's go to the emergency room," I pleaded with Suzanne on the way home. She refused. I begged harder. She gently shook her head. When we arrived home, I telephoned members of her family. Maybe they could talk some sense into her. They could not.

Clearly, something was wrong. The next day, Suzanne was still sluggish. She complained that whenever she tilted her head, she felt liquid flow from side to side. Her head felt heavy.

Once again, I begged her to let me take her to the emergency room. We still had time. We were scheduled to take a flight to Chicago to attend Ryan's graduation at Roosevelt University the next day.

"You cannot get on that plane with a concussion, Suzanne! It will kill you!" I resorted to drama.

"Would you *please* let me rely on God?" she asked. She left my bedroom. I stood there shaking my head. I did not know what else to do.

I was in my bathroom, blow drying my hair after a shower when the Lord gently rebuked me. In His eyes, I had acted faithlessly.

"Now, go get your oil," He instructed.

I walked to the kitchen to tell Suzanne what happened. I told her I was supposed to pray for her healing. I led her to the living room. I took a chair from the dining room table and placed it in the bright sunlight. I placed Suzanne in it. Then, I anointed her head with oil—just above the gash. I retrieved my spiritual warfare book, found an appropriate prayer, and laid my right hand on Suzanne's head. With the book in my left hand, I began to read my prayer.

"In the name of Jesus, any sickness or infirmity caused by an accident or trauma—"

"Oh, I'm healed!"

"You are?" Suzanne jumped up from the chair.

"See!" She started dancing and shaking her head from side to side. A broad smile lit up her face. The healing was instant! One minute she was sluggish and dragging, the next minute she was as animated as a cartoon character. She told me she felt the difference immediately.

I stood in the middle of the living room, mouth agape, with half blow-dried hair, wondering what just happened. The next day, we could barely see the wound and, the day after that, it was completely gone!

The Lord made it a joy to work for Him. While working in the kitchen at New Destiny, we began to salvage the leftover food the chefs were throwing away after their Sunday meals to the homeless. They always cooked too much. We knew God arranged it that way.

In the beginning, Suzanne and I would take what was left over each week, add a little of our own, if necessary, and serve it to the homeless on Friday evenings. Gradually, that shifted. In two years, we would be cooking full course meals on our own with food from a food bank.

It was illegal to serve the homeless in Orlando's public parks, and many people tried to discourage us, including Christians. But the Lord never allowed us to be arrested. We would pray for protection, among other things, and then head out. Members of another organization were arrested. They fought the case all the way to the Federal Supreme Court and ultimately lost.

The Lord started us off small at first, to train us, and then He grew our guest counts exponentially. The very first time Suzanne and I ventured out, we served three peanut butter and jelly sandwiches, three bananas—cut into six halves—and six small bottles of water to six homeless men. The food ran out in two nanoseconds.

We were being shown the ropes by an outreach team at New Destiny, who served the homeless once a month. Suzanne and I had no idea what we were doing. I even wore high heels and a skirt the first time I participated. But after that first night, she and I agreed we could do much better.

We decided we would take a lot more food—real food—and go every Friday, not just once a month. We would go earlier in the evening around dinnertime. We agreed to take printed literature about Christ and New Destiny's service times and, most importantly, we would tell no one.

People were always reminding us that what we were doing was illegal. We would always remind them that the devil was the prince of this world, and he was the one who instituted wicked laws. If God said, "Go," we were going. She and I agreed that we would stop only if God stopped us.

While working for "Hope for Destiny," Suzanne and I also served the elderly, disabled, infirm, unemployed, and working poor through New Destiny's food pantry program. Every Monday, New Destiny distributed boxes of groceries to approximately 400 poor families. It was one of the largest food pantry programs in Central Florida.

Suzanne and I were there every Monday. We usually started around 10:30 a.m., along with 25 to 30 other volunteers and didn't get home until

5:30 p.m. I would come home dog-tired and would have to soak my muscles in a hot steamy bathtub with Epson Salt. My muscles ached from lifting all day. But the work was so gratifying.

Deacon Chris, who headed the food pantry program, was extraordinary. That was not just my opinion. It was God's. The Lord gave me a vivid dream once, in which I saw scores of screaming fans—men and women—behind a roped off area, waiting for a single backstage door to open. They had camera phones, pens and pencils raised high with their notepads, hoping to get an autograph. I was right in front, trying to catch a glimpse of who would come through that door.

Finally, the door flung open. A security guard came out, followed by a line of men and women. Deacon Chris, dressed in a denim jacket and pants, was third in line. He smiled and blushed the entire time as he followed behind the others to a staging area. Just as I woke up, I distinctly heard God's Voice—"*My* Rock Stars!"

Deacon Chris knew about our ministry to the homeless. He always inquired about how many we fed the prior week. He would nod with approval. Then, he would direct food—produce, meat, drinks, bread, desserts—to be given to us for our ministry. He encouraged us to keep up the good work. He also introduced me to Mark Anthony at Bread of Life Fellowship, a Christ-centered food bank.

One day, Deacon Chris and I ran into each other at the Second Harvest Food Bank of Central Florida. He sensed God had arranged our meeting. After I was done, he asked me to follow him to Bread of Life. He wanted to make a personal introduction.

The first time I met Mark, he conducted an impromptu test. "Okay, I'm a homeless man in need of Christ. What would you say to me?" I had been well trained in evangelism at Wayside Baptist Church. I began to share the Good News of Jesus Christ with him.

When I was done, Mark said, "Okay, you can come every other week to start." Mark ended up giving Ephraim tons of free food and drinks for several years to help us feed the homeless. I felt so grateful and indebted to him and his ministry.

Once I gave a donation to his ministry—a $2,500 diamond ring that Michael had given me during our first marriage. It was a small token of appreciation for what he had done for Ephraim. The ring was a fragile antique from the 1800s. It was all I had to give.

Mark graciously accepted the ring, put it away, and then gave it back a year later. His kind gesture worked to give me the illusion that I was giving back a tiny portion of what I had been given. Now that I can, I make a point of sowing into Bread of Life Fellowship whenever I visit.

God made all kinds of provision for us. He just needed us "to go" and when we arrived, we would always discover He went ahead of us. He seemed to always give us more than we expected.

I will always be grateful for New Destiny Christian Center. I do not know what I would have done with myself those first months after I left Corporate America—the only world I knew for more than three decades. I learned at New Destiny, the importance of sacrificial service—how to give myself away. In giving myself away, I found myself—a new and better me.

New Destiny helped birth The Ephraim Project and my new destiny. I am especially thankful for the late Pastor Tims and Pastor Riva Tims, who left Baltimore with their children to start New Destiny Christian Center in Apopka, Florida. God raised them up just in time to meet me there and show me the ropes.

Chapter 35
Growing Our New Vineyard

When Suzanne and I started feeding the homeless we had very little money. We worked mostly from food donations. One day, at a family funeral gathering, Suzanne circled the room and asked each of her relatives to help us feed the homeless: "Nothing's too big and nothing's too small. Anything you can do to help will be appreciated."

We left there with nearly $100 in cash. We put the money in a glass jar and pulled from it only when needed. We marveled how God never allowed the money in the jar to run out.

During our first few weeks of operation, we managed totally on in-kind donations and the token cash. After two months, a donor sent us a $150 check and asked for a receipt. Up until that point, it never dawned on me that The Ephraim Project, set up as a charitable, private foundation to serve poor Ethiopians, could also be used to serve the homeless in the United States. Our mission was to serve "the poorest among us." Who was poorer in the U.S. than the homeless? We transferred the cash in the jar to Ephraim's tiny bank account and never looked back.

I remember our first sizable donation. I stumbled upon it totally by accident. I called a local Walmart to see if they carried a certain size to-go cup. I was prepared to purchase them. I introduced myself as the president of a ministry that serves the homeless. The woman who answered the phone automatically transferred me to the woman in charge of charitable contributions. I told that person who I was and what I was looking for. She asked me if I had proof that I was a nonprofit organization. She also asked me for a letter on our letterhead, detailing our need for cups.

I hung up the phone a little confused. Nevertheless, I prepared the letter, grabbed our tax exemption certificate, and headed to the store. A woman in customer service paged her for me. I was instructed to go to the back of the store to wait for her.

After 15 minutes, the woman I had spoken to over the phone burst through the double swinging doors with two shopping carts filled with to-go cups. She handed me a sheet of paper.

"Fill this out," she instructed.

"What is this for?" I asked.

She looked at me perplexed. "It's for the big check."

Suddenly, I realized I was about to get everything in those two shopping carts for free *and* a monetary donation! I resolved to say as little as possible. I did not want to undo whatever God was doing. Clearly, He was in charge, making it all happen. I quietly completed the double-sided application right there in the store and turned it in.

A few weeks later, I received a call from the store. The check was ready. I could pick it up. I could not drive to the store fast enough. The moment I opened the envelope and saw the amount, I knew Ephraim would never fail. God would only grow and prosper us.

During the first year of operation, Suzanne and I did all the work. We named our ministry to the homeless Project New*Start*. The first three years, everything was done out of our home. Although we only served food in the beginning, we felt God calling us to do more. He wanted us to restore hope and lives, to help people begin again. He wanted us to help give people a fresh start, like He gave us.

In our second year, Ryan, a published author, came to live with us. She joined the ministry as our communications specialist. It took her 12 hours to build our new website. I wept when she presented it to me. I caught a *real* glimpse of what God was doing through us and it was superb in my eyes.

As the number of people we served grew, God also grew our volunteer base. The handful of homeless people we served half-sandwiches to that first Friday would, in time, swell to more than 300. Scores and scores of volunteers, in time, would join Suzanne and me.

Ryan wore other hats too. She produced a system for tracking our food and paper inventories. Her second year with us she brought a sense of order to our haphazard distribution of toiletries and related items. We provided everything a homeless person needed to stay fresh, clean, and odor-free.

At one point, we offered weekly laundry services through a downtown laundry. Ryan oversaw this program. The homeless could present a voucher or have their names placed on a list to do a load of laundry for free every week.

As our client base expanded, God sent more workers. Suzanne, who used to cook all week on our home stove in order to be ready by Friday, was joined by a core of dedicated cooks. Some were trained chefs.

After we broke our residential stove from overuse, God moved our cooking operations to a commercial kitchen at First Alliance Church, located a few minutes from downtown, where we served the homeless. The Lord also moved the heart of a major donor to renovate the kitchen at St. George, so we could cook our meals there every fourth Friday of the month.

The fourth Friday of every month became known as "Orthodox Friday." Members of Orthodox churches throughout Central Florida—Greek, Antiochian, Egyptian Coptic, and Ethiopian Coptic—came to cook and serve the homeless. The fourth Friday was always our busiest. If any of the homeless people qualified for food stamps, their benefits were depleted by the fourth Friday of the month.

Another Orthodox church, Holy Trinity, periodically provided meals for us, using its state-of-the-art kitchen. But its main ministry focused on keeping food on the tables of the scores of families we removed from the streets. Sometimes, they gave so abundantly we had enough groceries to also supply a small congregation of poor Haitian families *and* the families of Mexican American migrant workers.

In 2009, we were given a large warehouse by Keith Greenwood, a New Destiny church member, who sold high-end, luxury cars. The London-born businessman leased the warehouse for a year, but then decided he no longer needed it. He turned the space over to us.

We were surprised when he and his wife, Glynis, renewed the lease a second year just for the ministry. Before we knew it, the warehouse was brimming with donated clothes, shoes, blankets, backpacks, small household items, and all kinds of other goods. We hardly had space to walk.

Eventually, all those things were transferred to our Family Clothing Closet that we set up at the Downtown Baptist Church of Orlando. We started with two big rooms. Today, we have 14 large rooms, spanning 30,000 square feet. These rooms are devoted to the "clothing the naked" sector of our ministry. We have become the go-to place for homeless families, battered women and, the working poor to get clothes, shoes, blankets, linens, toiletries, and other items, free of charge.

Gradually, the Lord moved us into casework. One of the most important things homeless people need is identification. Without an ID, they are stuck. They cannot search for employment. They cannot apply for Social Security benefits. They cannot get into a shelter, motel or hotel. They cannot rent storage space. They certainly cannot lease an apartment. They can go to jail without an ID!

If a case demanded we obtain an ID quickly, we worked to get it ourselves rather than go through IDignity—a local ministry that secured IDs for the homeless on a mass scale. Once we had a client's ID in hand, we could work to get him or her off the streets.

We helped people prepare resumes and dress for interviews and work. We provided everything from suits and ties for office jobs to steel-toe work boots for day laborers. We provided many with simple black pants, a belt, a white shirt or blouse, and slip-resistant shoes for restaurant work.

We bought them prepaid phones or put minutes on their phones so potential employers could reach them. We provided an address where they could receive mail related to their cases. We also had them set up email accounts if they did not have one. They could use the computer services for free at the public library.

We transported clients to and from job interviews or provided daily bus passes. For those who lived in their cars, we would put gasoline in their tanks. For those who secured employment, we provided a monthly bus pass, so they could get back and forth to work until they earned their first paycheck. We also provided monthly bus passes in special cases. For example, we provided a monthly bus pass for a homeless college student to get back and forth to school. In one instance, we paid for a student's books.

Some of our clients were too physically or mentally challenged to work. In these instances, we helped them apply for food stamps. Then, we fought for their Veterans or Social Security benefits. This took a lot of time and work.

Since 2009, Liz Hall, our senior caseworker, and I have worked 40 such cases. Neither of us had a lick of training when we started. We just moved, and God went before us. We have assisted 21 homeless men and women in winning their cases, amassing more than $1.1 million in benefits for them. The figure includes any authorized lump-sum payments to clients plus 5 years of annual benefits.[5] We do not envision any of these people being homeless ever again. Some cases were won within three to four months; others took more than a year. There were no fees for our service. Our work was free.

---

[5]*The $1.1 million in benefits is a conservative estimate. Most recipients will receive these benefits until they pass away.*

Each case required multiple visits to the Veterans Administration or the Social Security Administration and sometimes several trips to doctors' offices. In some cases, we paid for the doctors' visits. Social Security required professional medical and psychiatric diagnoses to support claims of physical or mental disability. In some cases, if our clients were denied benefits, we hired a lawyer to work on their appeals.

I was livid when I learned some people who were not homeless stole the Social Security benefits of those who were, simply because they could. Nobody was there to stop them. We had clients who required a third party to manage their funds because they were incapable of doing it themselves. In such cases, they signed documents, allowing a relative or friend to receive the funds on their behalf; they had to trust the relative or friend to pay their rent and other living expenses. Some payees did that faithfully, some did not.

We had one client who signed over her benefits to a friend who would not return her phone calls for months. This client suffered from excruciating back and leg pain, stemming from a hit-and-run car accident many years earlier. She used alcohol to numb the pain and eventually became an alcoholic. This resulted in severe, short-term memory loss.

She was too poor, too crippled, and too incapacitated to fight for her money, which was more than enough to put her in a permanent home. She had no phone, no friends, and no money. Many people wrote her off as crazy.

Having no means to get across town to the Social Security office or to the payee, she just gave up. We found her sleeping in the park with all her belongings in a shopping cart. The day we found her we took her straight to Social Security. The Ephraim Project became her Payee.

The Social Security representative informed us it was too late to retrieve the final check that would be sent to the former payee. But just before we left, the agent slipped me a piece of paper. On it, she had handwritten the address and phone number of my client's "friend."

I tossed and turned in my bed for two days, praying to the Lord about what to do. Finally, I hit upon an idea. The Lord led me to prepare an official-looking, threatening letter on our ministry stationery.

While I had no sanctioned power to do anything and no money to hire an attorney, I warned the woman in the letter that if she did not return the full amount of the last check to Social Security by a certain date, we would prosecute her to the fullest extent of the law. I included a stamped, self-addressed envelope for the check to be sent back to Social Security—to the attention of an agent's name I spotted on a name plate the last time I was there. If she returned it, I knew it would get to the right person.

Against all logic, but infuriated by the injustice of it all, I went to the woman's home. That was not the original plan. My plan was to mail the packet from the post office. But I found myself driving pass the post office. The next thing I knew, I was knocking on the woman's door. She was not home. She was with her parole officer. I spoke to her mother. I told her who I was, handed her the packet and told her what was inside.

The mother was terrified. She woke up her son, the woman's brother, who was napping in the back. He looked to be in his forties. They both assured me the check would be returned. They did not want any trouble. I could tell by the way our conversation went that the whole family knew my client's monthly check was being stolen.

While we waited for the check to be returned, we put our client in a hotel and brought her food and looked for a place for her to live. The check was returned within the time allotted, and we used it for her security deposit and first month's rent.

We went on to manage her bills for a year. Eventually, we turned her case over to a company that now pays her monthly living expenses and cuts her a weekly allowance check so she can buy food and other items. Presently, we are the payee for four formerly homeless clients, but we have managed as many as eight. This service is free as well.

God backed us into the prescription-filling business. We had many homeless clients who needed medication, but they had no money to get it. We filled all manner of medical and eyeglass prescriptions. We had one woman who was released two days after having open-heart surgery. She did not have insurance. This was alarmingly common. Many would be in agonizing pain after injury or surgery. But the hospitals discharged them regardless. Often, they ended up with a handful of prescriptions with no money to fill them and no place to go.

For cases such as these, we would fill the prescriptions and then pay for them to stay in an emergency shelter or hotel. For those who were not sick enough to be hospitalized, but still in grave pain, we would whip out our anointing oil and pray for God's supernatural healing. God always answered. In fact, the Lord gave me a dream once, in which He showed me His version of my "calling card." It was a humorous take off a late 1950s TV western, "Have Gun–Will Travel." The card read: "Have Oil–Will Travel."

Ephraim assisted 141 families in finding emergency, transitional or permanent housing. We are particularly focused on pregnant women and families with children. In many instances, we provided people with one-way bus tickets home. Once there, they connected with family and friends who helped them secure work or housing.

In several cases, we simply took our homeless clients into our homes because God made it clear that was His will. In two instances, one of our volunteers, Melody Gardner, took in families. One family of three, she took in for six months; the other, a family of five, she took in for two months. Both families are on their feet today.

Suzanne, Ryan, and I took in no less than eight homeless people at different times. The most extraordinary one was Megaraaj Jhadav. He lived with us for six months as God solved his case.

I saw Megaraaj in a dream many years before I ever met him! Teasing the Lord one night, I asked Him to show me Himself in His "earth suit."

"C'mon, Ishi, put on Your earth suit and let me get a good look at You, Mary's Boy!" That night, He gave me a dream. I saw Megaraaj. I asked the Lord to let me see Him in Person, and He showed me Himself in one of the "least of these" (Matthew 25:40).

Megaraaj used to build helicopters for McDonnell Douglas during the Gulf War, but when we took him in, he could not even button his shirt, brush his teeth, or work a microwave oven. He suffered a stroke that severely restricted the use of his left hand. It also stole his memory.

Suzanne, who became his primary caregiver during those six months, prepared him scrumptious meals to order. When necessary, they even went to the store together to get just the right cut of meat. It was nothing for him to wake up in the wee hours of the morning and complain he had not eaten dinner. No amount of our *telling* him he had eaten helped. Suzanne always had two peanut butter and jelly sandwiches in the refrigerator waiting for him when this happened. It happened a lot.

From what we could glean from his story, after the Gulf War, he and thousands of other workers were laid off from McDonnell Douglas. Megaraaj had no family to speak of. His former boss invited him to Seattle, Washington in hopes of helping him secure a job with Boeing.

The day Megaraaj arrived, Boeing laid off 13,000 employees. Unable to find work, he became despondent. He gave up and, eventually, lost everything. Megaraaj ended up in a homeless in a shelter in Seattle, Washington.

After several years of homelessness, Megaraaj's biggest dream was to get to San Diego, where he heard the weather was perfect. He had already moved from Seattle to Los Angeles. But Los Angeles proved to be too cold. Before he could make his way to San Diego, he had a stroke. That stroke brought him to Orlando.

He told us, "The bus people couldn't understand my speech." It had been slurred from the stroke. They put him on the wrong bus. Instead of putting him on a bus to San Diego, they put him on an Orlando-bound bus. But it was the bus God wanted him on. Once in Orlando, he ended up in our serving line. He begged us to help him. Clearly, he qualified for Social Security disability benefits.

The day we called the Social Security Administration, a representative requested we bring him to their offices immediately. Once there, we learned Megaraaj had nearly $50,000 in unclaimed Social Security checks! He was eligible to receive more than $1,700 monthly. The man had no reason to be homeless. He could easily afford a home and the care he needed. He just needed help.

The problem was Megaraaj had no recollection of ever applying for his Social Security benefits, nor did he remember where he instructed Social Security to send his checks. Social Security's records refuted his claim. The agency had proof that he himself had applied for his benefits. But that was all the information Social Security was willing to give us. It would not disclose where the checks had been sent, nor would it allow us to cancel the checks. It was against policy. The checks would remain good (and cashable) for a year.

We took Megaraaj into our home and fought for weeks to become his payee. Eventually, we won. Social Security was reluctant to let just anyone manage that amount of money for another person. We understood that. We also set out to find his lost checks.

Megaraaj did not believe for one minute he would ever see a dime of it and, therefore, requested that we put him on a plane to San Diego, which we did. He asked us to place him in a shelter there, which we did. The logistics were elaborate because he would be traveling alone.

His memory was selective at best, so we had to coordinate extensively with the San Diego shelter that agreed to take him in. Megaraaj needed an escort to help him board the plane and one to meet him when he disembarked. We also plastered him with notes that explained who he was and where he was going. We bought him a cell phone and programmed our numbers into it.

In less than a week, he begged us to bring him back to Orlando, which we did. He claimed San Diego was just as cold as Los Angeles. "Besides, you're the only family I know," he said.

While he was gone during that week, we kept up the fight on his behalf. Miraculously, we finally tracked down the missing checks. We traced them to the general mail delivery of a homeless shelter in downtown Seattle.

Megaraaj was an avid reader. He could read a 400-page book in a day. He would start in the morning and finish at 2 or 3 o'clock the next morning. We took him, almost weekly, to the book exchange, where he purchased or exchanged five to seven books.

Before he left for San Diego (and returned), he happened to be reading an espionage book. In it, he came across the name Boeing. The name triggered his memory! Suddenly, he remembered he lived in Seattle. He had gone there looking for work. He lived somewhere near water. Prior to that, he adamantly denied ever visiting Seattle or living there.

A quick Internet search of Seattle homeless shelters yielded one that was located downtown near a body of water. I called the shelter's general mail facility for several days and left messages. I never received a return phone call.

Finally, one day the Lord prompted me to call the shelter's executive director. He answered the phone on the first ring. I told him what we were looking for. He promised to investigate the matter and get back to me.

Later that day, he verified the shelter had seven Social Security checks made out to Megaraaj Jhadav. A staff member forwarded them to us. By the time the checks arrived, Megaraaj had returned. The day we received the checks we opened an account in Megaraaj's name.

We sought all kinds of medical treatment for Megaraaj as we searched for a permanent home for him. We eventually placed him in an assisted living facility that had medical personnel on staff 24 hours a day, seven days a week. There, he could get the round-the-clock attention and care he needed.

As with Megaraaj, God had us take others into our home. Other volunteers, like Tim and Liz Hall, did so as well. The Halls took in two homeless men at separate times, helping each one win his Social Security disability case.

In another instance, Tim became the health surrogate for a homeless man named Bob, who had not seen his family in 19 years. Just after Liz won his Social Security disability case, Bob collapsed in the street from an aneurysm.

The Halls eventually tracked down Bob's family. Two of his sisters flew to Orlando to visit him. It was a blessed reunion. They thought Bob had died years earlier. They asked Tim to remain as Bob's health surrogate. Bob now lives in a nursing home in Daytona Beach, Florida. God made us walk out each case by faith and, by His grace, we discovered something good in the end.

After we pulled our clients from underneath expressways, abandoned buildings, parks, doorways, and cars, we lent a hand in furnishing their new homes with donated items. We also purchased used furniture, small appliances, and other household items like dishes, silverware, pots and pans, and linens. In some cases, we paid for their rental and utility deposits. In one case, we assisted an elderly widow, evicted from her home and suffering from diabetes, pay for her insulin. Then, we moved her things off the street and into a storage facility. We paid for her storage until she could.

We performed every bit of our casework on our laptops in public parks, local fast-food restaurants and cafés, the downtown library, and church parking lots. We worked wherever we could pick up a Wi-Fi signal. Our vans became "mobile offices" because we did not have a building.

Since 2009, we have helped 280 families, impacting 437 individuals. Every case has been different. But in every instance, we tried to help each client understand that Jesus Christ was the lasting answer to his or her homelessness. Many received Christ for the first time, and many rededicated their lives to Him. For those who wanted no part of Him, we still walked alongside them in love. We provided for their needs with the hope that Christ would woo them to Himself through us.

Chapter 36
The St. George Connection

After Suzanne and I, and later Ryan, mastered a certain level of service, God sent us more people to serve. We would stay at a level for two, three or four weeks. Then, the Lord would increase the number. That was exciting and troublesome. It was exciting because we were reaching people and we saw God's hand making everything happen. We were not growing the ministry, He was. The growth was troublesome because we began to attract the attention of downtown condo and business owners.

Serving hordes of homeless people week after week near a business or condo invited the ire of the owners. (We had grown too big to try to surreptitiously serve in public parks.) We realized our constant presence could easily hurt a business or bring down property values.

The time soon came when we had to leave the centrally located business district. We moved our open-air operations several blocks away, to what we thought was a private, tucked-away street.

On that street, we started in front of a church that ran us off the first day. Then, we moved across the street to serve in front of another church. They let us stay for a while. Then, they requested we move because the homeless scared their parishioners and our food shares interfered with their Friday wedding rehearsals.

From there, we went back across the street to serve in front of the downtown post office. We served in front of the post office for nearly a year. Our numbers grew so large that on Fridays, at dinnertime, we blocked both sides of the streets. Cars could not get through, nor could pedestrians get to the bus stop or into the post office.

God warned me in a dream that the post office officials were about to come down on us; but in the process, I would be introduced to a man, referred to in my dream as "Your Eminence." The man wore a priest's collar. Apparently, he would help us.

Sure enough, less than a week after that dream, a tall African American woman stormed our vans the minute we pulled up.

"Who's in charge here?" she asked. I came forward. She asked me if I had permission to do what I was doing.

"Yes," I said, thinking of a letter I had received from the Mayor's office, commending us for our service to the homeless.

"Alright! Next week, bring that letter," she said. "I'm bringing the federal authorities, and we'll just see." She stomped off. My volunteers were shaking in their shoes, but I was thrilled! She looked *exactly* like the woman in my dream who introduced me to "Your Eminence!"

Adding to the intrigue, God had shown me a parking lot in a recent dream. I felt He wanted us to have it. So, the prior Sunday, on our way home from church, Suzanne, Ryan, and I stopped by the parking lot and walked its perimeter. As we walked, we asked God to give it to us, if it was for Ephraim.

After the woman from the post office left, we finished serving the homeless. Then, a small group of volunteers and I walked two blocks south to the parking lot I saw in my dream. We formed a little circle, held hands, and prayed. We asked God to give us the parking lot for our ministry as Susan, Ryan, and I had done the week before. I knew we could not show up at the post office the following week.

"You gotta talk to Father John!" a man yelled. I looked around. *Who was that?* The person spoke again. "You gotta talk to Father John!" I looked up. There was a homeless man looking out of the window of a vacant building just above us. I would later learn his name was "Mike the Biker." Mike saw our little group praying in the parking lot.

"Who's Father John?" I shouted back.

"He's the priest of that church." He pointed to the church on the other side of the parking lot. I looked at the church and looked back at him.

"What church is that?" I asked.

"St. George!" I started screaming!

God told me many times that my old address on Royal Saint George Drive was a sign to me. For years, I did not understand why. Now, I was standing in the parking lot of St. George, asking God to bless the poor with it. I later learned it was an Orthodox church, and its patron saint, St. George, was a defender of the poor and infirm!

I knew nothing about Eastern Christian Orthodoxy. But at that moment, on that evening, I was confident Father John would agree to let us come. (Author's note: The significance of the Green Dragon Street address is revealed in *The Late Great United States, Book Three.)*

Sure enough, Father John and I hit it off like two peas in a pod. At our first meeting, I showed him a copy of an email my friend Gina Hockaday sent me six weeks earlier. She told me, while she had been praying for me, God spoke to her. She wrote: "There's a man who looks like he's working for the City, but he's not. God will use him to open a way for you to get a building for the homeless. His name begins with a 'J'—it's either John or Jonathan."

Father John read the email and just smiled. I learned at that meeting he had, indeed, been working with the City of Orlando and several area churches for a year. Their desire was to turn part of the vacant building across from the church into a drop-in center for the homeless. The church owned the building. The project had not gone anywhere.

Father John decided at our Thursday breakfast meeting to join forces with The Ephraim Project. He gave us permission to serve the homeless in the church's parking lot. The next day, Friday, September 11, 2009, we had volunteers waiting in front of the post office. They directed the homeless to our new home, the St. George parking lot. We converted it into an open-air, mass dining hall.

A week later, First Alliance, gave us a 10-foot wooden cross. We tried everything we could think of to get the cross into St. George. The base was too big. So, we tried to store it in the building next door. Again, we had the same problem. The wide base, needed to support the height of the cross, prevented it from going through the doors. We had only one choice—to place the cross in the corner of the parking lot.

In time, we figured out that was exactly where God wanted it! At our meal service, we would say, "All of you who need prayer or need someone to talk to, come meet us at the cross. Someone will be there to talk or pray with you." People would get out of the food line and head to the cross for prayer.

As time went on, we glimpsed God's larger purpose. God had a reason for exposing us to the monsoon rains in the spring, the hot scorching sun in the summer and the frigid temperatures in winter. We became a church without walls—literally!

The open-air parking lot became the gathering place for people who ordinarily would not cross paths. People came to serve one another. The homeless benefited the "haves" just as much as the "haves" benefited the poor.

Our homeless ranks were comprised of men, women, and some families with children. They were from virtually every race and nationality. Some were mentally challenged, some were physically challenged; some struggled with drug and alcohol addictions, some would not touch a cigarette or even sip a cup of caffeinated coffee; some were skinny as a rail, some were morbidly obese; some were agnostic, some were atheist, many were Christian; some were skilled, gifted, and quite extraordinary, some were lazy and not the least bit ambitious; some had high IQs, some could not string together two thoughts; some had been homeless for years, and some were newly homeless; some were suffering from self-inflicted wounds; and some had their lives upended by Providence. Such was the case of Patricia and Raphael Robinson and their beautiful family of three small children.

The couple had to make a tough choice. Should they continue to make mortgage payments or pay for their son's surgery? Their two-year-old son, Solomon, needed an operation. Their medical insurance refused to cover the procedure. After much prayer, the two decided to stop paying their mortgage, and Solomon had his much-needed surgery. Today, he is a healthy, active, vibrant child.

But months after Solomon's operation, Patricia, Raphael, Solomon, and their other two children—ages 5 and 6 months—lost their home. Suddenly, the family found themselves among the ranks of the homeless. They tried unsuccessfully to get on their feet in Alabama. But, eventually, they wore out their welcome staying with Patricia's relatives. With nothing else to lose, they packed their three children and everything they owned into a 1996 Chevy Impala and headed for Florida.

The family ended up in downtown Orlando at St. George in our food sharing line. Our Project New*Start* volunteers spotted the children right away. That night, we found a temporary home for the family with a volunteer. We immediately began working with the husband and wife to find employment.

A few days after pulling the family off the street, a volunteer coached Patricia through a Disney online application and electronic screening process. We were elated when Disney invited Patricia for an in-person interview.

Our next task was to help her make a good first impression at her interview. We took her to Ross, a retail clothing store, and purchased an interview outfit. (This was before we established our clothing closet.) We were "over the moon" when Disney offered her the job.

The family rented a furnished trailer home in Kissimmee near Disney. For several months, Raphael watched the children while Patricia worked to help put the family back on its feet. Raphael, a machinist with 15 years of experience, eventually landed a good-paying job. He was soon earning enough to support the family, enabling Patricia to quit her job and stay home with the children. The last we heard from them she was pregnant with their fourth child.

Our volunteer ranks were just as diverse as the homeless we served. They were composed of men, women, and children of all ages; elementary, high school, and college students; the employed, underemployed, and unemployed; rich and poor; those with homes, those without; Protestants, Catholics, Christian Orthodox, Messianic Jews, Baptists, Charismatic Pentecostals, Independents, Seventh Day Adventists; Jehovah's Witnesses; Blacks, Whites, Hispanics, Asians, Native Americans and others.

Even *within* the Orthodox faith, we had Christians who were Lebanese, Egyptian, Ethiopian, Russian, Greek, Romanian, Syrian and Iranian—all serving alongside one another. God craftily orchestrated the pan-Orthodox movement within Ephraim, using St. George as a springboard.

Interestingly, we also had an Iranian Muslim volunteer who came every Friday to serve the homeless. He never missed a feeding. He was the president and CEO of a very large and successful retail and import-export grocery business. We did not stop him from serving alongside us because his faith was different from ours. We embraced him in Christian love. He liked being around us. It was clear to us that God sent him.

A wealthy businessman, he distributed hundreds of dollars' worth of merchandise to the homeless every week. They loved him and always rushed to help him unload whenever he pulled into the lot. Almost every week, he gave us 40 pounds of rice, a case of beans, and other items before he left.

The Lord simply blurred all the lines of difference between us. He did it without us ever realizing it. When we finally caught on, some of our volunteers started wearing T-shirts that read: "The church has left the building!"

Today, we average 148 food-service volunteers per month. No one is paid. We are 100% volunteer based. We still operate solely from cash and in-kind donations from local churches, businesses, schools, humanitarian organizations, and individuals.

One of our biggest financial supporters is my old college roommate, Brenda, who does not even live in Orlando. She lives in Atlanta, Georgia. The tithing miracle I experienced in college was not lost on her. She tithes to Ephraim every two weeks, selflessly giving to the poor.

We have never received a government grant of any kind. Churches, businesses, and humanitarian organizations support our efforts. But the backbone of our ministry is made up of many little donations from ordinary people.

Because no one is paid at Ephraim, approximately 95 percent of our cash and in-kind donations—valued in 2012 at more than $190,000 and expected to exceed $500,000 in 2013—are invested in direct services to the homeless. That is a long way from $100 in a glass jar.

Eventually, I left New Destiny Christian Center and settled into the rhythm at St. George. We were serving the homeless at St. George, and God needed me to minister to them there. He had poured and poured into me at New Destiny. Now He needed me to pour into others. I never attended New Destiny again.

Chapter 37
The St. George Serving Center

On April 12, 2011, the U.S. Court of Appeals finally ruled that it was illegal to serve the homeless in Orlando's public parks. While the case was being appealed in the higher courts, the City suspended all arrests. But after the ruling came down, ministries that had been using the parks suddenly had nowhere to go. Father John's phone began to ring off the hook. St. George's parking lot was private property.

One-by-one the ministries followed The Ephraim Project to St. George. By that time, Ephraim had been at St. George for more than a year. Father John and I had partnered together to grow the ministry. He had come to know and trust me, and I him. He knew my family. I knew his. He placed The Ephraim Project in charge of all the other ministries, forming the St. George Serving Center.

Today, 11 ministries serve the homeless at St. George, doing what The Ephraim Project does and more! A different ministry serves on the lot every day of the week. We all serve the homeless, but since we are gifted differently, God tends to employ our service programs differently.

For example, one ministry is particularly gifted in praying for the sick. Healings frequently occur on its day of service. According to some reports, one man actually got out of a wheelchair and walked! Another ministry is highly evangelical. Just recently it had 12 men and women come to know Christ at one of its food shares. One ministry focuses on helping those with drug and alcohol addictions. They have been blessed to help remove people from the streets and place them in rehab programs. Another ministry started a church. Still another just opened a thrift store as a means of employing the homeless they serve; all revenue, after expenses, is poured back into the ministry.

Three other ministries that used to serve at St. George branched off into specialty areas. One now serves the homeless near University of Central Florida, enlisting the help of college students. Another serves the homeless and poor families on the weekends in and around Casselberry, Florida. Still another raises awareness and food for the hungry through rock concerts. God, in His manifold wisdom, set and positioned each of us in His body, based on our talents and gifts.

Together, we serve a total of 1,500 guests weekly. Orlando's homeless know St. George is a place where God's people stand ready to provide a good meal and other humanitarian assistance. On Sundays, we at St. George invite the homeless to worship with us and then join us for a meal and Bible discussion in our Fellowship Hall. Surely, God is using the St. George Serving Center to restore the hope and lives of people whom the world forgot.

At a recent conference in New Orleans, Bishop Antoun Yssa Khouri, who presides over the Anthiochian Orthodox Christian Diocese of Miami and the Southeast, asked each of the 39 parishes to submit their plan to serve the poor in their communities. Completely smitten with St. George's role in helping the homeless in Orlando, he asked each priest to submit their plans by June 2014. At the conference, the diocese appointed a vice president—a member of St. George—to coordinate and oversee the effort.

Chapter 38
Ephraim Living Isaiah 58

On November 4, 2012, God gave me a dream. In it, He helped me see what He had accomplished up to that point through The Ephraim Project. He showed me our five streams of ministry. We were so busy doing the work Christ called us to do, none of us realized we were doing *exactly* what God called Israel to do in Isaiah 58. He told them to feed the hungry, clothe the naked, shelter the homeless, lift heavy burdens, and set captives free.

I have always looked at Isaiah 58 as God's, I-am-*really*-fed-up speech to Israel! I imagine Him saying: *"I'm sick of it! Do you hear Me? Sick of it! I've had it up to here! You claim you love Me. You want to be near Me. You want to hear from Me, so you fast. Your fasts are a sham! On the day you fast, you manage to find pleasure for yourselves. You even exploit your workers. You fight and argue. And you expect to hear from Me?*

"You want to know what pleases Me—what really thrills Me? You really want to know? Why don't you try sharing your bread with the hungry? Huh? Why not put some clothes on the naked? Why don't you shelter the poor and homeless—take them into your own houses, if you have to. Why don't you try lifting someone's heavy burden? Try to break a few yokes off the backs of people. Try to set some captives free! Loose the bonds of injustice for them.

"Do you love Me? Do you really love Me? Then, try doing what I ask! Do these things and I guarantee you will hear from Me! You will hear from heaven! Before you can finish your prayer, I will say, 'I'm here! What do you need?'"

Without ever realizing it, Ephraim, by God's grace, was living Isaiah 58. And just as He promised, God was in our midst, answering prayers left and right. Yes, we were doing what He called His people to do and more.

We did not forget the prisoners. When some of our homeless charges ended up in Orange County jail or another Florida prison, we visited them to see what we could do. We brought clothes or Bibles or deposited money onto their books. We contacted their loved ones. We wrote others on their behalf.

Ephraim also supported two out-of-state prisoners—one in Memphis, Tennessee and one in Bennettsville, South Carolina. The Lord brought both to my spiritual doorstep right after I resigned from Denny's. They, too, were signs.

God told me that we were "chained together" and that I was to pray for their release. In due season, the three of us would be released from our "prison pits" like Joseph was released from his. Between the three of us, we have probably exchanged more than 150 letters. They both are an inspiration to me.

In 2011, a modest donation from The Ephraim Project to House of Israel International Ministries helped build a small school for orphans in Ethiopia. And the Lord also gave us the opportunity to support widows through programs started by Susan and George Mamboleo in their tribal village in Kenya, Africa that had been devastated by famine. A small donation of just $100 bought seeds for women in their famine-ravaged village. With the seeds, they planted gardens and supplied food for their families. Finally, we channeled as much food and clothing as we could to the families of poor migrant farmers, who lived in deplorable conditions.

These three initiatives and our ministry to out-of-state prisoners had nothing to do with helping Orlando's homeless. But I quickly realized God presented these opportunities to allow us to walk in His commanded statutes. His Bride must also be mindful of widows, orphans, prisoners, and the "aliens among you."

God started The Ephraim Project with two people. Contrary to what everyone thinks, Suzanne Judith Eustache, a Haitian immigrant, was the inspiration and visionary behind the startup of our homeless ministry. Suzanne was 74 years old at the time. She knew what it felt like to be thirsty, hungry, naked, and without shelter.

"Come on, my dear, let's try it! Somebody has to say something!" she coaxed. By that, she meant the homeless did not have a voice. Somebody somewhere needed to stand up and speak to the "haves" on behalf of the "have-nots."

"With what? We have no money!"

"God is not asking us to do big things," she said. "He just wants us to do little things with big love." I could not argue with her on that one. She shamed me into our outreach to the poor.

In time, "little things with big love" became our motto. It is how we assessed our progress within the measure of a day. At the end of each day, lying in bed, I would ask myself, "Okay, let's see. Who did I love today?" If I could not name at least one person, I felt the day was not well spent—even though I may have accomplished a mountain load of office or project work.

I realized God was using Suzanne to make my life count in this world. Together, she and I could make an eternal difference in the lives of many, by demonstrating Christ's love to others in the tiniest ways—tiny to us, big to them, massive to God. Oh, yes, God was answering my November Prayer!

Chapter 39
Andre—My Golgotha and Bridge

God had another reason for moving me from New Destiny to St. George, but He kept it hidden from me until the set and appointed time. Five months after we began serving the homeless at St. George, I met Andre, a man I saw in dreams 15 years earlier! We were married on September 18, 2010, by my brother Earl, who is also a pastor. My parents and family members attended. Because my mother and father were too frail to travel to Orlando, we wed in Detroit at the home of my younger brother, Carl.

Six weeks later, on October 31—All Saints' Eve—Andre and I recited our vows again at St. George for the sake of our church family and Orlando friends. Father John presided over the second wedding ceremony.

I had a secret I kept hidden from everyone. Only God and a handful of people knew about it. Andre was not among them. While Andre was smitten to the core, I had no desire to marry him. I had no desire to marry anyone. I was already married to Christ! I was happy with my life! Why did He have to change it? His request broke my heart.

God did everything to facilitate the union. I resisted His every move. He was persistent. I cannot recall ever before resisting the Lord's will so strongly. When I refused to relent, all of heaven broke loose over my head!

God played His ace in the hole. My belly started to grow! I ballooned from a size 8 to a size 12 in three weeks! *Is Joshua coming soon?* I wondered. *What if the Lord tarries in removing us? I can't be visibly pregnant and single. What would people think? It would hurt my witness! It would hurt Ephraim!* Suddenly, I needed a covering. God graciously provided Andre!

While I saw Andre as a cover, and he saw me as a wife, God referred to each of us as a bridge for the other. I did not realize it at the time, but

God was working on a plan that He had put in motion 15 years before I ever met Andre. I would have to live more life to discover it.

I married Andre out of sheer obedience to God ... *and* fear of being seen as a 57-year old, pregnant, single mother, leading a Christ-centered ministry! It was the hardest thing I had ever done in my life. Our union looked like a train wreck waiting to happen. Walking down the aisle, I felt like I was walking to my execution.

Although I married Andre without understanding God's purposes, God allowed me to vaguely understand this much: the marriage would be the death of me. I would have to walk out the marriage by faith to find out exactly what that meant. God only reminded me of a profound event that occurred 13 years earlier.

On July 2, 1997, I awoke at 2:50 a.m. with a strange desire to talk to the Lord about my "Golgotha." I sensed deep in my spirit that one day I would be called to die for my faith. I began to inquire of the Lord about the way I would die and for what specific cause. At the time, I sensed my death had something to do with demolishing the spiritual stronghold of racism within the body of Christ in America. But I was not certain.

I was not prepared for God's answer. About two hours after I inquired about my death, the Lord gave Suzanne a dream to relay to me. At exactly 5 a.m. that morning, she tiptoed into my bedroom to share the dream.

The Lord revealed I was to be married and that marriage would spell my death ... *and* that death would be "good news" for me. I cannot explain the depth of my confusion because I was already married to Michael! Neither of us had any intentions of divorcing. In fact, a key feature of Suzanne's dream was a line spoken by a heavenly voice: "This is good news for Mrs. Phillips!"

Less than a year later, Michael and I separated. Five years after that, we divorced for the second time. It would be seven more years before I met Andre. Periodically, the Lord would give me a vision of a frog that adored me; but I never wired up that vision to a future husband. The only other thing I knew about the impending union was that we would not be married long. Whoever the man was, he would one day suffer a lethal head injury. I witnessed it in a dream.

Before I met Andre, I pondered for years ... *who is the elderly White man in my dreams chasing me around a table?* Whoever he was, he was completely enamored with me. At the time, I had no way of knowing that one day I would meet Andre, who was raised in Orthodox Romania, and we would become husband and wife. In the Orthodox tradition, when a couple marries, the priest leads them around a table three times—one time for each Person of the Holy Trinity.

When I first saw Andre, and he saw me, there was no attraction between us. He was just curious as to how an African American woman ended up in an Orthodox church. I found him to be odd and a bit abrasive. Then, God stepped in.

On February 14, 2010, Valentine's Day, at my chrismation into the Orthodox Church, Andre—my sponsor—took hold of my hand. When he did, God sent something akin to a lightning bolt from my hand to his hand. It traveled the length of his arm and nearly knocked him over. I would learn of this weeks later. At the time, he thought the same thing had happened to me. It did not.

From that point on, he behaved like the smitten man in my dreams. Again, that was a problem for me. I had absolutely no desire to be in a romantic relationship with him or any other man.

One would be hard-pressed to find a couple odder than the two of us. I had to grow accustomed to the strange stares and perplexed faces. In time, they tickled and amused me.

Andre was born in Bucharest, Romanian and grew up under strict Communism, which greatly impacted his religious upbringing. Steeped in Eastern Christian Orthodoxy, Andre rarely read the Word of God. He wholeheartedly, without question, embraced the traditions of the "Church Fathers." Whatever the priest said was "The Law."

For example, taking the law to an extreme, he was convinced he would go to hell if he ate meat on Wednesdays. I was born in the ghetto of Detroit, Michigan, the granddaughter of a Baptist preacher with strong leanings toward the charismatic. God raised me to be keenly suspect of the traditions of men, period. The stiff-necked Pharisees who claimed to love God, put their traditions before Christ and, thus, missed the time of His visitation. I had come from a long line of stiff-necked people—some may have even been Pharisees! So, if I could not back up a tradition with Scripture, I rejected it out of hand.

Even putting religion aside, Andre and I were polar opposites in almost everything. He liked to be cold. I liked to be hot. He was extraordinarily messy. I was highly organized. Andre wore the virtue of patience like a cloak. I was completely void of it. He smoked like a chimney. I detested cigarette smoke. Andre loved cats. I was allergic to them. Andre kept things for years. I regularly threw out or gave away anything not being used. Andre was a poor money manager. At no time was I unaware of the state of our finances. I knew the whereabouts of every last penny. Andre loved beef and pork but hated fish and chicken. I could go months without touching red meat. I preferred fish and poultry. He could consume large portions of rice, pasta, and potatoes for days on end. I steered clear of those carbohydrates as much as I could. I craved collard greens, spinach, and cabbage, none of which he could stomach. Andre liked big, old-fashioned luxury cars. I liked small, compact ones. Cooking was his favorite thing to do. I would only go in the kitchen if it was absolutely necessary. Andre's pace was glacial at best. I moved at lightning speed. I could accomplish more in one afternoon than he could in a week. He was highly social. I was perfectly content being alone.

It became a joke between us. If he really liked something, we both knew I would not and vice versa. Amazingly, we grew to respect each other's differences and adjusted accordingly.

However, there was something we both had in common, besides the love of a good cup of coffee—mine decaffeinated, of course. We both grew up poor. We marveled how my upbringing in the ghetto of Detroit, Michigan was not that different from his upbringing in Bucharest, Romania.

Both are bustling cities, filled with poor people trying to survive by whatever means possible. Whenever I did something bold or brazen, Andre would tell me, "Honey, you would fit in just fine in Romania." Once Andre watched me cut palm branches from publicly owned property to distribute to my friends at church on Palm Sunday. He marveled, "I tell you, Honey, you are more Romanian than the Romanians!"

One afternoon in the spring of 2010, before Andre and I were married, I visited his efficiency apartment. It was the filthiest place I had ever laid eyes on. Junk was everywhere. His apartment had not been cleaned in two years, since the day he moved in because of his physical challenges. I saw what was coming in slow motion.

"I will not be the one to clean his house, Ishi! No, no, no ... I will not!" The Lord remained quiet.

That afternoon, Andre and I talked on his balcony—the only clean place we could find to sit. I spent the afternoon explaining to him my wild and wondrous predicament. I did not want to be accused of deception. He needed to know the full story, so he could make an informed decision.

If he was from God, then God would prepare his heart to receive me. I even showed him my growing belly (that stopped growing after we were married!) He noticed how I had gone from being skinny, by Romanian standards, to being chubby in a few short weeks.

Surely, God went before me. Andre was completely open and eager to embrace any miracle God chose to send his way. We were married in the fall. Because I would return to his apartment and not the townhouse I shared with Suzanne and Ryan, I recruited two friends to help me clean his efficiency. We threw away almost everything he owned except his clothes. It took us 12 hours to clean that little space.

I knew the marriage would be difficult for me. Years earlier, Andre had suffered from a diabetic stroke that left him with only one leg, one arm, and one eye. He walked on a prosthetic leg. Most of his teeth were rotten. We eventually had them pulled and replaced with a full set of dentures. No one believed Andre was only 60 years old when we married, not even the priest. He was only two years older than I, but he looked 75!

During his lifetime, Andre never denied himself anything. He lived all over the world. He worked hard and played harder. His devil-may-care lifestyle took a toll on him in his later years. The Lord gave me a song one evening that summed up Andre's life to that point: *Yesterday, When I Was Young*. It was the sad song about a wasted, selfish life.

I was not physically attracted to Andre in the least. I also realized he would require a great deal of attention and assistance. How would I juggle the ministry's demands with his?

As taxing as that might prove to be, surprisingly, it was not my chief concern. What troubled me most about our union was that Andre happened to be the most cantankerous person I had ever met. He professed to love Christ and would kiss His icon and pray dozens of times a day, but he could be quite mean-spirited, especially behind people's backs. He was often rude to friends, neighbors, and strangers without even realizing it. Some of it was cultural, but most of it was his brusque personality.

He knew, deep down, something was off with his relationship with Christ. I lost count of the times he asked me and others to pray that Jesus would come into his heart in a real way. He asked several times every week.

A former English professor in both Romania and the U.S., Andre spoke seven languages and was well-read. As a young adult, he was crowned the undefeated *Jeopardy* champ in Romania. This all made it difficult to teach Dr. Petrescu anything. He felt he knew it all.

We often clashed over my ministry to the homeless. He exhibited a general lack of mercy or grace toward people who could do nothing for him. I would see red when he painted them all as deadbeats, not worthy of my time or effort. He saw the ministry as a threat. It took me away from him.

Living in a Communist regime while growing up, he knew very little about Scripture, so I bought him a Bible with giant type, thinking that would help. He read it periodically, but I saw no real fruit. However, I knew he adored God. Going to church on Sunday was the highlight of his whole week. He looked forward to it.

Andre smoked incessantly before our marriage, which I protested. He stopped long enough to say, "I do." Afterward, he resumed his 40-year habit. He would go outside on the balcony to smoke all hours of the day and night. I cannot express how much I detest the smell of cigarette smoke. No matter how hard he tried to keep it from me, I caught whiffs of it all day long.

Andre had already been married twice and divorced twice. The same was true for me. Still, I thought I pulled the real short end of the stick. *How could the Lord have done this to me?*

As we began to live together, the revelation God gave me 13 years earlier started to come to pass. The time had finally arrived. I was looking "my Golgotha" in the face. God would use the relationship to bring me to an utter and complete end of myself.

In a Golgotha, someone surrenders his or her life so someone else can live. Someone dies and is buried like a seed in the ground to one day produce a harvest. Andre was the tool God used to bring about my total death to self. I am ashamed to confess it, but I had to be dragged to my funeral.

Interestingly, Andre was an internationally known professional bridge player before his stroke. He still plays online with people from all over the world. Even more curious was his website, designed by a friend in France. In it, he is referred to as "The Toad-Playing Bridge Player!" As time unfolded, I learned Andre, a master bridge player, would serve as a bridge for me in more ways than one.

First, our marriage separated me from Ryan and Suzanne. The three of us were inseparable. I was my daughter's best friend. I had been for years. In like manner, Suzanne and I were convinced only death could separate the two of us. She was my spiritual mother and mentor.

However, the Lord showed me that His call on my life and His call on theirs would require us to travel different roads. My new Kingdom role-to-come did not involve them. Theirs did not involve me. Thus, my marriage to Andre facilitated the necessary break. He would be my bridge from one kind of life with them to another.

More importantly, God promised that I would experience a wondrous resurrection *after* my "death and burial." I would be catapulted into a new kingdom assignment for His glory. But first I had some dying to do. I was not yet fully dead.

Only by experience would I discover the things I had yet to relinquish. On the outside, I looked as if I had surrendered everything. But there were some things God knew I thought were still mine—my body, for example.

"Date nights" with Andre were the worst for me because he was not my soul mate. But I lay with him because he was my husband. That was a part of the marriage covenant. During those times, I would have to remind myself how our Lord selflessly gave Himself away to fulfill His earthly call. Yes, God would use this man to bring me to an utter end of myself. Only after I kissed myself goodbye could I expect a personal revival.

God always lavishes us with more than we expect. On December 11, 2011, Deone Adams, one of my homeless charges, invited Andre and me to the last performance of the "Singing Christmas Tree" at First Baptist Church of Orlando. Deone attended church there and managed to procure three free tickets.

Surprisingly, Andre's favorite part of the entire evening was not the live performance. Because the concert rivaled a Broadway musical, he was convinced the singers and dancers were all hired professionals. (They were not.) Andre's favorite part of the evening was the pastor's invitation to receive Christ. He listened intently.

At the end of the production, the pastor gave the testimony of a wealthy businessman. The man confessed to him over lunch one day that he was afraid to die. Right there at the table, the pastor shared the Gospel with the man, who decided that afternoon to invite Christ into his life.

That was 11 years earlier. The pastor had just attended the man's funeral and his children informed him of their father's graceful transition into eternity. He had no fear of dying.

"That's what I want!" Andre shouted sitting next to me. "That's what I *always* wanted!" I started to remind him that he prayed with me almost a year earlier to invite Christ into his life.

"Be still," the Lord whispered. I shut my mouth in mid-sentence.

Andre bowed his head. I could hear him praying out loud with the pastor. He asked Christ to enter his heart. When the offering plate passed, we turned in the card that had been given to us when we first entered the church. It informed the pastor and staff of Andre's decision.

The audience started gathering their things. Just when we thought everything was over, the choir suddenly began to sing *Handel's Messiah.* Andre jumped up and down in his wheelchair yelling, "The Halleluiah Song! The Halleluiah Song!" We looked at him. We thought he had lost his mind. At that moment, Andre *knew* he belonged to the Lord.

We did not know Andre had secretly prayed to the Lord for a sign. He told the Lord, *"If You have finally come into my heart, then have them sing the Halleluiah song before we go."* That was a long shot because the song was not on the program.

Days later, as I worked out at a gym, God began to speak to me about that evening. As God's plan began to slowly dawn on me, I could not stop sobbing. Through sobs, I kept blubbering, "Like the thief on the cross! Like the thief on the cross!" At the beginning of our union, God told me Andre would be like the thief on the cross, but I never made a connection. What did that mean? Now I understood.

Andre spent most of his life engaged in worldly pursuits. Now his life was nearly spent. But God so dearly loved him. He desired that Andre spend eternity with Him. God planned everything from the beginning.

It would take an arranged marriage to pull this man into His kingdom. God knew He needed to send someone into Andre's life, someone who knew Him intimately and who would serve this broken man, who would model what a true believer looked like. There was no other way.

In the fullness of time, God summoned me to relinquish my life—to lay it down, so Andre could cross over into eternity to be with Him. Just as Andre was my bridge to the other side, I was his. God asked me to give away my life, so Andre could live.

Since it is more blessed to give than to receive, the Lord knew I would receive a bountiful blessing in return. Finally, I understood that cleaning Andre's grimy apartment was a metaphor for how God would use me to help Him clean up Andre's life! Now I saw it as an honor, not a chore.

I have heard and read testimonies of God's extraordinary mercy in people's lives. Countless times, I have experienced His boundless mercy in my own life. Nothing spoke to me more profoundly, more powerfully, about God's mercy toward His children than my union with Andre. God will do whatever is required to bring His chosen ones into His fold.

When I finally understood that God used me to help woo Andre to Himself, my heart grew big and stout toward Andre. That, of course, propelled our relationship to a whole new level. After that, I heard all day long, "Yes, I do! I really, really do! In case you're wondering, I really do!" It was Andre reminding me all day long that he loved me.

Also, it became his custom to kiss my feet every morning when he woke up and every night before he went to bed. I could not stop him. God knows, I tried. Some mornings, the first thing I heard was, "Where are they? Where are they?" I would raise my toes, so he could kiss them. Then, he would go happily about his day. It was the same routine at night. He could not go to sleep without first kissing my toes.

In 2012, there was a shift in our marriage that I ignored for months. Andre would have these spontaneous outbursts of anger, triggered by the tiniest, silliest things. Then, on the night of November 17, 2012, I cried out to God for two straight hours, asking Him to reveal what was behind these sudden tirades. It did not take long for Him to answer. The next evening, Andre and I got into a colossal argument over the most ridiculous thing, but it ended up being a catalyst for a frank discussion between us.

Andre had been confined to a wheelchair for months. It hurt him to walk on his prosthetic leg because of an open wound on his stump. The wound had become infected with Mercer Disease—a highly resistant, contagious strand of bacteria. We had hoped the free antibiotics from Publix would clear up his condition, but they did not. He needed to see a wound care specialist.

Complicating matters, the relentless pain in his ghost leg kept him up for days. He got very little sleep. Every few minutes—*for days*—he would grip his ghost leg and scream in pain. So, in addition to a wound care specialist, he also needed to consult an orthopedic surgeon about the botched amputation he had in Romania years earlier, during which they failed to deaden his nerve endings.

Andre also desperately needed to see an endocrinologist for his diabetes, a urologist for a persistent bladder infection, and an ophthalmologist to care for his one remaining eye. He had not received any medical attention for 18 months, except for the limited care during our periodic emergency room visits at the local hospital.

We were told by Social Security nine months into our marriage that Andre no longer qualified for Medicaid or Social Security disability benefits; my monthly pension of $1,274 disqualified him. We exceeded the threshold to receive assistance by roughly $100.

We tried, on three separate occasions, to have his Medicaid reinstated, but only managed to get a "share-of-cost" designation. That qualified us to receive help only after we exceeded $1,017 in medical expenses each month. Sometimes we managed to do this; other times, we did not. Andre kept trying to get someone to hear his plight.

Finally, he was told by a Social Security representative that he would be eligible for full Medicaid benefits if he could prove I lived at a different address. Upon learning that, I moved out within seven days, and Andre began the application process. As the case unfolded, another Social Security representative asked to see actual divorce papers. I provided these within 30 days of the request.

God used the very thing that caused us so much pain and struggle in our marriage—the inaccessibility of medical treatment for Andre—to open an unexpected door for me. In God's eyes, I had completed my assignment to lead Andre to Him. After securing his soul, the Lord attended to Andre's physical needs.

The Lord has not revealed to me when He will take Andre away. I do not want to know. He has informed me that I will cry many tears when He does. Andre has confessed to me that he has absolutely no fear of dying. I have resolved to simply take each day as it comes. We are still good friends. I am confident when God takes him, I will see him again on the other side. *(Postscript: Only July 1, 2014, Andre suffered a massive brain aneurysm. He lost the use of his left arm, left leg, and right stump as a result. Although unable to move by himself, his mind remained strong and alert until he passed courageously into eternity on October 27, 2016.)*

Chapter 40
A New Season

I walked away from a lucrative-paying career and dissolved a highly profitable business. I had faced my giants, and God slew them all, one by one. I tackled two foreclosures and lost virtually every earthly possession. I weathered homelessness, the insane bureaucracy of the IRS, and an arranged marriage—all under the relentless, withering attacks of the enemy. There was not much else that could rattle me, and God would prove it.

The same week I left Andre in late 2012 to move into my own apartment, my mother died of fluid on the brain. We had a shunt put in her head three times to drain the fluid, and three times, the area around the shunt became infected. Each time, the infection spread throughout her frail body. My mother was unwilling to have a fourth surgery.

Forever the fighter, she confessed she was tired and asked that we stop. As her designated health surrogate, I would not let the doctors perform any more surgery. My siblings concurred. She died the day before Thanksgiving.

A week after my mother passed, Suzanne, my spiritual mother, left the ministry. We had been together 30 years. Two other friends and I helped her move four hours away, to Miramar, Florida. There, she became a nanny for a little 11-year-old girl whose single, working mother traveled a great deal. Suzanne cried the day I left her in Miramar. It was a sad day for both of us.

Two weeks after Andre and I officially divorced—60 days after my mother passed—my father died of cancer in the back, bone, and prostate. He also suffered from late-stage dementia. The last few months of his life he kept telling us, "I have to get a job! I have to get a job to take care of my family! I have to get a job!" Even at that late stage in life, he was still consumed with "making bricks in Egypt" to support his family.

Countless times, I tenderly told him he had done enough, and we had enough. We were all grown and well-provided for. I assured him he and mom had done a good job. We had all turned out well. He was 90, now. It was time to rest. I cannot describe how it broke my heart to see my dad in that state. At his death, he weighed only 92 pounds.

The Montford Pointe Marines bestowed upon my dad a most decorous military funeral. At the cemetery, before we entered a stately white rotunda, we saw seven Marines dressed in full uniform, standing at attention with rifles at their sides. The hall was lined with Marines—Black and White, men and women—on both sides as family and friends filed in and took their seats.

One of the most profound moments of the service was when two young Marines walked slowly and solemnly to the front—one Marine down each aisle. They met at the casket. Together, they gently removed the flag from the casket and carefully folded it.

The flag was given to my brother Earl. One soldier presented it to him on bended knee with outstretched arms and a bowed head. Outside, at that very moment, we heard the 21-gun salute. The seven Marines shot their rifles in perfect unison three times. It took my breath away. A brave soldier had gone home.

During this time of great loss, immense sorrow, and widespread upheaval, the Lord lavished me with a sweet, inexplicable peace. I also experienced a deep abiding joy and strength I never knew I had.

I told Him countless times that He could not have done anything more to prepare me for the passing of my parents. Just before they became deathly ill, He showed me them in dreams. They were in heaven. At the time, I could not understand why they were so young, serene, and beautiful—more stunning than I had ever known them to be.

Weeks before I was called to Detroit to help sort through their financial and medical affairs, the Lord put an old Quincy Jones song in my spirit, *Everything Must Change*. I had not heard the song in decades. I simply woke up one morning with a lyric playing in my head: "*Everything must change. Nothing remains the same. The young become the old and mysteries do unfold.*"

I heard the song repeatedly, day after day, week after week. At first, I did not understand why God put it in my spirit. But after my first night in Detroit, having seen the deteriorated state of my parents, I knew He was gently preparing me for their transition into eternity.

A year before any of this happened my siblings and parents agreed I should have Power of Attorney over all their affairs. We prepared all the necessary documents and tucked them away. At the time, I did not realize how invaluable they would be and how soon I would need them.

The Lord did something else as well. During that same period, He kept putting spellbinding books in my hands about people's near-death experiences. The books did more than just reinforce what I already knew by faith. They allowed me to glimpse heaven. By all accounts, it was a glorious, wildly fascinating place to be. I would be joining them sooner than I realized. God showed me this in several dreams.

Joy amid sorrow sounds crazy—contradictory, even. But it is not. Had I not experienced it firsthand, I would have not believed it was possible. Last of all, during these massive life changes, the Lord gave me every indication I would soon experience that promised resurrection. My long winter was over.

APPENDIX

Author's Five Dominate Areas of Strength (Kingdom Perspective)

Strategic

I am strategic only in that I am laser-focused on the eternal. It has taken my entire lifetime for God to detach me from the things of the world. In that process, the last 17 years have been the most painful. Now, if I cannot see the eternal value of something, I shun it. To me, it is wood, hay, and stubble. I do not like to waste time on things I consider irrelevant to God's chief goal—the salvation of human souls.

God has taught me to listen to Him before I listen to people. I do not lean on my own understanding or the understanding of others. I take to God virtually all my ideas, questions, challenges, and issues because I love talking to Him and He knows everything. Conversing with Him is my most favorite thing to do. I delight in His company, and He has given me every evidence that He delights in mine.

The Lord imparts to me knowledge and wisdom in a wondrously witty and winsome manner, which often makes me laugh and fuels my desire to learn more from Him. Although God speaks to me through His Word, I also hear His voice. It is nothing for Him to instruct me for hours at a time.

I have had the pleasure of hearing God's voice for 22 of the last 29 years I have known Him. He has taught me to question what many Christians automatically accept as truth or fact. At the same time, He has taught me not to debate inconsequential matters of doctrine with other believers. It detracts from His work.

He has shown me that most believers walk lockstep with the culture surrounding them and not according to His Word. Further, they cannot discern the difference. I am not to follow them or judge them. I am to love them and simply do as His Spirit or word instructs. I am not their Holy Spirit. I am not the Author and Finisher of their faith. He is. They are His workmanship, not mine. This frees me to love.

God is brilliant beyond all imagining. Therefore, as I follow His directives, I often appear to be clever, resourceful, and inventive. By God's Sovereign choice, I see and hear in the Spirit what most miss or dismiss, so when I act on what the Spirit reveals, I seem strategic, original (and sometimes crazy). God shows me things in dreams and visions that greatly impact how I perceive the world and interact with it and others around me.

Achiever

Like Joseph, the Lord continually blesses the work of my hands so that no matter where I go or what I do, I rise to the top for His glory, often against great odds. I have a large, God-given capacity for work, and I can do the work of two or three people. Most of my bosses have called me a "workhorse." I am lightning fast and can do many things at once. I strive to do them all well.

I am highly, intensely focused, and not easily deterred from my goals. When I decide to do something, I do it with great vigor and passion and with bulldog tenacity. I do not give up. I loathe wasting time or having my time wasted. I have eight clocks in my tiny one-bedroom apartment.

The belief that God has given me much (revelatory knowledge) and, therefore, expects much of me, drives me. I believe I can do anything Christ calls me to do because His Word says so. He will always give me everything I need, no matter the task. Over the past six years, God has worked out of me a keen competitive streak—stoked by 30 years in Corporate America. There is neither competition nor Lone Rangers in the kingdom of God.

Adaptability

I go with the flow. God has made my life a great adventure for His glory. For this reason, I treasure spontaneity. I cannot stand for my time to be tightly scheduled either by myself or others.

I resist the notions of luck, chance, and happenstance. I am convinced God controls all things. There is not a random or maverick molecule in the universe. The Lord knows where I am, at every fraction of every nanosecond, in relationship to everything else in Creation, including every human being, sparrow, ant, and cockroach.

His will for me unfolds before me "as I go" by faith. Therefore, I like to leave plenty of room in my day for the Lord's Spirit to direct my path, to place me where I am supposed to be at each precise moment, per His ordained plan for me and others. If God blows up my schedule, it is because it needed to be.

The Lord orders my steps daily for His glory. He exhorts me to "stay in the day," and to look back at my past only to fuel present moments. He forbids me to race ahead of Him to the future. I take great satisfaction in being spiritually agile. I welcome unexpected changes and challenges. They are clues and cues in this great adventure I am living with Him.

Belief

The Holy Spirit has apportioned me an enormous amount of faith. I believe the Bible is the inerrant Word of my Creator and Savior, who loves me more than I can ever comprehend. His Word directs and guides everything I do. If His Word says it, that settles it. It does not matter what the situation looks like or what others say.

I believe the most important thing I can do is to love my God with all my heart, soul, and mind and to love others as I love myself. This love must show in my actions. Mercy is an action word. Talk is meaningless if it is not backed by action. My obedience to my Lord shows that I love Him, and my mercy toward others shows that His love flows through me.

I believe nothing is impossible for God, and He can do anything in and through me. Therefore, I live most of my life outside my comfort zone and the comfort zone of others, so much so that I often risk being seen as irrational. I am fearless because of my trust in God. I walk by faith in Him, not by what I see or what the experts say.

Like my Savior, I am on this earth to serve, not to be served. God has shown me that my life is a sacrifice to Him, so I devote vast amounts of time, money, and energy serving others. For the sake of the gospel, I routinely put others before myself. It is not because I am all that nice;

it is because God asks me to. I feel a great deal of responsibility toward people—even strangers.

I am zealous about the things I believe. In the earthly realm, my beliefs have cost me much. Early in my walk with the Lord, I sensed I would, one day, die for my beliefs.

Input

I love to learn. I crave information as it relates to what God has put me on earth to do. I have a passion for history, especially as it relates to Scripture because God has shown me "what has been before shall be again." Rarely do I allow information unrelated to my call to consume my time. God removed all televisions from my home more than six years ago.

I enjoy studying patterns and types since God works in these. They help me understand His plan for the world and me. I have an ardent interest in other cultures as well as the rise and fall of past civilizations because "what has been before shall be again."

The Lord loves it when I discover new things. I can feel His delight when I connect His cosmic dots. It gives me immense pleasure, too. Since 1986, I have tried to record the revelations the Lord has given me, some of which would astound Christendom as well as the secular world. For years, I could not understand why God deposited in me these terrible and wondrous mysteries. It has taken my entire lifetime to understand who I am in the Lord and my Kingdom call.

www.ingramcontent.com/pod-product-compliance
Lightning Source LLC
LaVergne TN
LVHW020526100826
845148LV00010B/1361

9780615907437